NICOTINE DEPENDENCE

NICOTINE

Understanding and Applying the Most Effective Treatment Interventions

DEPENDENCE

Charles E. Dodgen

American Psychological Association
Washington, DC

Published by
American Psychological Association
750 First Street, NE
Washington, DC 20002
www.apa.org

To order
APA Order Department
P.O. Box 92984
Washington, DC 20090-2984
Tel: (800) 374-2721; Direct: (202) 336-5510
Fax: (202) 336-5502; TDD/TTY: (202) 336-6123
Online: www.apa.org/books/
E-mail: order@apa.org

In the U.K., Europe, Africa, and the Middle East, copies may be ordered from
American Psychological Association
3 Henrietta Street
Covent Garden, London
WC2E 8LU England

Typeset in Goudy by Page Grafx, Inc., St. Simons Island, GA

Printer: Data Reproductions, Auburn Hills, MI
Cover Designer: Aqueous Studios, Arlington, VA
Technical/Production Editor: Peggy M. Rote

The opinions and statements published are the responsibility of the authors, and such opinions and statements do not necessarily represent the policies of the American Psychological Association.

Library of Congress Cataloging-in-Publication Data
Dodgen, Charles E.
  Nicotine dependence : understanding and applying the most effective treatment interventions / Charles E. Dodgen.
     p. cm.
  Includes bibliographical references and index.
  ISBN 1-59147-233-4
  1. Tobacco habit—Treatment. 2. Nicotine. I. Title.

  RC567.D63 2005
  616.86'506—dc22

                                                              2005001047

British Library Cataloguing-in-Publication Data
A CIP record is available from the British Library.

Printed in the United States of America
First Edition

In loving memory of Dr. Thomas J. Lynaugh
and Veronica M. Jaeger

CONTENTS

ACKNOWLEDGMENTS

Because I work primarily as a clinician in private practice, most of my professional attention is devoted to direct patient care. This means that the time needed to complete this project was taken from that which would otherwise be considered personal time. Practically speaking, for a married father of two children, I had to take precious time from the family. For their tolerance of this, I am indebted to my wife, Lisa, and children, Danielle and Christopher.

I would also like to thank Phillip M. Sinaikin and Raymond F. Hanbury, both very busy professionals themselves, for reviewing the manuscript and providing valuable suggestions. I want to express my gratitude to the library staff at Saint Barnabas Medical Center in Livingston, New Jersey: Sylvia Barrasso, Chris Connor, and Mila Lungun were very helpful in obtaining resource materials for the book. Finally, I would like to acknowledge the assistance provided by Phuong Huynh, my development editor at American Psychological Association. Her feedback, and the comments from the peer reviewers that she arranged for, improved the manuscript considerably.

NICOTINE DEPENDENCE

INTRODUCTION

Although known for decades, at least since the surgeon general's initial findings were published in 1964 (U.S. Department of Health, Education, and Welfare [USDHEW], 1964), the hazards of smoking have only recently begun receiving the attention they deserve in the popular media and in general public discourse. Previously, discussion of the adverse medical consequences of smoking was more or less confined to medical and health-related publications. Recent legal rulings against tobacco companies may be interpreted as recognition of the harmfulness of tobacco products and as a reflection of the American public's growing intolerance toward the damage they cause. Smoking is far from a casual, pleasurable activity for many users. Although legal (if the user is of legal age), nicotine consumed via cigarettes appears to be one of the more addictive, as well as destructive, substances of abuse (U.S. Department of Health and Human Services [USDHHS], 1988). It is a well-established fact that most, if not all, smokers desire to stop at some point in their histories (USDHHS, 1988); often this is motivated by concerns about health.

PURPOSE OF THIS BOOK

There are currently available many products designed to aid smokers in their efforts to quit. In fact, pharmaceutical companies now advertise these products directly to consumers, and they have made some medications available without prescription, which has both positive and negative consequences. On the positive side are easy access and availability to the consumer. On the negative side is the fact that the former gatekeepers of pharmaceutical products, physicians, have been removed from the equation. Physicians traditionally have served a protective function, learning about the appropriate use of pharmaceutical products and monitoring the patient's use of and response to the product. Without physician involvement, consumers are left on their own to evaluate smoking-cessation products (some of which still do require a prescription) and programs. Consumers typically lack the information, or the objectivity, to make a fully informed, balanced decision regarding treatment. Rather, they are left to respond to the usually narrow and incomplete claims of the products' advertisers.

That there is a tremendous market for products to assist smokers to stop their use of cigarettes is apparent to anyone who goes into a pharmacy, physician's office, clinic, or supermarket, or turns on the television to see advertisements for products such as Nicorette, NicoDerm CQ, and so forth. Smoking cessation has become a $450 million industry (Howell, 2000); although this helps to explain the business interest in the products, it also suggests the presence of a need. Smokers are searching for methods to assist them in their efforts to quit. In addition to pharmaceutical products, there exists a substantial market for literature on smoking cessation written for the lay public. Much of the literature may be fairly characterized as self-help, assisting the reader to develop a personal quit program. The behaviorally oriented self-help books typically discuss important concepts such as the establishment of a quit date, development of appropriate expectations for the process of quitting, management of emotions and stress, maximizing motivation, relapse prevention, and so on. However, the objective evidence undergirding their treatment approach is often lacking. If a smoker is to make a decision about treatment, he or she should possess all of the relevant information before deciding on a plan, and not just the claims of one or another pharmaceutical manufacturer or book author.

A book that compares the evidence supporting the various treatment interventions and products is a necessity for the psychologist interested in helping smokers who want to maximize their chances of successfully mastering their smoking addiction. Clinicians of various disciplines in the mental health and medical fields will also greatly benefit from this information. This simple rationale serves as the basis for the publication of this book.

Although the logic is straightforward enough, to provide clinicians with current information about treatment techniques that have been determined to be valid for nicotine addiction is not as simple a matter as one would hope. In current technical terminology, we are interested in identifying empirically validated treatments (those supported by scientific studies). The problem is that there is much controversy over the methods that should be used in psychotherapy outcome research to establish the validity of a given treatment technique. Which treatment techniques are judged valid, therefore, may in part be a function of the method used in a given study. Therefore, one cannot simply look up the "best" intervention for smoking cessation, because it depends partially on the perspective from which the intervention is viewed. The tension between researcher and clinician is well known in psychology and perhaps most evident in the area of psychotherapy outcome research (Abramson, 2001; Beutler, 2000; Goldfried & Wolfe, 1996; Kazdin, 2001; Kendall & Hudson, 2001; Nathan, Stuart, & Dolan, 2000; Seligman, 1995; Wampold, 1997). Few would challenge the need to identify valid treatment techniques. Using scientific standards for the establishment of safe, effective treatments seems a reasonable alternative to the practice of using techniques simply because they exist, or because people think they work based only on personal experience (anecdotal evidence), strong belief, or adherence to a favored theoretical model (Beutler, 2000). On the other hand, techniques developed in a laboratory setting may be of limited or no value when used in clinical settings. It is interesting to note that the impetus to seek empirically validated treatments appears to have been provided by sources outside of psychology (Goldfried & Wolfe, 1996). Managed health care organizations and government agencies have effectively issued mandates to provide scientific evidence of the value of services they are paying for. Additionally, biological psychiatry, with impressive advances in the development of pharmaceutical treatments for psychiatric problems, has exerted indirect pressure for practitioners of psychotherapy to demonstrate its effectiveness.

Care must be taken to attempt to reconcile the sometimes conflicting perspectives of the researcher and clinician; the issue of considering the concerns of both when evaluating treatment interventions will be discussed more fully in chapter 7. Suffice it to say for now that valid treatment interventions need to balance both the scientific requirements of the researcher and the requirement of practical application mandated by the clinician. It must also be stated that even the best technique, like any tool, is of dubious value in the hands of an unskilled, poorly trained, or otherwise incompetent therapist. We know that successful psychotherapy involves much more than the application of specific techniques, not the least of which is what occurs in the domain of the therapist–patient relationship. There is no substitute for the experience, skill, and judgment of a competent therapist; for this reason outcome research evaluating treatment interventions should inform, not dictate, treatment (Goldfried & Wolfe, 1996; Stricker et al., 1999). Clinicians may rightly employ certain techniques that have not been empirically validated; it must be remembered that although a technique is not currently empirically validated, this does not mean that it is invalid, or that it never will be validated. So we must always keep techniques in the proper context as tools to be used to aid treatment; they are not the sum total of treatment.

Treatment guidelines for nicotine addiction, derived from state-of-the-art research methods, currently exist which are published by professional associations (e.g., American Medical Association, 1994; American Psychiatric Association, 1996; British Thoracic Society, 1998) in addition to those from a consortium of seven federal government and nonprofit organizations (USDHHS, 2000b). The question may then legitimately be posed, "What else needs to be stated about smoking cessation?" The guidelines serve as an excellent starting point for the discussion of smoking cessation. However, the guidelines, impressive as they are, are insufficient for many purposes. For starters, the recommendations are largely (although not solely) based on findings from efficacy studies (i.e., well-controlled, laboratory-like studies). The foregoing discussion was provided to support the point that guidelines based on efficacy studies should not be the sole source of information on the treatment of nicotine addiction. There are other reasons that one must seek information to supplement the guidelines. For instance, since the major guidelines have been published, new information continues to come out that requires consideration.

Another reason to look beyond the existing guidelines is that except for those of the American Psychiatric Association, they are written with a focus on primary care medical practitioners as the main audience. The role of a physician or nurse is similar to that of a psychologist, but also significantly different. Some recommendations in the guidelines are geared toward the physician in an active role of adviser, a position not automatically assumed by psychotherapists. For physicians, dissemination of information, including rendering of advice and guidance in a brief treatment encounter, even when not requested by the patient, is consistent with their professional role. Consideration of the patient's readiness, tolerance, or general reaction to the medical recommendations seems secondary to the offering of the information. By contrast, psychologists, with more of an explicit focus on the relationship and the establishment of a positive therapeutic alliance, may not be able to easily implement some of the recommendations in the medical guidelines. Although the major guidelines can be of use for psychologists (Wetter et al., 1998), they are not entirely applicable. To be sure, the guidelines do recommend that the primary care medical practitioner assess an individual's motivation to quit smoking and promote motivation for cessation in those not currently motivated. Realistically, though, the assessment strategies and interventions that can be applied in a typical psychotherapy session of 30 to 50 minutes are significantly different from those used in the typical encounter of 3 to 5 minutes between a physician and a patient.

Furthermore, guidelines are just that—outlines. Psychologists need to know much more than can be contained in any set of guidelines to be able to competently treat a given patient interested in smoking cessation. For example, knowing that nicotine replacement therapies are efficacious is useful information but hardly sufficient for a therapist to support a patient's use of them.

Traditionally, the study of tobacco use and its effects on the human body has been conducted by the medical profession. The devastating consequences on the health of tobacco users are undeniable. However, although the ultimate effects are physical, the *use* of the substance causing the damage fits well with the addiction/disease model (USDHHS, 1988). The addiction model is very different from the acute disease medical model, in which someone gets sick or is injured, receives treatment, and fully recovers. Nicotine addiction, like other chronic medical conditions such as diabetes and obesity, is more like typical mental disorders than acute medical conditions in several ways. First, complete cure in the traditional sense is not a goal; rather, effective management is pursued. Even someone abstinent of nicotine for a long period of time is not thought of as cured any more than a diabetic would be thought of as cured of the diabetes when he or she was asymptomatic and good blood sugar control was achieved. With both conditions it is understood that if behavior were to change back to previous form (the person smoked a cigarette or blood sugar management deteriorated), the condition could again be evident. Second, much responsibility for management of the condition is in the hands of the affected individual and typically requires significant lifestyle changes. Finally, the burdensome requirements of changing behavior and maintaining these changes over the long term often means there will be episodes of treatment noncompliance and resumption of previous unhealthy behaviors (with nicotine addiction this would be referred to as a relapse). In medicine, treatment noncompliance is a nuisance to treatment and often results in compromised care; if nicotine addiction is treated like an acute condition, it may appear to the clinician (as well as the patient) as though relapse is evidence of treatment failure. In psychotherapy, the study and improvement of treatment compliance often *is* the treatment (most apparent in the burgeoning field of behavioral medicine).

Psychologists, therefore, are in a uniquely strong position to treat nicotine addiction and, as has been noted (e.g., by Wetter et al., 1998), are well qualified to do so for multiple reasons:

1. Nicotine dependence is recognized as an addiction and mental disorder, both of which are commonly treated by psychologists.
2. It co-occurs with other mental disorders.
3. With the availability of nonprescription pharmacotherapies, psychologists are no longer at a competitive disadvantage compared with medical providers.

In addition, nicotine dependence is a leading cause of premature death and illness in patients, making it a relatively urgent problem to address in treatment.

In the treatment of nicotine addiction what may be suggested is a reversal of roles between physician and psychologist. In the past, medical models have effectively been applied to help explain and guide the treatment of psychological disorders (i.e., the so-called "medicalization" of psychotherapy); with respect to the treatment of nicotine addiction, the "psychologizing" of a traditional medical condition may be in order. Psychotherapy models exist that can effectively assist the clinician to address the behavioral, motivational, emotional, and cognitive aspects of the addiction, in addition to the physiological components that are the focus of medical and pharmaceutical interventions. Indeed, psychotherapies have demonstrated efficacy similar to those of nicotine replacement therapies in the treatment of nicotine addiction (Wetter et al., 1998). There should be little doubt that psychologists possess knowledge and skills that nicely complement those of medical practitioners and that allow them to be collaborative partners with these practitioners in the treatment of nicotine dependence.

CONTENT AND ORGANIZATION OF THIS BOOK

This book is aimed primarily at clinicians who treat patients for nicotine dependence. It is appropriate for psychologists, psychiatrists, social workers, physicians, nurses, substance abuse counselors, and school counselors. Before proceeding, a word on terminology: Currently, the term "dependence" is sometimes used in place of the previously popular word, "addiction," although the two are synonymous and interchangeable (and both are used in this book). The term "dependence" appears to be preferred by some professional organizations for a couple of reasons: "Addiction" is so overused that it may be losing meaning (e.g., addiction to sugar, sex, work, video games, etc.), and "dependence" is less stigmatizing a term than "addiction" (Henningfield, Cohen, & Pickworth, 1993).

In reviewing the literature on tobacco use and nicotine dependence, it is immediately plain that there is no shortage of information on the subject. For example, the U.S. government has amassed a tremendous database of all tobacco-related research that includes tens of thousands of studies. Actually, there may be too much information to be of practical use to the busy clinician. In a publication by the British Thoracic Society (1998), it was aptly noted that what was needed was not necessarily more data, but more high-quality summaries of the data for use by clinicians. In this spirit I have aspired to provide information on nicotine addiction and its treatment, informed by scientific and clinical publications and clinical experience, that will be of practical value to the clinician. In order for the book to be user-friendly, and in consideration of the enormity of the database on nicotine addiction, some process had to be used to streamline the presentation of the information. The major organizing principle guiding selection of material was, "What would a psychologist (or other clinician) want and need to know to best help a smoker seeking treatment?" In additional consideration of the reading audience, the tone of the presentation is collegial, clinician-to-clinician, reflecting practical experience and insight gathered from this experience; an endless recitation of studies and facts from studies that exist would be boring and of dubious value. The literature is used to support key points, but the points of discussion are clinically driven. Because

almost all tobacco consumed in the United States (about 95%) is via cigarettes (Ma, Shive, Legos, & Tan, 2003), smokers are the primary targets of
nicotine dependence research and treatment. Likewise, this publication is
directed to the treatment of smokers, although the same interventions used
for smokers may also be applicable to users of noncigarette tobacco products
(USDHHS, 2000b).

This book aims to present everything a clinician needs to know to
understand and effectively treat this prevalent, yet treatment-refractory,
condition. The book starts with a review of the consequences of nicotine
use (chap. 1), including the well-known physiological damage, as well as the
less obvious but nonetheless real psychosocial damage. It then (chap. 2) discusses psychological processes, namely denial and ineffective coping styles,
that are associated with and provide fertile ground for the development of
nicotine dependence. Following this, a discussion of the pharmacology of
nicotine (chap. 3) helps provide an appreciation of the role of the drug, and
its action in the body, in nicotine dependence. The ensuing presentation
of the evidence supporting the addictiveness of nicotine (chap. 4) answers
the crucial questions: What is addiction? and How does nicotine use fit with
the general addiction model? Discussion of assessment (chap. 5), including
the use of informal clinical methods as well as formal psychometric tools to
guide treatment, precedes a comprehensive review of counseling and pharmacological treatment interventions for nicotine dependence (chap. 6). The
clinical and research support for specific interventions is reviewed (chap. 7)
to identify valid treatment methods. A relatively short list of efficacious and
effective interventions recommended for use in the treatment of nicotine
dependence is selected from the comprehensive list discussed in chapter 6.
The importance of relapse prevention training (chap. 8) to combat cravings
and extend the influence of treatment beyond the formal treatment period
is explained. Special treatment considerations are described that apply to
the specific, at-risk smoking populations (chap. 9) of substance abusers and
psychiatric patients, racial and ethnic minority members, and women, in
addition to perhaps the most important population, adolescents (chap. 10).
Adolescents are discussed in a separate chapter because most smoking for
any subgroup begins in this stage of life, and because one entire set of treatment interventions available for adults (pharmacotherapies) is not currently
accepted for use by adolescents. Finally, in the appendix, an assessment and
treatment model is presented that integrates the material presented earlier in
the book and that may be used to assist the clinician to develop and apply an
individual treatment plan for nicotine dependence. A detailed, step-by-step,
10-session model is described.

Techniques used for smoking cessation are discussed throughout the
book. In some cases a description of the intervention is sufficient to allow the clinician to administer the treatment (e.g., pledging, described in
chap. 6). With other interventions, a description, a sample form, and a case

example are presented to facilitate understanding and proper application of the intervention (e.g., the "What Smoking Does to Me" form and accompanying case example in chap. 1). The forms that I use in my practice and present in the book consist of simple, face-valid exercises designed to educate the patient and actively involve him or her in the treatment process. The knowledge presented in this book will allow a clinician to provide sound treatment, or to evaluate treatment programs if a referral is preferred. The reader is reminded that to be effective, the generic treatment model must be skillfully applied and adapted as appropriate to the characteristics of each individual case.

1

NEGATIVE CONSEQUENCES OF CIGARETTE SMOKING

The purpose of this chapter is to provide the reader with information about the known negative consequences of cigarette smoking. In addition to medical problems, and even premature death, significant psychosocial damage may result from cigarette smoking. Being aware of the full range of problems caused by smoking places the clinician in a position to share it with the smoker, at the proper time and in the appropriate amount and manner, to enhance motivation to stop smoking.

PHYSICAL CONSEQUENCES

It is difficult to imagine that there is an adolescent or adult in this country who does not know that smoking harms health. Most people could probably go a step further with their knowledge to state that smoking causes lung cancer in humans (Weinstein, 1999). Despite this overall awareness of the harmfulness of cigarette smoking, it is still important for those who treat patients for nicotine dependence to be fully informed about the negative consequences of smoking. Smokers can benefit from a reminder that they are not alone in experiencing problems from smoking and that it is an addictive disorder with predictable medical, mental health, financial, social, and familial consequences. Although he or she may have a general idea that smoking is dangerous, the average person may not know the full extent of the damage smoking can cause to smokers, their families, and society. Because health concerns are the most common reasons cited for seeking to stop smoking, it is good for the treatment provider to be familiar with all the available information for the purpose of sharing it with patients as appropriate. Most people seem to have little or no awareness of the psychosocial consequences of smoking, so being able to provide this information in treatment may help create an additional incentive to stop smoking. Awareness of the negative consequences of smoking is the foundation of treatment. If there were no negative consequences of smoking, what would be the motivation to stop? With increased awareness of the harmfulness of tobacco use, the smoker will have a more accurate idea of the chances of being injured by smoking and of the low likelihood of deriving benefits from smoking (Hansen, 1992); the net effect should motivate interest in cessation of use.

U.S. Surgeon General's Initial Report

The surgeon general's reports are an excellent source of information on the health consequences of smoking; the initial report was published in 1964, and since 1969 there have been mandatory annual reports dedicated to cigarette smoking and its health consequences. In the surgeon general's landmark first report (USDHEW, 1964), Luther L. Terry noted that the relationship between tobacco consumption and human health had been the subject of much concern for some time, dating as far back as the early 16th century. With improving sophistication of experimental design came increasing scientific evidence of the danger of cigarette smoking. Surgeon General Terry (USDHEW, 1964) noted that in the early 1900s an increase in the rate of lung cancer was observed, which may have been the starting point of the modern investigation of cigarette smoking. Although cigarette smoking was suspected of being a health-injuring habit, it was still a source of controversy, and the question needed to be answered with objective, scientific evidence. In keeping with his office's commitment to protect the health of the American people, Surgeon General Terry felt compelled to form a committee to study all available evidence relating to smoking and human health. The committee evaluated evidence of three types: (a) animal experiments; (b) clinical and autopsy studies comparing smokers and nonsmokers; and (c) population, or epidemiological, studies relating smoking histories to diseases and mortality.

Exceptional care was taken so as to yield valid, high-quality conclusions. Incidentally, the report is still a very interesting read, which is a tribute to its excellence. The major findings published in the first surgeon general's report (USDHEW, 1964) are presented in Table 1.1.

TABLE 1.1
Comparison of the Major Findings Regarding Smoking and Health From the 1964 and 1989 U.S. Surgeon General's Reports

Health consequence	Year	
	1964	1989
Mortality	Increased death rate in men	Increased death rates in men and women
Cancer		
Lung	Causes lung cancer in men	Major cause of lung cancer in men and women
Oral cavity	Causes lip cancer (pipe smoking)	Major cause of oral cancer (lip, tongue, mouth) in men and women
Larynx	Causes cancer of the larynx in men	Major cause of cancer of the larynx in men and women
Esophagus	Correlation between smoking and cancer of the esophagus in men	Major cause of cancer of the esophagus in men and women
Urinary bladder	Correlation between smoking and cancer of the bladder in men	Contributory factor for bladder cancer in men and women
Kidney	No information	Contributory factor for cancer of the kidney in men and women
Pancreas	No information	Contributory factor for cancer of the pancreas in men and women
Stomach	No information	Correlation between smoking and cancer of the stomach in men and women
Cervix	No information	Correlation between smoking and cancer of the cervix
Nonneoplastic respiratory diseases		
Chronic bronchitis	Cause of chronic bronchitis	Major cause of chronic bronchitis in men and women
Emphysema	Correlation between smoking and emphysema	Major cause of emphysema in men and women
Cardiovascular disease	Higher death rate in men from coronary artery disease	Major cause of coronary artery disease in men and women. Cause of stroke
Other conditions		
Peptic ulcer	Correlation between smoking and peptic ulcer	Cause of peptic ulcer
Maternity/ fertility	Correlation between smoking and lower birth weight	Cause of intrauterine growth retardation. Probable cause of reduced fertility in men and women

continues

TABLE 1.1 *(Continued)*

Health consequence	Year	
	1964	1989
Smoking and accidents	Correlation between smoking and death from fire in home	No information
Involuntary smoking	No information	Secondhand smoke is a cause of disease in healthy nonsmokers
Tobacco habit	Determined by social and psychological factors	Smoking is addictive and nicotine is an addictive substance

U.S. Surgeon General's 1989 Report

The surgeon general's 1989 report (USDHHS, 1989) reflects on 25 years of progress in the effort to reduce the health consequences of smoking since the surgeon general's original report. In documenting the damage resulting from cigarette smoking, it was noted that a quarter of a century of research had not only failed to invalidate the major findings of the original report but also reinforced them. In addition, other health consequences from smoking had been identified since 1964. The principal findings of the surgeon general's 1989 report are summarized in Table 1.1. It is clear from a comparison of the two surgeon general's reports that in the time since the original report, cigarette smoking has been established as a major cause of premature death, cancers, respiratory conditions, cardiovascular disease, and other illnesses in men and women. Chronic cigarette smoking has also become recognized as an addiction to nicotine.

Other Health Statistics Related to Smoking

Although the surgeon general's reports are excellent sources of information regarding cigarette smoking, they are not the only ones. Information is readily available, free of charge, from the American Lung Association, the American Heart Association, and the American Cancer Society. On the basis of the information culled from the surgeon general's reports, it is obvious that cigarette smoking is responsible for serious damage to many areas of the human body. The facts presented below, which were obtained from the preceding organizations, give some idea of the death and morbidity toll of smoking on the American public.

- Smoking is the number one preventable cause of premature death in the nation.

- Smoking causes approximately 430,000 deaths per year in the United States.
- Smoking kills more people than cocaine, heroin, alcohol, fires, auto accidents, homicides, suicides, and AIDS combined.
- In 1996, smoking-related illnesses cost the nation more than $100 billion (50% in medical expenses and 50% in related costs).
- Environmental tobacco smoke ("secondhand smoke") causes 53,000 deaths per year in nonsmokers.
- People who have never smoked but live with a smoker are 30% more likely to have a heart attack.
- The Environmental Protection Agency has designated environmental tobacco smoke a Group A carcinogen (a classification that includes such materials as asbestos and radon).
- Environmental tobacco smoke elevates the risk of sudden infant death syndrome.
- Environmental tobacco smoke is responsible for 150,000 to 300,000 cases of lower respiratory infection and 400,000 to 1 million attacks of asthma in children of smokers annually.

There is also recent evidence to suggest that smoking is a risk factor for breast cancer in women (Al-Delaimy, Cho, Chen, Colditz, & Willet, 2004; Reynolds et al., 2004). Earlier investigations yielded inconsistent results, but more recent, better-designed studies are finding that risk of breast cancer in women is related to duration and amount of smoking.

The facts speak for themselves: Smoking destroys the body. Some smokers may be unfamiliar with the more common respiratory disorders caused by smoking. Chronic obstructive pulmonary disease (COPD) is a term used to refer to the conditions of emphysema, chronic bronchitis, and asthma. COPD refers to a condition of generalized obstruction of the small airways; the term was adopted because the three conditions often coexist so that it is difficult in any individual case to determine which condition is causing the obstruction (Berkow & Fletcher, 1987). COPD affects 15 million people in the United States, and it is rare in nonsmokers (Howell, 2000). Emphysema is a condition resulting from destructive changes in the alveolar walls of the lungs that causes diminished lung functioning. Symptoms include difficulty breathing, shortness of breath, diminished activity, and fatigue. Chronic inflammation of the alveoli in the lungs due to irritation from smoke is thought to be the major cause of the condition.

Chronic bronchitis is a condition associated with prolonged exposure to bronchial irritants such as cigarette smoke. The bronchial tubes (tubes connecting the windpipe to the lungs) become inflamed, with resulting reduction in airflow to the lungs. Symptoms of chronic bronchitis include copious production of mucus, frequent infections, and persistent cough.

Some warning signs of lung cancer that may be helpful to smokers to be on the alert for are persistent cough; chest pain; hoarseness; weight loss, loss of appetite, and altered taste; nausea and vomiting; fatigue and weakness; blood in sputum; shortness of breath; and fever without a known reason (Gift, Stommel, Jablonski, & Given, 2003; Howell, 2000).

Ingredients of Cigarette Smoke

What is in cigarette smoke that so badly damages the body? Most people do not give too much thought to the biochemical compounds contained in cigarette smoke. The makeup of cigarette smoke helps to explain the havoc that smoking wreaks on the human body. Some smokers may benefit from knowing what it is that they are putting into their bodies. The estimated number of known compounds that make up tobacco smoke exceeds 4,000; some of these specific compounds are known to be toxic or carcinogenic (USDHHS, 1989). Tar is one toxic substance in tobacco that is also known to cause cancer; it is additionally responsible for respiratory problems and the staining of teeth and fingertips (Howell, 2000). Tar itself is chemically complex, consisting of such dangerous substances as formaldehyde, arsenic, cyanide, and benzene. Other chemicals found in tobacco smoke are the pesticide DDT, ammonia, nickel, acetylene, acetone, carbon monoxide, and, of course, nicotine, the substance responsible for addiction to cigarette smoking. Some of the chemicals in tobacco smoke other than nicotine are responsible for much of the physical damage caused by smoking. Carbon monoxide is probably the compound most responsible for heart disease. Carbon monoxide replaces oxygen in the blood and tissues, causing damage to the tissue of organs such as the heart (Howell, 2000).

Benefits of Smoking Cessation

Increasing the awareness of smokers to the dangers of smoking carries some risk of frightening them into greater denial. It seems important also to make smokers aware of the health advantages of smoking cessation. There is much evidence available that with cessation, there are correspondingly positive changes in the body that make it worth the effort to stop. The surgeon general's entire 1990 report (USDHHS, 1990) was devoted to the health benefits of smoking cessation. The report was clearly written in an effort to remind readers of the value of smoking cessation. The five major conclusions are discussed below:

1. The first conclusion addressed the questions of "Who benefits from smoking cessation?" and "How soon after quitting will benefits be realized?" The answer provided to the first question was, in short, all smokers. That is, smokers of either sex and of all ages can improve their health by stopping. This

is particularly important for older smokers, who may feel as though it is too late to expect any gains from smoking cessation. Benefits are also achieved whether or not the person already has a smoking-related disease. Those who have a smoking-related disease may feel as though the damage is already done, so what's the use in stopping now? Research shows that stopping smoking arrests the progress of diseases and allows for improvement in many conditions caused by smoking. In addition, for those who do not show symptoms of smoking-related diseases, the risk for developing those diseases is reduced by stopping. Thus, those smokers who are not yet stricken with a disorder may also derive benefits from stopping.

2. The issue of mortality was also addressed. The encouraging news is that former smokers live longer than continuing smokers.

3. Morbidity was the subject of the third conclusion; risks of many of the serious diseases caused by smoking are reduced by cessation, including lung and other cancers, heart attack, stroke, and chronic lung disease.

4. Infant birth weight was discussed in the report's fourth major conclusion. The risk of having a low-birth-weight child can be reduced to normal levels if the mother stops smoking either before pregnancy or by the third to fourth month of pregnancy. More recent research (Ashmead, 2003) shows that cessation in the third trimester (up to the 30th week of gestation) can produce benefits in terms of infant birth weight. In general, the sooner in her pregnancy a woman stops, the better in terms of infant birth weight.

5. Finally, the report addressed impediments to smoking cessation: weight gain and psychological duress resulting from quitting. These are important considerations because fear of weight gain is a significant barrier to success at cessation, as is avoidance of psychological distress. Smokers may be helped to know that the average weight gain related to smoking cessation is only about 5 pounds, and that the adverse psychological effects from withdrawal are usually only experienced in the short term. Furthermore, with more prolonged abstinence, the negative feelings are usually supplanted by positive ones relating to changes in self-esteem, a sense of mastery, and freedom from withdrawal symptoms.

The American Cancer Society (2000) publishes an interesting fact sheet that relates specific improvements in health to specific time periods from last cigarette smoked:

- After 20 minutes, blood pressure and pulse rate drop to normal.
- After 8 hours, carbon monoxide level in the blood drops to normal, and oxygen level in the blood rises to normal.
- After 24 hours, chances of heart attack decrease.
- After 48 hours, abilities to taste and smell improve.
- After 72 hours, bronchial tubes relax and lung capacity increases.
- After 2 weeks to 3 months, circulation improves and lung functioning improves up to 30%.
- After 1 to 9 months, respiratory symptoms of coughing and sinus congestion decrease; fatigue and shortness of breath decrease, and overall energy increases.
- After 1 year, excess risk of heart disease from smoking is halved, and after 15 years it is nearly that of never-smokers (persons who have never smoked).
- After 10 years, precancerous cells are replaced by normal cells and risk of cancers decreases.
- After 15 years, death rates for ex-smokers are nearly the same as those for persons who have never smoked.

PSYCHOSOCIAL CONSEQUENCES

When discussing the negative consequences of smoking, it is typical to think only, or at least primarily, about the potential medical impact of cigarette use and not about the negative psychosocial consequences of smoking. It seems that people, even clinicians in medical and mental health professions, are accustomed to thinking about psychosocial damage resulting from abuse of other substances, but not so much about the damage from nicotine dependence. For example, job loss, emotional disturbance, marital and other family difficulties, and financial and legal problems are well-documented sequelae of dependence on substances such as cocaine, heroin, and alcohol. Although the negative psychosocial consequences of nicotine addiction may in most cases be less obvious or dramatic, they nonetheless exist and can be quite serious. Therefore, they deserve discussion not only for the sake of rendering a complete inventory of the damage caused by chronic smoking but also because of the potential treatment implications. Exhibit 1.1 presents the psychosocial consequences of smoking that are discussed below.

Increase in Dysphoria, Stress, and Depression

An idea that enjoys both intuitive appeal and empirical support is that smokers derive some emotional and cognitive benefits from smoking

EXHIBIT 1.1
Psychosocial Consequences of Cigarette Smoking

- Increase in dysphoria, stress, and depression
- Negative impact on self-esteem
- Secondary emotional reactions to physical problems caused by smoking
- Increased risk for use of other substances
- Handicapping effect on development of effective coping strategies
- Accidental injuries related to smoking behavior

(discussed in Carmody, 1989; Jarvik, Caskey, Rose, Herskovic, & Sadegh-pour, 1989; Parrott & Kaye, 1999). For example, smokers report that cigarette smoking reduces anxiety and stress, and they are observed to smoke more when under duress. In addition, smokers also report that smoking provides elevation of low moods and increases alertness and concentration. As Carmody put it, nicotine is used by smokers for the purpose of affect regulation (affect regulation being any attempt to cope with negative mood states). He further describes two categories of affect regulation: inhibitory and excitatory. Inhibitory affect regulation involves the reduction of arousal and negative mood states, including anxiety, fear, and anger. Excitatory affect regulation refers to the increase of arousal to alter negative mood states such as depression, feelings of sadness, low energy, and boredom.

The anxiolytic and mood-improving effects of cigarette smoking are indisputable. That smokers self-medicate with cigarettes is not news. A perhaps surprising, yet very convincing, angle to the self-medication hypothesis, however, has been advanced by Parrott and his associates (Parrott, 1999; Parrott & Garnham, 1998; Parrott & Joyce, 1993; Parrott & Kaye, 1999): The ostensible beneficial effects from smoking derive mainly from the reversal of unpleasant abstinence effects. In other words, the stress that is being attenuated by smoking is created by smoking in the first place! Parrott and Kaye discussed two rival models proposed to account for the observed positive effects of cigarette smoking on anxiety and on alertness and cognitive functioning: the Nicotine Resource Model (NRM) and the Deprivation Reversal Model (DRM). The NRM proposes that the ostensible benefits gained from nicotine use are real; the DRM purports the opposite. That is, the DRM suggests that improvements in mood and cognitive functioning seen with cigarette smoking result from reversal of the irritability and impaired concentration that characterize nicotine withdrawal. Parrott and his associates have conducted research and obtained results in support of the DRM. For example, they found that average daily stress levels for smokers and nonsmokers did not differ, but smokers did exhibit predictable changes in stress ratings during the day in relation to smoking status (Parrott & Joyce, 1993). More specifically, reported stress for smokers followed a pattern: It was high prior to smoking, low after smoking, high prior to smoking, and so forth. This cycle repeated throughout the day. Smoking did not improve mood except to reverse the effects of nicotine withdrawal.

In additional support of the DRM, it was found that deprived smokers (current smokers who were abstinent overnight for purposes of participating in the study) reported significantly more emotional disturbance in the form of stress and irritability, cognitive symptoms of diminished concentration and alertness, and increased restlessness than smokers (nondeprived) and nonsmokers (Parrott & Garnham, 1998). When they were allowed to smoke, formerly deprived smokers' moods improved in comparison to other smokers' and nonsmokers' moods. Further support for the DRM comes from research showing that through the course of a day, deprived smokers' self-rated moods, arousal, and pleasure were lower than those of nondeprived smokers and nonsmokers (Parrott & Kaye, 1999). In addition, the deprived smokers reported more cognitive failures (e.g., forgot to do something, felt confused, felt easily distracted) than smokers and nonsmokers. Smokers and nonsmokers reported similar self-ratings through the course of the day, so no advantages in mood or cognitive functioning were found from smoking. Instead, only deficits were observed, in terms of alertness and cognitive and emotional functioning, in deprived smokers.

In addition to the results directly obtained in their studies, Parrott and Kaye (1999) cited two findings from longitudinal studies that lend more support to the DRM: (a) instead of decreasing, self-rated stress increases in adolescents as they become regular smokers, and (b) once beyond the initial acute withdrawal period immediately following cessation, smokers report significantly less stress after successfully quitting smoking. If smoking reduced anxiety, the opposite trend would be expected.

This research strongly supports the idea that cigarette smoking is *anxiogenic* (i.e., anxiety-causing) rather than *anxiolytic*. There is also evidence that cigarette smoking is depressogenic (i.e., depression-causing). An association between cigarette smoking and depression has been established (Balfour & Ridley, 2000; Choi, Patten, Gillin, Kaplan, & Pierce, 1997; Daeppen et al., 2000; Glassman et al., 1990; Hall, Munoz, Reus, & Sees, 1993; Patten et al., 2001; Wang, Fitzhugh, Westerfield, & Eddy, 1994). In cross-sectional studies of the general population (Glassman et al., 1990) and of subjects seeking mental health (Patten et al., 2001), smoking cessation (Hall et al., 1993), or alcohol treatment services (Daeppen et al., 2000), a significant correlation is observed between cigarette consumption and depression. Although these studies help to establish a relationship between smoking and depression, they are only suggestive because of the correlational nature of the investigations. A step closer to establishing a causal relationship, by longitudinal study that allows for observation of the order of emergence of smoking and depressive symptoms, was provided by Choi et al. (1997). In this study, it was found that among adolescents not reporting significant depressive symptoms at baseline, smoking status was the most significant predictor of the development of depressive symptoms at follow-up, 4 years from baseline.

Also related to mood, smoking has been found to negatively influence physical activity. Adolescents I have treated for nicotine dependence have tended not to be physically active relative to nonsmoking adolescents; they are usually involved neither with organized sports at their schools nor in informal athletic activities. Although this may reflect the influence of several factors, it should not be a surprise, because smoking results in a number of consequences that would serve as a deterrent to physical activity (USDHHS, 1994). Young smokers report the increased experience of respiratory symptoms, including shortness of breath, coughing spells, phlegm production, and wheezing; they report overall diminished physical health and fitness. Smoking during adolescence has been found to retard lung development and reduce maximum lung function (Fagerstrom, 2002). Physical activity has been associated with depression such that rates of depression are lower among the physically active and sports players (Paffenbarger, Lee, & Leung, 1994). Because cigarette smoking and depression are both complex and multifaceted, the relationship between the two is not a simple one. It may perhaps best be described as reciprocal (Wang et al., 1994). That is, smoking results in increased risk for depression, and depression results in increased risk for smoking. Choi et al. (1997) suggested several mechanisms by which smoking may result in depressive symptoms. Dysphoria may be the result of an inability to stop smoking. An absence of effective alternative coping strategies may enhance vulnerability to depression. Either through consumption of nicotine or from withdrawal processes (or both), alteration of neurochemical functioning may increase the development of depressive symptoms. Smokers are at increased risk of engaging in other health-compromising behaviors (e.g., other substance abuse) that may increase the risk of depression. Finally, Choi et al. considered the possibility that the relationship between cigarette smoking and depression may not be causal, but the result of shared genetic or environmental dispositions. For example, a family history of depression is predictive of both depression and smoking in adolescents. In addition, certain personality characteristics and behavioral tendencies may predispose someone to both cigarette use and depression, such as high emotionality (person is easily distressed), low soothability (unable to manage dysphoria), and impulsiveness.

Negative Impact on Self-Esteem

Smoking is a behavior not without personal or social implications. As public sentiment becomes increasingly negative about cigarette smoking, smokers will be viewed differently, both by themselves and by others. Compared with 30 years ago, smoking is less common and the smoker statistically more deviant. Dermer and Jacobsen (1986) found that smokers are viewed more negatively by others than nonsmokers are. Gibson's (1997) review of the literature on the perception of smokers revealed that nonsmokers' cognitions, feelings, and behaviors are significantly more negative for smokers than for other nonsmokers. For example, nonsmokers perceive smokers less favorably than they perceive other nonsmokers with regard to such dimensions as intelligence or wisdom, likability, morality, manners and consideration, sophistication, self-discipline, insecurity, hyperactivity and nervousness, calmness, honesty, imagination, and maturity. Nonsmokers also perceive smokers more negatively in terms of attractiveness and desirability as dating or marriage partners, close friends, employees, coworkers, or students. Smokers are also perceived as more sexually active. In short, the reviewed research showed that nonsmokers perceive smokers more negatively in terms of almost any dimension, demonstrating that a strong negative stereotype exists (Gibson, 1997).

The existence of a negative cognitive set on the part of nonsmokers toward smokers is not the entire story. There are also corresponding aversive emotional reactions aroused in nonsmokers when interacting with smokers or exposed to smoke (Gibson, 1997): increased anxiety and fatigue as well as hostility. In addition, decreased arousal and mood are experienced by nonsmokers in interaction with smokers.

Not unexpected, given that nonsmokers have negative thoughts and feelings about smokers, it has been found that they also behave more negatively toward smokers (Gibson, 1997). Nonsmokers show more aggressive behavior, decreased helping, and increased interpersonal distance when exposed to smokers or secondhand smoke. Taken together, these findings convincingly demonstrate that smokers have become a stigmatized outgroup (Gibson, 1997). The current antismoking climate in the United States appears to encourage an expression of antipathy toward smokers that may well handicap them personally, socially, and professionally. It should be added, however, that cigarette smoking may be a source of increased status in some adolescent groups that have nontraditional values. If an adolescent identifies more strongly with and receives support from one of these groups, it may protect him or her from the impact of negative appraisal by the nonsmoking majority.

Just as praise by others is esteem-boosting, negative valuation is esteem-lowering. In addition to the external, social appraisal that negatively influences self-esteem, one's sense of oneself is also lowered by engagement in behaviors that harm the self. Body esteem, or the way people feel about their bodies, is a component of self-esteem, and it is lowered by illness or injury (Mayer & Eisenberg, 1988). Miller (1987) noted that illness is often accompanied by shame and loss of self-esteem; smoking is responsible for much acute (e.g., coughing, infection) and chronic (e.g., emphysema) illness, as documented earlier in this chapter. Among adults rating self-perceived health (a global rating of their own overall health), physical condition was expectedly strongly related to the rating (Shields & Shooshtari, 2001). That is, those individuals with health problems or functional restrictions rated their health status lower than people without health problems or functional restrictions. It is important to note that the researchers also found that psychosocial factors such as heavy smoking also affected ratings. Heavy smokers (20 or more cigarettes per day) self-rated their health as lower than did others who were not heavy smokers, independent of actual physical status. The authors suggested that these findings indicate that people have an idea of how they should behave to be healthy, and when they do not behave in accordance with this idea, negative self-valuation results.

In an inpatient substance abuse treatment unit where I worked, it was apparent to staff and patients alike that the self-esteem of the substance abusers was badly damaged. I was asked many times, "How can I repair my self-esteem and feel better about myself?" One response offered was "Stop doing things to hurt yourself." It does damage to the self to injure the body, whether the damage is self-inflicted or otherwise. I observed across many cases that self-esteem significantly improved as mistreatment of the self was stopped by cessation of use of cigarettes and other drugs of abuse; this clinical observation, though shared by other clinicians I have spoken to, awaits support from more scientific study because it may be argued that self-esteem was low to begin with, thus instigating substance abuse, and after self-esteem improved for some reason, substance abuse was terminated.

Another clinical impression, which too may require more rigorous study to fully establish its validity, relates to statements made by abusers of substances. I have many times heard substance abusers in their 20s and 30s lament the fact that their parents did not do more to stop their initial use of cigarettes, and later, other substances. "Why didn't they clamp down on me more and make me stop when they knew I was using?" I believe that this is a statement reflecting a sentiment such as "Why did they not care enough about me to stand up and battle with me if that is what it would have taken?" Lack of parental intervention when engaging in self-damaging behavior appears to be experienced by abusers as an absence of caring about them at some level. Parental valuation is a significant influence on self-esteem. Hearing such complaints from substance abusers convinced me to advise parents to be very active in intervening at the earliest signs of cigarette or other substance use by their adolescents, rather than take a much riskier wait-and-see approach.

Secondary Emotional Reactions to Physical Problems

In addition to the elevated death rate of smokers, there is also increased morbidity, which was discussed earlier in this chapter. Smokers experience not only serious illnesses such as cancer, emphysema, and stroke but also increased problems of a more common variety, such as respiratory symptoms of coughing and wheezing. There is an old dictum in psychology about physical ailments: Illness breeds regression and depression. The latter is of concern for current discussion. Evidence supports the saying, as people with physical ailments are observed to have elevated rates of depressive disorders (Gill & Hatcher, 2001; Wool, 1990). In addition to the self-esteem-lowering effects of illness that make one more vulnerable to depression, there are other factors that contribute to elevated risk for depression, especially with the more chronic or life-threatening illnesses resulting from smoking. For example, with chronic physical conditions there are multiple levels of loss experienced: loss of functioning, loss of role, and loss of body image (Vilhjalmsson, 1998). In addition, at the level of life stressors, chronic conditions pose a threat to financial well-being, work, and social and family relationships (Vilhjalmsson, 1998). All of these potential consequences of physical disability resulting from smoking may be thought of as adaptive tasks for the affected person to cope with to maintain adequate and healthy levels of emotional, physical, and social functioning (deRidder & Schreurs, 2001). The extraordinary challenges involved place those with chronic physical conditions at risk of coping ineffectively, and of depression. Because risk of smoking-related illnesses is a function of duration and amount of smoking, this factor becomes more significant with longer smoking history. So it is now seen that in addition to cigarette smoking being directly depressogenic (discussed in an earlier section of this chapter), the illnesses it causes act as another depression-causing influence on the smoker.

Increased Risk for Use of Other Substances

Study of the initiation and progression of substance use typically focuses on adolescents because this is the time when most substance use begins (Dodgen & Shea, 2000; Swadi, 1992). In an attempt to first describe, then explain, the progression of substance use, researchers have developed stage, or sequential, models. A highly regarded and influential model is that of Kandel (1975), which is based on longitudinal study of adolescents. Kandel's model, which originally consisted of four stages and was later amended to six stages, is presented below (discussed in Bukstein, 1995):

- beer or wine use,
- hard liquor or cigarette use,
- marijuana experimentation,
- alcohol abuse,
- prescription medication use, and
- opiates and other illicit drug use.

Each successive stage is thought to represent a progression of substance use; the earlier the stage, the more adolescents are expected to use the substance, so that there should be progressively fewer adolescents using substances at each higher stage. Dodgen and Shea (2000) pointed out that epidemiological statistics on substance use support Kandel's model. For example, for lifetime prevalence statistics published for 1993 (percentage of adolescents who had ever used a specific substance in their lifetime) the following order was obtained: (a) alcohol, 87%; (b) cigarettes, 61.9%; (c) marijuana, 35.3%; and (d) opioids, 1.3%.

The prevalence results are in precisely the order predicted by Kandel's model; adolescents usually start with substances that are legal and available to adults—alcohol and tobacco. Alcohol and tobacco are referred to as "gateway drugs" because their use tends to precede movement to other substances (discussed in Bukstein, 1995). It is not suggested that alcohol use causes cigarette use, which in turn causes marijuana use, and so forth. However, the use of cigarettes may be thought of as behavior that is part of a risk syndrome (USDHHS, 1994) whose interruption may reduce risk for use of other substances. Conversely, allowing cigarette use to progress unimpeded places an individual at risk for other substance use, so there is good reason to attempt cessation if cigarette use is discovered by parents or clinicians. Moreover, health risk behaviors tend to cluster so that smokers as a group are more likely than nonsmokers to engage in other behaviors such as poor diet, low physical exercise, and greater alcohol consumption (Sherwood, Hennrikus, Jeffery, Lando, & Murray, 2000). There is some evidence to suggest that motivation to make one lifestyle change may carry over to other areas; however, doing nothing may tacitly encourage passivity with all risk behaviors.

Handicapping Effect on Development of Effective Coping Strategies

One thing common to all forms of substance abuse is that, at least initially, the substance provides some apparent coping benefits to the user. Many cocaine abusers, for example, report that in addition to the elevating effects on their mood, the enhanced mental agility they experience allows them to feel more self-confident and smarter. Using cocaine before a business meeting, or while socializing, is therefore desirable. As another example, the tranquilizing effects of alcohol make it another substance that abusers use for a seemingly positive purpose: to steady their nerves. However, there are a couple of obvious limitations of using substances as coping aids. One problem is that tolerance develops. An ever-increasing amount of the substance is necessary to achieve a given effect. Ultimately, the person is using the substance just to "feel normal," and the putative benefits are lost. This, of course, leads to addiction to the substance.

Another limitation is that because cigarettes are readily available coping aids that may be used throughout the day, there is no incentive to develop other coping strategies to deal with problematic situations or emotional reactions. With the vanishing effects of the substance (due to tolerance), the person is eventually left without effective coping strategies.

However the cigarette is being used in any individual situation—to calm anxiety, serve as self-administered reinforcement, or elevate mood; as a distraction from worries; and so forth—some other more constructive coping technique can and should be used. Why use a coping strategy that ultimately must fail and that *creates* many physical and psychological problems?

Unfortunately, to many people addicted to cigarettes or other substances, as long as the substance is available, alternative coping methods do not appear as attractive. To illustrate this point, a patient of mine in the course of therapy developed a plan to combat stress with exercise, psychotherapy, and better management of time, and by asserting himself more effectively at work. At one point in the treatment he commented, "Why go through all of this when I could just resume smoking to reduce the stress?" The trap of apparent immediate relief from discomfort is difficult to overcome and is a significant barrier to healthier, more effective coping. Educating smokers about the necessary failure of smoking as a long-term coping strategy, and about the physical and psychological consequences of attempting to use cigarettes for the long term, may help convince them to endure the short-term discomfort of cessation while developing more effective coping strategies.

Accidental Injuries

In reviewing the literature, Sacks and Nelson (1994) found that cigarette smoking was an independent risk factor for many types of injuries, including thermal injuries (i.e., caused by fires), motor vehicle accidents, occupational injuries, and suicide.

Injury from cigarettes causing fires should come as no surprise to anyone. However, the magnitude of the damage done is somewhat shocking (Sacks & Nelson, 1994):

- Fires were the fourth leading cause of death from injury in the United States for the year discussed (1988), taking a total of 4,835 lives.
- Cigarettes caused approximately 29% of the fire-related deaths that year and were responsible for another 3,766 nonfatal injuries.
- Specifically regarding residential fires, smoking was responsible for between 26% and 56% of deaths from residential fires, and 24% of nonfatal injuries; nonsmokers are harmed as well as smokers in these fires.
- The association between smoking and residential fires was found to be independent of alcohol use.
- Smoking paraphernalia (i.e., lighters and matches) are also a source of accidental injury, especially for children. For example,

in 1988, 4% of house fires were caused by children playing with these materials, and cigarette lighters caused in excess of 20,000 injuries in the same year.

Smokers carry a significantly higher risk of motor vehicle accidents than nonsmokers even when the research is controlled for such factors as age, driving experience, level of education, and alcohol consumption. Smokers are also significantly more likely than nonsmokers to be injured on the job. Finally, smokers are at significantly elevated risk of committing suicide. Although the causal relationship of cigarette smoking to fire-related injuries is self-evident, the reasons for the association of smoking with automobile and occupational injuries are more complex and less certain. Sacks and Nelson (1994) advanced several possible explanations. The direct toxic effects of nicotine or carbon monoxide may impair cognitive or psychomotor performance. The evidence for this possibility appears strongest in explaining nighttime motor vehicle accidents due to the impairment of night vision resulting from accumulation of carbon monoxide in a closed vehicle. Another possible factor is distraction of the driver or worker due to preoccupation with the lighting or holding of the cigarette, obscured vision due to smoke, or excessive eye-blinking and coughing due to the presence of smoke. Associated medical conditions resulting from cigarette smoking (such as respiratory or cardiovascular diseases) may also negatively affect performance. Confounding factors such as the use of other psychoactive substances or the presence of personality traits such as risk taking, greater emotionality, and nervousness may predispose to both smoking and injury.

The association between cigarette smoking and suicide has been recognized by several authors (e.g., Miller, Hemenway, Bell, & Rimm, 2000; Paffenbarger et al., 1994). The correlational nature of these studies does not allow for certainty in establishing a causal relationship between smoking and suicide. An obvious possible line of thought is that because cigarette smoking is known to increase depression, and depression is a contributing factor in suicide, smoking is an indirect cause of suicide. As with the other types of injuries, it is impossible at this time to rule out the possibility of the use of other harmful substances or the presence of confounding personality factors, or the possibility that depression causes people both to self-medicate with cigarettes and to commit suicide (Miller et al., 2000).

NEGATIVE CONSEQUENCES FORM
AND CASE EXAMPLE

Presented in Exhibit 1.2 is a form ("What Smoking Does to Me") that I created for use in my practice to raise awareness and facilitate discussion about negative consequences of smoking.

EXHIBIT 1.2
Form for the Assessment and Discussion of
Negative Consequences of Smoking

WHAT SMOKING DOES TO ME

Instructions: Below are lists of negative consequences that people may experience as a result of smoking. The lists are divided into two categories, short-term and long-term consequences. Please review the lists and answer the questions. If you can think of any consequences not on the lists, please feel free to add them.

Question 1. What negative consequences have you experienced as a result of smoking? Please list them in order of importance to you (i.e., most important first).

_____
_____
_____
_____
_____

Question 2. What negative consequences do you think you might experience if you continue to smoke, and when do you think you will experience these consequences?

_____
_____
_____
_____
_____

Short-Term Consequences

1. Smell (of clothes, car, house, body, breath)
2. Expense of smoking
3. Disapproval from boss, parents, school officials
4. Rejection by peers
5. Discoloring of teeth and fingers
6. Harm to athletic performance
7. Increased incidence of respiratory infections
8. Increased coughing and shortness of breath
9. Addiction to nicotine
10. Increased depression
11. Increased anxiety
12. Lowered self-esteem
13. Contribution to other drug use (including alcohol)
14. Cause of accidental injuries (e.g., from fires)
15. Exposure of others around me to smoke
16. Aggravation of asthma

Long-Term Consequences

1. Cancers (lungs, lips, tongue, mouth, larynx, esophagus, bladder, kidneys, pancreas, stomach, cervix)
2. Respiratory conditions (chronic bronchitis, emphysema)
3. Heart and artery disease resulting in heart attack or stroke

continues

EXHIBIT 1.2 *(Continued)*

4. Peptic ulcers
5. Maternity problems (low-birth-weight children); fertility problems for men and women

Benefits of Smoking Cessation

You may be surprised and pleased to learn that the negative consequences you identified above as current or future concerns can be improved or prevented by cessation of smoking. In fact, all of the short-term and long-term consequences of smoking can be improved or avoided by stopping. Anyone benefits from smoking cessation. Male and female smokers of any age who quit live longer than continuing smokers and, regardless of smoking history, experience other health improvements by quitting. If a smoking-related illness is present, its progress can be halted by quitting, and if you are not suffering from a smoking-related illness, your risk of developing one is reduced. The body begins to repair itself after smoking stops. The positive impact of cessation begins within a day, and the longer someone is abstinent from smoking, the more benefits will follow.

Note. From *Stop Smoking System*, by C. E. Dodgen, 2004, Florham Park, NJ. Unpublished manuscript. Reprinted with permission.

Having the consequences in front of them on the form may help stimulate cognitive activity about smoking in respondents beyond what would take place if the smoker were asked to respond verbally or to an open question. Note also that the respondent is requested to rank consequences in order. This tells the clinician which consequences are most important to the smoker. Questions are also asked about anticipated consequences if smoking should continue. Some smokers may not yet be experiencing smoking-related problems but by considering the questions may be more mindful of potential future problems.

A section on the benefits of smoking cessation is included in the form. Attention to the positive outcomes resulting from quitting smoking can be motivation-enhancing.

In Exhibit 1.3 is a case illustrating the use of the "What Smoking Does to Me" form.

CONCLUDING COMMENTS

This chapter has presented the adverse consequences of smoking. For adolescents and adults, concern about the health consequences of smoking is a commonly reported reason for desiring to stop smoking. Clinicians need to be familiar with the physical and psychosocial consequences of smoking. Knowing this information is necessary, but there is more that is required. It is also necessary to be able to present the information in a manner most

EXHIBIT 1.3
Case Example: Tameeka A.

BRIEF BACKGROUND AND SMOKING HISTORY

Tameeka A. is a 62-year-old married mother of two children. She came to treatment because of distress experienced from the loss of a job and related financial concerns. Marital strain was also evident and contributing to the emotional duress she was experiencing. In response to my usual inquiry during intake about the use of substances (including nicotine), she reported an approximately 4-year history of smoking. She estimated smoking two to two-and-one-half packs of cigarettes (40–50) per day. She reported no past quit attempts despite a vague, long-standing desire to stop. When asked about current interest in smoking cessation she again expressed a desire, but no plan. She also offered the concern that because she was already feeling poorly, this might not be a good time to stop smoking; furthermore, she felt that having smoked so much for so long she might not be able to stop. Several months into treatment she experienced what turned out to be an episode of acute anxiety. She went to the hospital emergency room thinking she was experiencing a cardiac problem and was informed it was a panic attack. At this point in the treatment, now scared about the possibility of heart trouble from smoking, she agreed to attempt to stop smoking.

SMOKING-CESSATION INTERVENTIONS

Mrs. A. completed the "What Smoking Does to Me" form. She identified a future heart attack as a potential long-term consequence that she feared, and she was surprised to learn from the form that smoking could increase depression and anxiety and lower self-esteem, all areas of current concern. She also reported the financial burden of smoking as a source of stress.

COMMENTS

Awareness of the negative short-term psychosocial consequences (increase in depression and anxiety, lowering of self-esteem, cost) and concern about cardiac health strengthened Mrs. A.'s resolve to quit smoking, and cessation became one element of the treatment to improve her mental status and health. Identification of those consequences most important to the individual provides information for the clinician to use to help maintain the commitment to behavior change. In the case of Mrs. A., when she expressed a desire to smoke, I would ask her how she thought that might affect her anxiety and depression, her heart health, or her financial problems.

relevant to the individual. If a patient reports in the initial appointment that one reason for wanting to stop smoking is having been advised by a doctor that smoking is aggravating his or her asthma, it is a good idea to focus on the negative consequence of smoking. It would not be advisable to go into all of the other negative consequences of smoking—cancers, depression, and so forth. At the most, it may be appropriate to inquire whether the individual is aware of other problems smoking may potentially cause, and whether he or she would be interested in knowing more. However, in general, clinicians should be familiar with all this information because they will not know in advance which pieces will be relevant for a given individual. The total inventory on negative consequences should not be forced on every patient as a matter of course, but shared with sensitivity to readiness and tolerance. This principle applies in all cases and with all of the information in this book. The person seeking treatment is not an empty receptacle to be filled with facts, but a person presenting in varying degrees of readiness to change. Clinicians who do not work in this context might just as well hand the patient a book on smoking cessation that contains all of the facts on the subject.

SUMMARY

The U.S. surgeon general's office has been a world leader in documenting the adverse consequences of smoking. Smoking causes premature death (430,000 deaths per year in the United States) and a long list of diseases, including the following: (a) cancer (lung, oral cavity, larynx, esophagus, bladder, kidney, pancreas, stomach, and cervix); (b) respiratory conditions (COPD—chronic bronchitis and emphysema); (c) cardiovascular disease (heart attack and stroke); (d) fertility and obstetric problems; and (e) peptic ulcer. Smokers usually have some awareness of the physical damage caused by smoking but are often completely unaware of the psychosocial problems caused by smoking. Smoking actually enhances anxiety and depression. Because anxiety and depression are probably the symptoms most frequently reported to mental health professionals, information on the exacerbation of these symptoms from smoking can be invaluable in establishing a reason to stop smoking. Additionally, smoking damages self-esteem, is increasingly socially deviant, places an individual at risk for use of other substances of abuse, discourages effective coping with stress, and is associated with various types of accidental injury.

Smokers are sometimes curious about what it is in cigarettes that damages one's health, and they may be under the misconception that nicotine is the offending substance. It turns out that chemicals other than nicotine are responsible for much of the damage. There are over 4,000 known compounds in tobacco smoke, some of which are known carcinogenic agents or otherwise toxic.

In addition to helping the individual understand the dangers of smoking, it is also helpful to provide hope: Stopping smoking has many benefits. All smokers profit from cessation; individuals who have not yet developed a serious illness will experience reduced risk of doing so, and those already symptomatic can derive the benefit of arrested progress of the disease.

2

PSYCHOLOGICAL PROCESSES
AND SMOKING

Smoking is a complex behavior with many possible determinants. This chapter reviews statistics regarding the prevalence of current smoking and the initiation of new smokers, which indicate that although decreased from decades ago, smoking remains a serious problem. Factors associated with the initiation, progression, and maintenance of use are discussed. Psychological processes that support smoking, particularly the defense of denial and ineffective coping, are highlighted. It is hoped that the clinician will gain a better understanding of the internal and external factors that contribute to smoking behavior and be better able to address them in treatment.

OVERVIEW

Chapter 1 reviewed the evidence of the deleterious effects cigarette smoking has on humans. I purposely used findings from the surgeon general's initial report (USDHEW, 1964) as the starting point to emphasize the fact that high-quality, scientifically derived evidence has been available for over 35 years. The evidence has mounted and only gotten stronger since then. Although there are many people who may not know the full extent and details of the harmful effects of smoking, few are completely unaware of the dangers inherent in smoking. Discussion of the risks of tobacco use is a standard component of health classes and Drug Abuse Resistance Education (DARE) programs in schools. Because of the widespread availability of this information, personal denial is necessary to support smoking. Without the psychological defense of denial, smoking would be, from the standpoint of the smoker, a naked act of self-destruction. Unfortunately, personal denial has been buttressed on other levels. Despite the enormity and seriousness of the smoking problem in the United States, tobacco companies, government programs, and even health care professionals have acted in ways that appear to have minimized the problem for many years. This culturewide denial is not only shameful but supports the denial of individual smokers. In addition to the psychological defense of denial, more conscious coping mechanisms appear to be involved with cigarette smoking. To the extent that smoking represents an attempt to cope with stress, maladaptive as it is, coping strategies are of interest to clinicians attempting to assist smokers to stop. By helping smokers to develop more effective coping strategies, they may render smoking unnecessary as a technique of stress management.

Ultimately, smoking decisions (to start or not, to stop smoking once started, or to resume once discontinued) are personal and individual, and psychological processes influencing these decisions, such as defense mechanisms and coping strategies, must be discussed. Although the consideration of risk factors for cigarette smoking is extremely important, particularly for prevention efforts, we know that relatively static risk factors (e.g., socioeconomic status, parents' smoking status) alone cannot tell us why only certain at-risk individuals actually become smokers. Furthermore, regarding the potential for treatment, individual cognitive and emotional factors are potentially changeable, whereas some risk factors are not.

PREVALENCE OF CIGARETTE USE

One of the more disturbing facts about cigarette smoking is that despite all of the published information that is available in the United States, smoking continues for many adults, and there are new adolescent smokers every day. The prevalence of adult cigarette smoking showed a trend of steady increase from the early 1900s until the mid-1960s. The surgeon general's initial report (USDHEW, 1964) is credited with facilitating health concerns and a downward pattern in smoking. For example, prevalence of smoking among adults was 40% in 1965 and 29% in 1987 (USDHHS, 1989). An American Cancer Society fact sheet reported that 22.9% of U.S. adults smoked in 1998 (representing approximately 48 million Americans).

Bukstein (1995) reviewed trends in adolescent smoking (as well as use of other substances not relevant to the present discussion), using as a primary source of information the National High School Senior Survey (NSS, also known as the Monitoring the Future Survey). The NSS is an assessment sponsored by the National Institute of Drug Abuse that was started in 1975 and is conducted annually. Different levels of substance use are assessed by the NSS, including (a) lifetime prevalence (i.e., the percentage of students who ever used a specific substance), (b) 30-day prevalence (i.e., the percentage of students who used a specific substance in the last 30 days), and (c) prevalence of daily use (i.e., the percentage of students who used a specific substance on a daily basis in the 30 days prior to the survey). Before reviewing prevalence statistics, it bears mentioning that a notable limitation of the NSS is that the assessment is conducted with students who are present in school to complete the survey. School dropouts, for example, are excluded from the survey, and they are known to have extremely high smoking rates relative to those who remain in school (Wang, Fitzhugh, Eddy, & Westerfield, 1998).

Smoking, overall, decreased from 1975 to 1993 on all three levels of use measured by the NSS: (a) lifetime prevalence in 1975 was 73.6%; in 1993, 61.9%; (b) monthly prevalence in 1975 was 36.7%; in 1993, 29.4%; (c) daily use prevalence in 1975 was 26.9%; in 1993, 19.0%. From a public health standpoint, although encouraging because numbers were moving in a positive direction, prevalence rates were still unacceptably high. To make matters worse, there was a reversal through the 1990s such that an overall increase in cigarette smoking was observed in high school students (Centers for Disease Control and Prevention [CDC], 2000). The CDC analyzed data from the National Youth Risk Behavior Survey (YRBS). The biennial survey assesses health risk behaviors of U.S. students in grades 9 through 12. Levels of use assessed are similar to those described in the NSS: (a) *lifetime smoking* was defined as the percentage of students who had ever smoked; (b) *current smoking* was defined as the percentage of students who had smoked in the 30 days preceding the survey; and (c) *frequent smoking* was defined as the percentage of students who had smoked 20 or more of the 30 days preceding the survey. The prevalence numbers of the YRBS are not exactly comparable to the NSS because of the inclusion of younger adolescents than the senior-only NSS. Results from the YRBS were as follows: (a) lifetime prevalence was stable from 1991 to 1999 at 70.4%; (b) current smoking went up significantly, from 27.5% in 1991 to 34.8% in 1999; and (c) prevalence of frequent smoking also rose significantly, from 12.7% in 1991 to 16.8% in 1999.

INITIATION, PROGRESSION, AND MAINTENANCE OF CIGARETTE USE

As the prevalence statistics above demonstrate, cigarette use overall has dropped considerably since the mid-1960s. Education has had a very positive impact. However, smoking has not disappeared, so there must be factors at play other than the ignorance of smokers. It would be naive of anyone to think that education alone could single-handedly eradicate the problem, because smoking, like other addictions, is a complex, multiply determined behavior. Substance use typically begins in adolescence. Use of substances has been linked to developmental processes (Bukstein, 1995). Substance use may for some adolescents facilitate identification with peers, independence from authority, and autonomy, and allow for experimentation with adult roles. Many risk factors for use and abuse of psychoactive substances have been identified. For example, Bukstein summarized research on adolescent risk factors for use and abuse of substances and identified 38 factors. The factors were grouped into five categories and are presented here.

1. *Peer factors* associated with substance use are peer substance use and strong attachment to peers.
2. *Parental or family factors* such as parental substance use and tolerance of adolescent substance use are some of the variables associated with substance use in this category.
3. *Individual factors* such as poor impulse control, low self-esteem, poor coping skills, poor academic performance, anxiety, depression, and antisocial personality are examples of factors associated with substance use.
4. *Biological factors* include inherited dispositions to substance use.
5. *Community/social/cultural factors* include low socioeconomic status, deviant norms condoning the use of substances, and high unemployment.

The relative influence of a specific risk factor is thought to vary depending on the stage of use (Bukstein, 1995). For example, a stage model has been developed illustrating that the degree of substance dependence is a function of different factors (Leeds & Morgenstern, 1996). Experimentation and nonproblematic use of substances are a function of more external cultural and social factors (Factors 1, 2, and 5, above). More internal, psychological problems and ego deficits appear to underlie progression to mild dependence (Factor 3 above). Further movement to moderate to severe levels of dependence results from biobehavioral processes such as classical and operant conditioning, alteration in functioning of brain centers for pleasure and pain, neurotransmitter changes, withdrawal states, and drug cravings (Leeds & Morgenstern, 1996).

The preceding discussion of risk factors and the stage model of progression of substance use provides some basis for understanding the addictive process in general. Risk factors specific to the initiation of cigarette smoking, as opposed to all substances, have also been identified (USDHHS, 1994) and are summarized in Exhibit 2.1.

A stage model of child and adolescent use has been described that is specific to cigarette smoking (Flay, 1993). The stages are presented and

EXHIBIT 2.1
Factors Associated With the Initiation of Smoking

Sociodemographic factors

- Socioeconomic status (SES). Low SES predicts initiation of cigarette smoking.
- Parental education. Less formal education of parents has a weak relationship to initiation of smoking.
- Number of parents living in the home. Children in single-parent homes are more likely to start smoking.
- Developmental stage of adolescence. Ages 11–15 are high-risk for initiation of smoking.

Environmental factors

- Availability and acceptance of cigarettes. Communities that allow tobacco advertising and do not restrict access to cigarettes (e.g., by allowing access to cigarette machines) encourage the initiation of smoking.
- Interpersonal factors. Parental smoking is an inconsistent predictor of smoking; older sibling smoking increases the risk of smoking; peer smoking is a very important risk factor (perhaps the single most important factor, especially if the bond with peers is strong).
- Perceived environmental factors. Adolescents who smoke overestimate the prevalence of smoking; those who perceive that peers approve of their smoking are more likely to smoke. Adolescent perceptions that parents are generally unsupportive and/or indifferent to their smoking are more likely to smoke.

Behavioral factors

- Academic achievement. Poor academic performance is associated with smoking.
- Risk-taking and rebellious behaviors are associated with smoking.
- Refusal skills. Inability to resist pressure to smoke is associated with smoking.

Personal factors

- Knowledge of long-term health consequences appears to have no significant effect to deter smoking.
- Functional meaning. Adolescents who perceive benefits from smoking (e.g., helps manage feelings, peer identification) are more likely to smoke.
- Self-esteem. Low self-esteem is associated with smoking.
- Self-efficacy. Perceived ability to resist offers to smoke is negatively associated with use.
- Psychological well-being. Depression is associated with smoking.
- Smoking as a risk factor. Those adolescents already smoking are at risk to progress in their use. Those adolescents who intend to smoke are likely to smoke.

Note. Adapted from *Preventing Tobacco Use Among Young People: A Report of the Surgeon General* (p. 123), by the U.S. Department of Health and Human Services, 1994, Atlanta, GA: Author. In the public domain.

described, and psychosocial factors particularly relevant to a given stage are also mentioned (discussed in USDHHS, 1994). The five stages are the preparatory stage, trying stage, experimental stage, regular use, and nicotine dependence. The preparatory stage is the earliest stage of the smoking model, at which there may not even be any smoking behavior yet. During this stage attitudes and beliefs about smoking are formed, and the child or adolescent may consider the positive functions of smoking. Psychosocial risk factors yielding the most influence at this stage are tobacco advertisements and role models (adults or older siblings) who smoke.

In the trying stage, actual smoking behavior has occurred, although only a few times. Social reinforcement is important in shaping the perception of the smoking experience and in encouraging further use. Peer use, the misperception that smoking is normative, and availability of cigarettes are important factors at this point in the process. Repeated smoking, although not in a regular pattern of use, takes place in the experimental stage. Use is characterized as episodic and tends to be connected either to a particular person (e.g., boyfriend or girlfriend, or close friend who smokes) or a particular situation (e.g., a party). Social situations in which smoking takes place, smoking peers, low self-efficacy to resist peer pressure, and availability of cigarettes are relevant risk factors for this stage of smoking.

In the regular use stage, a more stable pattern of smoking occurs that is generalized across situations and people and happens at least weekly. Factors influencing smoking at this stage include having peers who smoke, the perception that smoking serves positive functions (e.g., reduces stress, strengthens bonds with peers), and few restrictions on smoking in school, at home, and in community settings.

Nicotine dependence and/or addiction is the final stage of the smoking model. At this stage the criteria for dependence are met. Tolerance, an inability to stop, withdrawal when cessation is attempted, and a compulsion to use are observed.

The average length of time from initial try to regular use is approximately 2 to 3 years (USDHHS, 1994). An alarming finding by DiFranza et al. (2002) is that nicotine dependence can develop well before regular use in adolescents. Symptoms of dependence can be seen after an adolescent has smoked only a few times. The authors concluded that adolescents are more vulnerable to nicotine dependence than adults, potentially becoming dependent early on and at low levels of nicotine exposure.

Documentation of the natural history of any condition is important for a variety of reasons, not the least of which is that it would be impossible to gauge the effectiveness of treatment without knowing how the untreated condition would naturally progress (Dodgen & Shea, 2000). Smoking behavior is stable over time, which is good news for nonsmokers and bad news for smokers (Chassin, Presson, Rose, & Sherman, 1996). Adolescent smokers tend to be adult smokers, even those who are only experimental smokers in adolescence. Smoking rarely starts after age 21, a finding with important implications for prevention efforts. It is also important to note that smoking behavior does not follow a course typical of other substances of abuse. The use of substances usually rises from adolescence into young adulthood, then declines in the mid-20s. Cigarette use also rises into early adulthood but does not show the decline seen with other substance use. Several factors may account for the unusual persistence of smoking behavior (Chassin et al., 1996): (a) tobacco use is legal; (b) health consequences are not experienced until later in life; (c) the pharmacological effects of tobacco do not impair daily functioning like other substances, so the ability to meet the demands of adult life is not obviously disturbed by smoking and pressure to stop is low compared with alcohol and other substances; and (d) nicotine has a strong addictive power.

MISPERCEPTIONS OF SMOKERS

Identifying the many correlates of smoking initiation clarifies why knowledge of health statistics alone is insufficient to prevent smoking. There are many potential influences and variables that need to be considered when attempting to account for the smoking decisions and behavior of any individual. In fact, perceptions of the health statistics themselves vary, depending on smoking status: It has been convincingly demonstrated that smokers and nonsmokers perceive risk of harm from smoking very differently. When compared with nonsmokers, adult smokers underestimated the risks of lung cancer, heart disease, and noncancerous chronic lung disease from smoking (Lee, 1989). Adult smokers were found to underestimate the personal risk of cancer or heart disease from smoking (Ayanian & Cleary, 1999). Furthermore, smokers perceived their own risks as smaller than those for the "average smoker," further minimizing their personal risks. A significant positive relationship between the number of cigarettes smoked and the likelihood of distortion or denial of the health hazards of smoking has been identified (Dawley, Fleischer, & Dawley, 1985).

Weinstein's (1999) excellent review article addressed the topic of risk comprehension with specific reference to cigarette smoking. In general, the assumption that underlies education efforts is that awareness of health statistics will allow people to make an informed decision about risks they should accept and those they should not accept or at least reduce. Other factors than knowledge of potential harm play an important role in decision making, such as emotions, personal values, social influences, environmental barriers, and economic constraints. Someone who is informed of risks may still choose an ill-advised behavior because of the influence of one or more of these other factors. Although for the individual knowledge of risks is not sufficient to determine his or her behavior, it is necessary to be armed with facts to effectively guide behavior.

People make decisions on health-related matters all the time; implicitly they are making risk evaluations. For example, they routinely make choices regarding diet, exercise, rest, use of alcohol or other drugs, management of stress, hygiene, and so forth. Yet, in making these choices people are not in possession of all available information relevant to making a fully informed decision. Therefore, the average person must have some way to evaluate risk in the absence of complete and accurate information. Weinstein (1999) suggested that there are three types of information (which he refers to as *risk dimensions*) that are minimally necessary for an individual to comprehend the risks of any behavior and to make a reasonably informed decision, in the absence of comprehensive data. The risk dimensions and relevant findings are discussed below with respect to smoking.

1. *Severity of potential harm.* Although the majority of people can report a vague appreciation of the fact that cigarettes are bad for health, they are much less able to identify specific ailments resulting from cigarette use. Furthermore, even if someone is aware of a particular disease or condition that may result from smoking, he or she may not appreciate such things as the poor cure rates, the ways in which smoking-related illnesses limit people's lives, and the aversiveness of many treatments. Adolescents are known to underestimate the harm from smoking compared with adults, which helps to account for their high-risk status.

2. *Estimation of the probability of harm.* Most health statistics on smoking are presented in terms of odds and percentages. Although these statistics are precise, it has been demonstrated that lay people have a very poor understanding of them and so may not be able to use the information in making decisions. For example, Weinstein (1999) reviewed research demonstrating that people rated cancer as posing a greater risk when it was described as killing 1,286 out of 10,000 people than when described as killing 24.14 out of 100 people. Or, when people were asked to estimate the risk of dying from three smoking-related illnesses, the total chance of dying typically exceeded 100%. Risk estimation, therefore, is far from objective and may reflect personal needs more than accurate mathematics. It is well-known that smokers estimate their personal risk below the risk of harm to other smokers, so that risk assessment for smokers appears to reflect more of an attempt to minimize personal vulnerability than to offer an objective appraisal.

3. *Difficulty of avoiding harmful consequences.* If people are aware of potential negative consequences and appreciate the difficulty in avoiding harm, this knowledge may serve as a barrier to initial use. With regard to smoking and the extreme difficulty of stopping, nonsmokers should be disinclined to start smoking. Unfortunately, but predictably, adolescents underestimate the chances of getting addicted and overestimate the ease of

stopping. For example, Colby et al. (1998) reported that very few high school students who are daily smokers (5%) expect to be smoking 5 years after graduation when, in fact, the majority (75%) will still be smoking.

A major implication of Weinstein's (1999) article is that a simplistic, unidimensional view of risk comprehension is inadequate. That is, it is not sufficient to inquire whether an individual is aware that smoking is bad for him or her. A clinician would be well advised to evaluate an individual on all three risk dimensions to be able to more specifically address missing information, inaccuracies, and distortions. People have a limited understanding of risk, so it is important to identify more precisely what they do and do not know about smoking.

DENIAL

The studies discussed above, which reveal that smokers underestimate the risks of smoking in general and, further, minimize their personal risks relative to other smokers, demonstrate that the impact of important information is being neutralized in the minds of smokers. This process of neutralization may be said to be evidence of defensive operation, specifically denial. Clinicians who work with substance abuse of any type are aware that the defense of denial is involved. It is necessary to understand more than the simple fact that denial is present, however, to appreciate its role in cigarette smoking and possible implications for treatment.

The topic of psychological defenses has been somewhat controversial outside of psychoanalysis. Cramer's (1991) review of the history of psychological defenses identified Sigmund Freud as the first to popularize the concept. Defenses were originally conceived as mental counterforces to the expression of instinctual drives. Anna Freud later expanded the concept to include the management of anxiety and guilt stemming from both internal (instinctual) and external sources. There have been many psychological defenses described in the literature. Laughlin (1983) identified 22 major (or primary) defenses and 26 minor (or secondary) defenses. The reader is referred to Laughlin (1983) and Cramer (1991) for more in-depth discussion of psychological defenses and their development and operation.

Despite the fact that the study of psychological defenses had diminished greatly in academic psychology by the end of the 1970s (primarily due to a rejection of the idea of unconscious cognition), it has been observed that many defense mechanisms are enjoying much clinical and research attention from cognitive and social psychologists, albeit under different names (Cramer, 2000; Vaillant, 2000). For example, the psychological defenses of projection, displacement, and denial have been investigated recently as the constructs attribution, scapegoating, and positive illusions (Cramer, 2000), respectively. It is now widely accepted that unconscious memories and thoughts exist that may influence conscious memory and behavior. Defense mechanisms are said to be unconscious processes used for various purposes: to resolve emotional conflict, to provide relief from emotional tension, to avoid or quell anxiety, to cope with consciously intolerable situations (Laughlin, 1983), and to protect other mental (ego) functions from the disorganizing and disruptive effects of excessive negative affect such as anxiety and guilt (Cramer, 1991). In other words, psychological defenses help to protect the smooth functioning of the mind, reduce cognitive dissonance, and maintain the emotional equanimity of the individual by resolving or reducing conflict that would otherwise generate much disruptive affect; this is accomplished outside of the awareness of the individual. Vaillant (2000) described defenses succinctly as automatic processes that reduce subjective distress by altering perceptions of internal and external reality. Defenses protect people from sudden changes in internal (affect, self-image, conscience) and external (relationships, reality) circumstances.

The psychological defense of denial has been defined as a primitive disavowal or negation (Laughlin, 1983). Denial is used to alter aspects of reality that would be disturbing if made conscious, as compared with the defense of primary repression, which protects the mind from potentially disturbing internal–instinctual processes (Cramer, 1991). Denial has been discussed developmentally from two distinct perspectives, horizontal and vertical (Cramer, 1991). From the vertical standpoint, defenses can be hierarchically ordered with respect to theoretical constructs such as degree of complexity or distortion of reality. Vaillant (1977), for example, categorized defenses hierarchically with respect to level of maturity or immaturity. Immature defenses, such as denial, are said to be more characteristic of early development; more mature defenses, such as sublimation, are thought to develop later. The use of immature defenses is associated with psychopathology, and mature defenses with psychological health and resiliency in adults.

The *horizontal perspective* refers to the chronological ordering of defenses. The study of children has revealed that denial as a defense is used early in childhood, and its use decreases with age as other defenses become more prominent (e.g., projection and identification, respectively). The use of denial is associated with childhood, immaturity (of ego development), and primitivity. The horizontal (longitudinal) study of defenses also allows for the study of specific defenses over time; defenses do not remain static, and each appears to have its own developmental course. It must be noted that with time, and ego and cognitive development, less severe forms of denial may be observed. It should be taken for granted that denial is present in cases of substance abuse; in most cases, however, this does not refer to a total disavowal of reality. This is particularly so in cases of tobacco dependence. Except for the rare case of a psychotic individual, smokers do not deny basic realities such as the obvious fact that they smoke. How, then, is denial operating in the typical case? Forms that denial may take are the physical or psychological withdrawal from painful situations, resulting in the ignoring of reality (as opposed to claiming reality does not exist, as in the more primitive form of denial). In addition, denial can be seen in the misperception or misinterpretation of the meaning of events. In other words, denial may be used to not perceive at all (primitive negation), to perceive but ignore, or to distort what is perceived. Research that reveals smokers' avoidance of information that relates smoking to health and their underestimation of risks from smoking is evidence of the less primitive forms of denial. Denial, then, is not a simple all-or-nothing process. In fact, in a summary discussion of denial, Lazarus and Folkman (1984) identified seven different types of denial: (a) denial of information, (b) threatening information, (c) personal relevance, (d) urgency, (e) vulnerability–responsibility, (f) affect, and (g) affect relevance.

It would be a mistake to automatically equate denial with psychopathology (Cramer, 1991; Lazarus & Folkman, 1984). Denial is normal under some circumstances, in which (a) external reality is overwhelming and cannot be changed (e.g., carrying on with life as if real catastrophic events such as acts of terrorism do not exist) and (b) the person, because of chronological immaturity, has no ability to modify the situation (e.g., a child living in severe poverty). The use of denial in these situations can alleviate distress when nothing constructive can be done to change the circumstances. Even in situations that may be altered, use of denial early on may help with the adjustment to difficult circumstances and allow for a phasing in of reality, rather than an abrupt and overwhelming transition (e.g., with the loss of a job, sudden illness, or other crisis situations).

There is another aspect of denial that is much less discussed than the alteration of perception of reality—the replacement of negative aspects of reality with positive ones. This is referred to as the construction of a personal fantasy (Cramer, 1991); the fantasy is constructed to take the place of an unpleasant reality. This aspect of denial is reflected in the perceptions of smokers, who not only downplay the risks of smoking, but also see positive functions and images resulting from cigarette use, such as being "cool," belonging to a desired group, and looking rugged and sexy. Tobacco companies make full use of these positive fantasies in their advertising, constructing images that serve as rivals and replacements for the more realistic view of cigarettes as "cancer sticks."

A problem with denial as it relates to smoking is that it is often used on a long-term basis with situations that may be altered. Denial blocks an individual from seeking other means to feel independent, to manage feelings, to look mature, or to fulfill whatever other functions the smoking serves for a given individual. Denial handicaps efforts not only to stop the smoking itself (it is difficult to treat a problem that someone feels is not a problem) but to address other deficient coping skills that the smoking is used to compensate for.

It is unfortunate, but true, that the denial of individuals has received strong external support from various sources, some expected, others quite surprising. That tobacco companies would attempt to deny the dangers of tobacco use is obvious; support of denial by the government, physicians, and mental health and recovery specialists is unexpected. Tobacco companies generate tremendous income from the sale of their products in the United States. For example, in 1996 it was estimated that the approximately 45 million U.S. tobacco users generated approximately $55 billion in annual sales (Gibson, 1997). Gibson raised a key question: How can tobacco companies continue to sell products when the products are proven to be lethal when used? There appear to be several explanations: (a) strong protobacco constituencies in the American South where tobacco is grown, (b) financial support of members of Congress by tobacco companies, (c) employment of protobacco lobbyists in Washington, and (d) effective public relations use of a strategy of denying health dangers.

Pollay (1997) described the denial tactics of the tobacco industry, which were initiated in the 1950s and originally used to attack medical studies documenting the link between smoking and lung cancer. The goal of such attacks is to create a perception of doubt and controversy over the medical findings that provides a basis to quell public concern and legislative action; the use of these counterarguments is also to provide a rationale for those individuals already inclined to smoke to challenge the medical findings. Since the 1950s this strategy of denial and of undermining the perceived validity of medical research has been used to challenge the findings concerning smoking and heart disease, dangers of secondhand smoke, nicotine addiction, the social costs of smoking, and the effects of advertising in the enticement of new (adolescent) smokers.

Tobacco companies rely very much on the recruitment of new smokers, and adolescents are very attractive as prospective smokers: They demonstrate tremendous brand loyalty, and being young and healthy, they have many years of smoking ahead of them (Pollay, 1997). Cigarette advertising imagery appeals to themes important to adolescents: independence, acceptance, sex appeal. Adolescents are generally more susceptible to the persuasion attempts of advertisers than are adults, who have more experience with their tactics. In general, the presence of cigarette advertisements creates a sense of familiarity, safety, prevalence, and acceptability that contributes to the perception that smoking is more common than it actually is. An interesting and clever example of "fighting fire with fire" with respect to tobacco companies is seen in Florida. In the state, an antitobacco marketing campaign has been instituted, referred to as the "Truth" campaign (Farrelly et al., 2002; Zucker et al., 2000). The program uses marketing techniques that have been effectively employed by tobacco companies for years. Whereas the marketing efforts of tobacco companies target youth and hide the addictiveness and negative health effects of smoking, the message of the "Truth" campaign (delivered via trendy television and print advertisements, T-shirts, stickers, a Web site, and more) is to expose the lies and manipulation of profit-driven adults in tobacco companies who are exploiting youth for their own gain. Research is finding that the campaign has been effective in changing adolescent attitudes about smoking (i.e., increasing antitobacco attitudes) and influencing behavior (i.e., reducing smoking; Niederdeppe, Farrelly, & Haviland., 2004).

The government's mixed attitude toward tobacco also helps to support individual denial. For starters, its designation of this deadly product as legal at all represents a message of approval of use. In addition, the subsidization of tobacco farming is a further show of support. Not all consumers are aware of the federal government's financial support of tobacco companies, but many are. One general public survey found that 55% of respondents thought that U.S. taxpayers subsidized tobacco farmers (Altman, Levine, Howard, & Hamilton, 1997). In contrast to the support for tobacco use demonstrated by deeming its use legal and subsidizing the growth of tobacco, the U.S. government has spent millions of dollars documenting the negative consequences of cigarette smoking and promoting treatment and prevention efforts, sending a conflicting, confusing message to the public.

Physicians may be accused of reinforcing denial by individual smokers when they neglect to address the matter as a medical concern. Patients can easily get the impression that if the one person entrusted to safeguard their health is not saying anything about their smoking, then maybe it is not all that bad. A minority of smokers are offered assistance to stop smoking by their physicians. One population-based survey reported that fewer than 15% of smokers were offered help in quitting smoking by their physician; only 3% had had a follow-up appointment to address the matter; and fewer still had received specific smoking-cessation advice (USDHHS, 2000a). Similarly, another study reported that smoking status had been assessed in only about 67% of clinic visits, and only 21% of smokers had received smoking-cessation counseling during clinic visits (USDHHS, 2000a). Reasons identified for the underidentification and undertreatment of tobacco use by medical practitioners are (a) inability of many clinicians to quickly and easily identify smokers, (b) lack of awareness by clinicians of effective treatments and how to apply them, (c) time constraints on clinicians, and (d) inadequate institutional support for routine assessment and treatment of tobacco use.

In addition, physicians may not be as comfortable working with chronic disorders requiring lifestyle changes as they are with acute illnesses. Cocores (1993), a psychiatrist, has suggested that physicians in general do not receive sufficient training in the assessment and treatment of substance use disorders, particularly with regard to nicotine. Perhaps even more troubling, he opined, is that psychiatric training at many levels (medical schools, psychiatric residency training programs, hospitals and clinics, publications, etc.) is lacking in the area of tobacco use, so psychiatrists do not receive adequate preparation for the assessment and treatment of nicotine dependence, despite the fact that the majority of their patients are smokers.

Cocores (1993) also noted that psychiatrists are not immune to denial about nicotine themselves, despite their professional training. Psychiatrists, like anyone else, can become addicted to nicotine. Naturally, this personal denial would affect one's attitude about a patient's use of nicotine, most likely in the direction of acceptance of it. I think it is fair to say that these observations about psychiatrists also apply to other health care and mental health professionals.

Professionals who treat addictive disorders have not been innocent regarding the reinforcement of denial about smoking. As an example, during the late 1980s and early 1990s, I worked on an adult inpatient substance abuse treatment unit in a private psychiatric facility. During this time, there was an attitude among the multidisciplinary treatment staff that to challenge nicotine dependence while treating other addictions was ill advised. The thinking was that the addiction to alcohol or other substances had brought the person to treatment, and this should be the focus of treatment. To attempt to also treat the nicotine addiction was thought to distract from the more immediate and serious problems. It was assumed that stripping persons of cigarettes at such a time would deprive them of a tried-and-true coping method and overwhelm them with stress at a time when they were already being asked to surrender other chemical aids to coping. It was like saying, "Cigarettes will kill them in 30 years, cocaine (alcohol, etc.) could kill them now." The staff comprised professionals of several disciplines, including nursing, psychology, psychiatry, social work, and substance abuse counseling, and this attitude was pervasive and not peculiar to any particular type of training. That our facility was not alone in this type of thinking was verified in discussion with clinicians in other inpatient and outpatient substance abuse treatment programs. One needs only to go to an Alcoholics Anonymous (AA) or Narcotics Anonymous (NA) meeting and see clouds of smoke above the attendees to see that even these fellowships have an attitude of acceptance of nicotine use (not to mention caffeine).

The inclination to delay the treatment of nicotine was a classic case of a reasonable idea guiding treatment without sufficient empirical support. As we have now learned, and as is discussed more fully in chapter 9, in most cases it is best to treat nicotine addiction simultaneously with the treatment of other substances.

COPING

When discussing psychological defensive processes (such as denial, discussed above), the topic of coping is also relevant. Because both psychological defenses and coping processes are thought to reduce stress and enhance adaptation and well-being, there is some overlap between and confusion about the two (Miceli & Castelfranchi, 2001). Differences between defenses and coping processes have been identified (Cramer, 2000). Critical factors for differentiating defenses and coping processes include distinguishing whether the psychological processes are unconscious (defense) or conscious (coping), and whether they are unintentional (defense) or intentional (coping). Therefore, in order for an adaptive process to be considered a defense mechanism, it must be both unconscious and unintentional (Cramer, 2000). An additional criterion has been suggested (Miceli & Castelfranchi, 2001): whether mental representations are manipulated (defense) or revised (coping). Manipulation is considered to be an unconscious process driven by an unconscious goal of rejecting a given mental representation to avoid the experience of negative affect. Revision is thought to be driven by a conscious goal of rejecting a mental representation but also constrained by the limits of reality (i.e., the individual explicitly acknowledges that reality cannot be changed by will). Two other criteria, considered noncritical and more a matter of emphasis (Cramer, 2000), used to differentiate defenses and coping processes are that defenses tend to be dispositional and coping processes situation-specific and that defenses can be arranged on a hierarchical scale and coping processes cannot.

Lazarus and Folkman's (1984) seminal book on coping is an excellent resource on the fundamentals of coping theory. In their work, they define stress from a relational perspective (between the person and the environment), as opposed to prior definitions emphasizing the stimulus or a stereotyped response of the organism. Stimulus definitions typically focus on external, or environmental, events normatively thought to produce stress, such as illness, loss, significant life changes, and so forth. An example of a tool designed to measure stress from this perspective is the Holmes and Rae (1967) scale, which defines and measures stress in terms of the occurrence of life events. Selye's (1974) classic work in stress is an example of a response approach; his description of the general adaptation syndrome describes a generic state of stress of the organism in response to any noxious agent or circumstance. The relational definition of stress takes into account both the environment and the individual; this concept is directly and explicitly analogous to the medical concept that illness is the result of a vulnerable organism meeting with a pathogen. Psychological stress is defined as "a particular relationship between the person and environment that is appraised by the person as taxing or exceeding his or her resources and endangering his or her well-being" (Lazarus & Folkman, 1984, p. 19).

Appraisal, a cognitive evaluative process, is integral to the experience of stress (or lack of stress). A relational definition of stress, dependent on appraisal, helps explain individual differences in the subjective experience of stress. Two people may react very differently to what appears to be the same circumstance; for example, one person may find the loss of a job a devastating defeat and experience much stress, whereas another may see it as an opportunity or challenge and experience little stress (or maybe even positive feelings of excitement). Cognitive appraisal is thought of as a process of categorizing events in terms of personal well-being. A distinction is made between primary and secondary appraisal (Lazarus & Folkman, 1984). Primary appraisal has to do with a judgment as to whether the person is being harmed by or benefiting from a particular circumstance. Secondary appraisal, similar to the concept of self-efficacy, relates to a judgment about the ability to do anything about circumstances under consideration. Situations judged to be irrelevant or benign-positive are of little concern for coping purposes. However, an appraisal of stress occurs when a situation involves harm or loss, threat, or challenge, and thus requires coping.

Coping, which involves processes used to manage situations appraised as stressful, is described as "constantly changing cognitive and behavioral efforts to manage specific external and/or internal demands that are appraised as taxing or exceeding the resources of the person" (Lazarus & Folkman, 1984, p. 141). There are two general types of coping: problem-focused and emotion-focused. *Problem-focused coping* is directed at management of problems, similar to problem solving but more inclusive, involving such processes as defining a problem, generating alternative solutions, and weighing alternatives. *Emotion-focused coping* is directed at managing the emotional response to the stressors and reducing distress, including processes such as avoidance and minimization, selective attention, and finding positive value in negative events. Generally speaking, problem-focused efforts tend to be applied in situations judged to be alterable, whereas emotion-focused coping tends to be used when a situation is determined to be unalterable.

Stress and coping are important processes to discuss in relation to adolescent smoking. Adolescence is well-known to be a time of high stress, when coping skills are severely challenged by developmental demands. Psychologists have long held a view of adolescence as a time of "storm and stress" (Arnett, 1999), a period of development characterized by conflict with parents, mood instability, and risk behaviors. A study designed to empirically assess stress and smoking behavior of Canadian adolescents focused on life strain (i.e., an enduring type of stress as compared with episodic, acute stress stemming from major life events; Allison, Adlaf, & Mates, 1997). The adolescents in the study identified four primary areas of concern (listed in order of frequency): (a) school strain, which included worries about homework, school rules, and relationships with teachers; (b) family strain, which reflected concerns about relationships with parents, parental rules, and relationships with other family members; (c) social strain, whereby worries were noted about appearance, peer relationships, and lack of money; and

(d) aggression strain, reflecting concerns about racial tensions, gangs, and encounters with strangers.

It was further found in this cross-sectional investigation that the coping strategies used by these adolescents related to smoking behavior. Smoking was positively correlated with passive coping behaviors such as sleeping, eating, watching television, and listening to music. Smoking behavior was negatively correlated with active coping such as exercise, improvement of self, and religious activity. It is noted that the passive coping behaviors are distractive and avoidant strategies similar to emotion-focused coping: They are directed at regulating emotion and not solving problems or addressing the stressors.

Results similar to the ones noted directly above have been obtained in other studies investigating the relationship between coping strategies and cigarette smoking (Dugan, Lloyd, & Lucas, 1999; Naquin & Gilbert, 1996; Vollrath, 1998; Wills, 1986). In Naquin and Gilbert's cross-sectional evaluation of American college students, smokers were found to have a significantly higher score for emotion-oriented coping than nonsmokers or former smokers. Vollrath's cross-sectional study of Swiss university students found a relationship between level of smoking and coping behaviors. Heavy smokers (those consuming 20 or more cigarettes per day) showed significantly less problem-focused coping and more emotion-focused coping strategies compared with nonsmokers or light smokers.

A study by Wills (1986) used cross-sectional and longitudinal analyses of American adolescents in the seventh and eighth grades. Significant relationships were found between coping and smoking. A positive relationship was observed between smoking and several coping behaviors: (a) seeking peer support; (b) entertainment (i.e., socializing with friends); (c) aggression; and (d) distraction (e.g., ignoring the problem). A negative relationship was found between several other coping behaviors and smoking: (a) behavior coping (i.e., active information gathering and problem solving); (b) relaxation; and (c) emotional support from adults or peers. Results were consistent across cross-sectional and longitudinal analyses. Longitudinal measurements demonstrated that coping styles preceded smoking (and not the reverse), which strongly suggests that coping influenced smoking behavior and not vice versa.

Dugan et al. (1999) also used both cross-sectional and prospective techniques in their analysis of English adolescents. In cross-sectional analyses, smokers reported less use of problem-focused, and more use of emotion-focused, coping strategies compared with nonsmokers. The results of the longitudinal analyses showed that those adolescents who changed smoking status from nonsmoker to smoker (in the interim from baseline to 6-month follow-up) reported more frequent use of cathartic (emotion-focused) coping strategies. Also, those already smoking at baseline who increased smoking at follow-up were found to be more likely to use a cathartic coping style.

TREATMENT CONSIDERATIONS

The results reviewed in the sections above on denial and coping lead to suggestions for the treatment of nicotine dependence. Denial is not a monolithic mental process to be frontally assailed and cracked with general medical facts. The manifestations of denial must be assessed and attacked in their specifics for a given individual; denial must be addressed before treatment can proceed. Coping styles broadly characterized as emotion-focused predate and predispose individuals to smoking behavior. The teaching of more effective problem-focused coping appears a necessary component of treatment.

Given the existence of a large number of psychosocial correlates of smoking (discussed throughout this chapter), nicotine dependence remains difficult to fully explain. Clearly, explanatory and treatment models need to be comprehensive. Psychosocial models of nicotine dependence treatment derived from cognitive and social learning theories are prominent today (e.g., Bandura, 1997; Marlatt & Gordon, 1985). Marlatt's treatment model, primarily identified with relapse prevention, is discussed in detail in chapter 8. Bandura's cognitive social learning model (summarized in Abrams et al., 2003) includes Pavlovian and operant conditioning principles, as well as cognitive processes such as outcome expectancies, self-control, and self-efficacy. Essentially, smoking is regarded as a behavior that is learned, with contributions from all three types of learning (Pavlovian, operant, and vicarious or modeling). Internal or external cues act as signals to smoke, and the delivery of nicotine is reinforcing by either removing negative symptoms or generating positive experiences (or both). Self-control processes are relevant in that if smokers desire to stop, they must be able to evaluate their own behavior, set realistic and achievable goals, and correct or guide their behavior as necessary. Outcome expectancies are involved because positive expectations of smoking are associated with the act of smoking. Self-efficacy, the subjective sense of confidence someone has in his or her ability to perform a certain task or meet certain demands, is most important in the application of treatment principles. A perfectly good treatment plan may show poor results for individuals who do not possess the confidence that they can execute the plan. The setting of achievable goals and practical success in applying skills learned in treatment help to bolster self-efficacy.

In this model, treatment is conceived to promote unlearning of smoking by disrupting the processes maintaining the behavior and developing and supporting healthier alternative behaviors. Only a cursory review of the treatment interventions identified as valid in chapter 7 reveals the omnipresence of the social–cognitive learning model in the treatment of nicotine dependence. Rapid smoking and contingency contracting derive from operant conditioning; stimulus control is based on Pavlovian conditioning;

cognitive processes are apparent in coping and cognitive procedures (pledging, norm-referencing, and values clarification); and social support reflects the value of social influences.

SUMMARY

Despite widespread dissemination of information detailing the negative consequences of smoking, people continue to smoke and new smokers are starting each day. Clearly, there are forces at play that diminish the impact of this information, which might otherwise be expected to serve a larger deterrent value and incline more current smokers to stop. Sources external to the individual have been identified that can act to explicitly or covertly encourage smoking and to function as counterforces to the messages about the evils of smoking: promotional and advertising activities of the tobacco industry; the government's mixed attitude about the tobacco industry; and undertreatment of nicotine dependence by medical, mental health, and addiction professionals.

Internal factors that contribute to the neutralization of information about smoking include the psychological defense of denial and use of certain ineffective coping strategies to alter how a person feels rather than to change a situation. Denial may result in an individual ignoring or somehow distorting information so that he or she is less conflicted or disturbed about smoking behavior. One rarely discussed aspect of denial is the construction of a positive fantasy; positive images of smoking allow individuals to identify with the images and feel good about themselves. In treatment, the clinician does well to remember the ostensible positive function of denial from the smoker's perspective, which will contribute to the reluctance to give it up. The individual will need help finding other, more constructive means to bolster self-esteem, to feel independent, to belong to a group, and so forth. For this reason, a frontal assault on denial is usually not helpful. It is wise to inquire about smoking and how the smoker feels it helps him or her, to get at what will need to be provided for that individual in treatment.

Coping skills have been found to relate to smoking behavior, especially during adolescence, when smoking behavior is being established. More specifically, adolescents who smoke tend to prefer emotion-focused coping methods. The implication is that smokers would benefit more from active problem-focused coping. It is not surprising that problem-focused types of interventions are found to be efficacious in smoking cessation studies (see chap. 7). The cognitive–social learning model has had a heavy influence on the treatment of nicotine dependence. The model is sufficiently comprehensive to explain the psychosocial influences on smoking, and to suggest relevant treatment interventions.

3

PHARMACOLOGY OF NICOTINE

Because it is now known that nicotine is the major psychoactive substance responsible for addiction to cigarettes and other tobacco products (USDHHS, 1988), an understanding of the pharmacology of this drug is necessary. The aim of the present discussion is to provide information on nicotine that clinicians may need to know to assist smokers they are treating; readers interested in more in-depth discussion of the pharmacology of nicotine are referred elsewhere (e.g., Benowitz, 1998; Blum, 1984; Henningfield et al., 1993). Frequently asked questions that occur in the course of treatment have included, What is nicotine? What are its effects on the body and brain? How does nicotine do what it does to the body and brain? What creates pleasure from its use? What are the symptoms of withdrawal, what causes these symptoms, and how long do they last? These questions as well as the all-important question of how nicotine creates addiction are addressed in this chapter; in addition, the addiction issue is the central topic of chapter 4.

Nicotine is a powerful drug. Because nicotine is legal, its potency may be underestimated by some users in much the same way as that of alcohol. Many of my patients have made statements to the effect that cigarettes (or alcohol) must not be as powerful as illegal substances such as cocaine and heroin or they would not be legal. This is surely not the case. Cigarettes alone are responsible for much more damage than all of the illegal substances combined. Nicotine is a substance that has been thoroughly studied and whose properties and effects on humans are well established. It can be stated with certainty that nicotine is a strong drug that affects many systems of the body, including the nervous system, cardiovascular system, musculoskeletal system, and endocrine system; these manifold effects undergird and contribute to the behavior of cigarette smokers and to nicotine addiction (Benowitz, 1996; Murray, 1990). The potency of nicotine has been established empirically. Potency is a gauge of the strength of a substance determined by measuring the amount of a drug necessary to produce a specific effect; the less of a drug necessary to produce an effect, the more potent that drug is. Readers may be surprised to learn that, compared with cocaine and morphine, nicotine is 5 to 10 times more potent in producing psychoactive effects in humans (Kozlowski, Henningfield, & Brigham, 2001).

The nicotine found in cigarettes is a naturally occurring chemical in tobacco. American cigarettes are a blend of four different types of tobacco, with exact formulas depending on the brand; each type of tobacco is processed differently and has different characteristics (Slade, 1993). Cigarettes are highly refined products reflecting decades of research and development. Cigarettes are not organic products that are plucked from the source in usable form like a fruit or vegetable. In addition to the blending of different tobaccos, many additives are included to enhance flavor and sweetness, to adjust pH, to reduce harshness, to maintain moisture, and to regulate burning of the tobacco and cigarette paper (Slade, 1993). The government does not force disclosure of additives to cigarettes, for they are treated by the government as trade secrets.

What kind of a drug is nicotine, and how does it compare with other drugs of abuse? There are different ways to classify drugs for purposes of description and comparison; one of the more commonly used methods is by pharmacological effects on the central nervous system (CNS), with the classifications presented here (Blum, 1984):

1. Narcotic drugs include opioids such as opium and heroin.
2. CNS depressants are substances including alcohol, barbiturates, and benzodiazepines.
3. CNS stimulant drugs include amphetamines, cocaine, and caffeine.
4. Psychotomimetics (also referred to as hallucinogenic or psychedelic drugs) are cannabinoids, LSD, and mescaline.

It is interesting to note that in the classification system above, nicotine does not fit easily into a category. Depending on the dose, nicotine may be considered either a CNS stimulant or a CNS depressant. Nicotine is sometimes classified by itself because of its biphasic effects (Dodgen & Shea, 2000). At low doses of consumption, nicotine causes sympathetic nervous system arousal, with attendant increases in heart rate and blood pressure (CNS stimulation); at higher doses, nicotine produces the opposite responses of slowing the heart rate and lowering blood pressure (CNS depression; Benowitz, 1998).

Quite naturally, nicotine must enter the body before it can have any influence. When discussing the introduction of any substance to the body, we are really discussing how the substance enters into the bloodstream of the user, the circulatory system being the mechanism by which the substance is distributed throughout the body. The route of administration of a substance, as it is often called, has significant implications for short-term effects (e.g., intensity of the "high") and long-term consequences (e.g., disease risk, addiction liability). In the literature on nicotine, the term *nicotine delivery system* is commonly used (Slade, 1993). Nicotine may be delivered in a variety of ways: It may be absorbed through the highly vascularized membranes of the mouth (pipe, cigar, powder snuff), nose (powder snuff), or lungs (cigars, cigarettes); nicotine may also be absorbed through the skin (nicotine patch). Nicotine is an alkaloid substance with a pH of 8.0; because of the pH of the mouth (approximately 7.0), nicotine is not easily absorbed there (Benowitz, 1998). Tobacco products used for oral absorption add substances (and use certain tobaccos) to raise the pH of the mouth to increase absorption. Tobaccos used in making cigarettes have an acidic pH of around 5.5; little is absorbed in the mouth, but the relatively large surfaces of the lungs allow for easy absorption despite the pH level of the substance. The form of delivery greatly influences the acute effects as well as abuse liability of nicotine. Inhaled nicotine from cigarettes gets into the bloodstream, and consequently to the brain, much faster than nicotine administered through the other methods; cigarette smoke delivers a more intense, more rapid, and briefer rush of drug to the brain. With nicotine, as with other drugs of abuse, users tend to prefer the more immediate and powerful rush of a drug to slower, more subtle effects. For example, cocaine users may have a long history of fairly casual, nonproblematic use when consuming the drug intranasally (IN). However, once it is smoked in the freebase form, or "crack" preparation, they lose complete control of their use, with very dire consequences: spending huge amounts of money, disappearing from work or home, engaging in ill-advised or even illegal behavior to get more money or drugs, and so forth. It is still the same drug, but when it is consumed through smoke inhalation, the high is more intense and appealing, withdrawal more aversive, and the desire to continue to consume much stronger. It is no surprise that cigarettes represent 95% of tobacco products consumed in the United States (Slade, 1993). Empirical studies confirm clinical observations that higher doses of drugs delivered more rapidly are both more appealing and more addictive to users (Henningfield & Keenan, 1993).

The course that nicotine takes when delivered through cigarettes is as follows (Kozlowski et al., 2001): Nicotine is vaporized through the burning process and is inhaled in smoke into the lungs, where it is absorbed into the bloodstream. From the lungs it goes to the left ventricle of the heart and is carried via arteries throughout the body. Because of its small molecular size and high solubility, nicotine passes easily through the protective blood–brain barrier. It takes only 7 to 10 seconds from inhalation to entrance to the brain; nicotine levels rise and fall rapidly so that despite the development of tolerance, resensitization to the effects of nicotine allows for the experience of some pleasurable effects even with successive cigarettes (Benowitz, 1996).

The elimination half-life of nicotine is approximately 1 to 4 hours, with significant individual variation (Benowitz, 1996). Half-life measures a substance's duration of action. Literally it refers to the time required to eliminate half the amount of a substance from the body (Johanson, 1992). Therefore, the longer the half-life, the longer the body takes to eliminate the drug, and the longer the duration of action. Substances with a shorter half-life are associated with a more intense high and higher abuse potential. With nicotine's average half-life of approximately 2 hours, and regular smoking throughout the day, typical smoking patterns result in an accumulation of nicotine in the system so that some amount of the drug is maintained all day even though smoking is not continuous (Benowitz, 1998; Henningfield et al., 1993).

Nicotine is metabolized primarily in the liver, with a small percentage metabolized by the lungs; some nicotine is urinated unchanged (Benowitz, 1998; Henningfield et al., 1993; Kozlowski et al., 2001). Nicotine is metabolized to nicotine oxide (4%) and cotinine (70%–80%; Benowitz, 1998; Slade, 1993). Cotinine has a very long half-life of approximately 16 to 20 hours, which makes it an excellent marker for detection of cigarette smoking.

A cigarette contains about 8 to 10 mg of nicotine (Henningfield et al., 1993; Kozlowski et al., 2001), although the smoker typically only receives 1 to 2 mg of nicotine per cigarette, with the remainder lost in smoke or trapped in the cigarette butt. It is recognized that the dose of nicotine actually delivered to the smoker cannot be determined simply by the nicotine content of a given cigarette. Smoking behavior is variable, and the nicotine yield from a cigarette depends to a large extent on individual smoking characteristics (Benowitz, 1998). Variables that have been identified include (a) puff volume, (b) depth of inhalation, (c) amount of dilution with air in the room, (d) rate of puffing, and (e) plugging of ventilation holes in the cigarette butt, which increases nicotine intake. Therefore, knowing the number of cigarettes smoked and the nicotine content of a given cigarette brand does not tell us precisely how much nicotine a person is taking in; to know for certain, blood tests would have to be given. For this reason, the levels of tar and nicotine in a specific cigarette may be irrelevant for determining the actual amounts of chemicals consumed and the health impact of smoking. Tobacco companies have marketed low-tar and low-nicotine cigarettes as healthier alternatives to high-tar and high-nicotine brands. Smokers have been shown to maintain very consistent blood levels of nicotine from day to day; in studies in which nicotine levels of cigarettes have been lowered without the awareness of the smoker, compensatory smoking behaviors have been observed to increase blood nicotine levels (Slade, 1993). For example, smokers may increase puff duration, puff volume, or puff frequency to increase nicotine yield from a cigarette. Consequently, low-tar and low-nicotine cigarettes, so-called "light" cigarettes, do not reduce the health risks of smoking (Kozlowski et al., 2001). Furthermore, because these "light" cigarettes are marketed as low-risk alternatives to conventional cigarettes, their use may actually deter people from quitting because they feel a false sense of safety from using them.

On the biochemical level, nicotine binds to receptors (nicotinic cholinergic receptors) in the brain, autonomic ganglia, and the neuromuscular junction; most relevant for the discussion of nicotine dependence is that receptors in the brain are found in the greatest number in the cortex, thalamus, interpeduncular nucleus, amygdala, septum, brain stem, and locus ceruleus (Benowitz, 1998). The activation of nicotinic receptors by nicotine results in the release of a wide array of neurotransmitters, including acetylcholine, norepinephrine, dopamine, serotonin, and beta endorphin (Benowitz, 1998). The release of dopamine in the area of the brain thought to be involved in the reinforcing effects of other drugs of abuse (nigrostriatal region) suggests a mechanism for nicotine addiction.

Nicotine affects the functioning of many systems of the body in addition to the nervous system (Benowitz, 1998). In the cardiovascular system, nicotine acts to stimulate the sympathetic nervous system and results in an increase in blood pressure, heart rate, and cardiac output (Benowitz, 1998; Murray, 1990). There is also an alteration in blood flow, including constriction of vessels in the skin, resulting in lowered skin temperature. Alteration of endocrine functioning occurs because nicotine causes the release of adrenocorticotropic hormone (ACTH) and of cortisol, which affects mood and contributes to osteoporosis. Nicotine also increases the metabolic rate of users and has an appetite-suppressing influence; it may also specifically reduce the desirability of sweet-tasting food. Weight is suppressed through diminished appetite and increased metabolic rate. Smokers are typically 5 to 10 lbs lighter than nonsmokers; weight gain subsequent to cessation of smoking is a known complication in the maintenance of abstinence. As for the musculoskeletal system, nicotine has the effect of relaxing many skeletal muscles.

A dose–response relationship has been observed with nicotine (Henningfield & Woodson, 1989). That is, as the dose of nicotine is increased, there is an increase in the magnitude of biological response (with a ceiling effect eventually being reached). Dose–response relationships are contrasted with threshold ("all-or-none") biological responses, such as the firing of a neuron. An example of another dose–response relationship is seen with human responses to alcohol; this relationship is so reliably observed that it serves as the basis for law-enforcement decisions (i.e., because impairment in motor functioning and judgment are found above certain blood-alcohol levels, arrest will result if the person is caught driving with a blood-alcohol reading exceeding the state-determined limit).

For naive users, the reaction to nicotine is usually strongly aversive, and the person may experience a racing heart, headache, light-headedness, nausea, vomiting, even a delusional state (Benowitz, 1998; Kozlowski et al., 2001). The reaction of the naive user is essentially a toxic reaction (i.e., a reaction indicating that the person has been overdosed or poisoned and is under the influence of the harmful, undesirable effects of the drug). The effects of nicotine are listed in Exhibit 3.1 (discussed in Dodgen & Shea, 2000).

Tolerance to some of the effects of nicotine develops rapidly, and through different mechanisms. The body reacts to defend itself from the toxic effects by increasing the number of receptors, thereby enhancing its ability to handle the nicotine; there is also decreased responsiveness of the receptors to the nicotine (Kozlowski et al., 2001). The inevitable consequences of increased tolerance are that greater amounts of the drug (and increased exposure to all of the poisonous chemicals in tobacco smoke) are then needed to gain a desired effect, and a physical dependency develops in which nicotine is needed to prevent the onset of aversive withdrawal symptoms (i.e., an addiction is created; Kozlowski et al., 2001). Unfortunately, in addition to the fact that tolerance develops rapidly, it also diminishes fairly

EXHIBIT 3.1
Effects of Nicotine Consumption

Acute psychological consequences

- Subjective feelings of relaxation, well-being, reduced fatigue, and enhanced attention

Acute physiological consequences

- Increase in heart rate
- Increase in blood pressure
- Vasoconstriction of the skin (lowered skin temperature)
- Suppression of appetite
- CNS changes suggesting increase in arousal and attention

Toxic state

- Nausea
- Vomiting
- Light-headedness, dizziness
- Weakness
- Respiratory paralysis
- Tremor
- Convulsion

Note. From *Substance Use Disorders: Assessment and Treatment* (pp. 11–12), by C. E. Dodgen and W. M. Shea, 2000, San Diego, CA: Academic Press. Copyright 2000 by Academic Press. Adapted with permission.

quickly with regard to the psychoactive and heart rate effects of nicotine, so although successive cigarettes throughout the day may yield less pleasure, a smoker begins each day with renewed sensitivity and responsiveness to the drug due to the several hours of overnight abstinence. The symptoms of the initial reaction are rarely ever experienced again, so tolerance of the toxic effects appears more enduring (Kozlowski et al., 2001).

It is wise to keep in mind that many factors contribute to the ultimate effect of a substance on an individual in addition to the pharmacological properties of the drug under consideration. Besides the pharmacological action of nicotine, the dose, the tolerance and general personality of the smoker, body weight, age, medical status, presence of other drugs in the body, gender, and emotional state of the smoker at the time the nicotine is consumed, as well as the social setting at the time of consumption, can all affect the response of an individual (Blum, 1984). The greater the amount of nicotine consumed (i.e., the larger the dose), the stronger the reaction. The higher the level of tolerance developed, the less reaction there is to nicotine. The personality of the smoker is a factor in terms of how smoking is used. For example, an anxious individual may find nicotine relaxing, but a depressed individual may find cigarettes energizing. Adolescents are especially sensitive to social setting; in a prosmoking environment, smoking is more likely, and the smoking experience is more positive. With respect to body weight, the heavier the person, the more nicotine that is necessary to produce an effect. Age is a factor in the sense that children and the elderly are generally more sensitive to all psychoactive substances. Because nicotine is primarily metabolized by the liver, liver disease will alter the response to nicotine. The presence of other psychoactive substances in the body will naturally alter the response to nicotine as well. Males tend to experience nicotine as more rewarding than females. Because nicotine is psychoactive (i.e., it changes mood and feelings), the emotional state of the user when nicotine is consumed interacts with the psychoactivity of the nicotine.

NICOTINE INTOXICATION

The *Diagnostic and Statistical Manual of Mental Disorders* (4th ed.; *DSM–IV*; American Psychiatric Association, 1994) does not list an intoxication syndrome for nicotine. This should not be taken to mean that there is no intoxication from the use of nicotine. Intoxication refers to psychological and behavioral influences of a drug, often considered positive by the user; such effects as relaxation, diminished fatigue, and increased alertness are cited by smokers as reasons for smoking. However, to meet the criteria for an intoxication disorder with respect to *DSM–IV*, in addition to there being substance-induced psychological and behavioral changes, there must be accompanying clinically significant impairment. As nicotine is typically consumed, there are no maladaptive behavioral or psychological changes (e.g., cognitive impairment, impaired social or vocational functioning, etc.) from it. Because of the absence of an intoxication disorder, cigarettes can be consumed in many settings and situations in which other substances cannot be (Slade, 1993), which is a problem in the sense that there is much public tolerance of smoking. Although nobody would blink at the sight of a group of factory workers taking a 10-minute cigarette break, people would naturally be shocked to see the same workers taking a beer break. This makes sense because of the immediate danger of working while consuming alcohol versus nicotine, but it also underscores the public tolerance of smoking.

PERFORMANCE ENHANCEMENT

There has been some controversy, alluded to in chapter 1, over whether there is any performance enhancement from nicotine use in humans. The main question is, Does nicotine confer certain mental or behavioral advantages, or are perceived benefits merely reversals of deficits caused by nicotine withdrawal? To address this question, Heishman, Taylor, and Henningfield (1994) reviewed studies published in scientific journals from 1970 to 1993. The majority of studies were conducted with the methodological flaw of testing nicotine-deprived smokers, so observed improvements in functioning with nicotine cannot be taken as absolute enhancement, but rather as restoration of normal functioning. Heishman et al. (1994) made the point that to demonstrate genuine performance enhancement, studies must show that nicotine improves functioning of nonsmokers or of nondeprived smokers. The authors classified nicotine performance studies they reviewed into four categories: (a) sensory (e.g., visual discrimination tasks); (b) motor (e.g., finger-tapping rate); (c) attentional (e.g., searching or scanning); and (d) cognitive (e.g., learning, memory). With nicotine-deprived subjects, most studies found a facilitating effect of nicotine on some measures of sensory, motor, and attentional abilities; only a minority of tests showed improvement in cognitive abilities. These results likely reflect improvements in withdrawal-induced deficits. Studies with nonabstinent smokers or nonsmokers indicated that nicotine improved only motor abilities (e.g., finger-tapping rate; motor responses on brief tests of attention). Because nicotine provides significant deficit reversal, it seems that its enhancing effects are more relevant in discussion of maintenance of use, and not initiation. Others (e.g., Perkins & Stitzer, 1998) have also concluded that nicotine's most important performance-enhancing properties are related to deficit reversal and that true enhancement unrelated to withdrawal is found only for simple motor or simple cognitive tasks (e.g., reaction time); effects on more important or complex skills are not reliably found. Taking up cigarette smoking to gain mental benefits is not advised.

NICOTINE WITHDRAWAL

Withdrawal is a syndrome precipitated by the reduction or cessation of use of a substance that causes significant distress or impairment in functioning; this includes behavioral, cognitive, and physiological components (American Psychiatric Association, 1994). Withdrawal is one of the cornerstones of the traditional physical addiction model (tolerance being the other). *DSM–IV* lists eight diagnostic criteria, presented in Exhibit 3.2. At least four of the criteria must be present within 24 hours of reduction or cessation of use of nicotine for the diagnosis of nicotine withdrawal to be made. In addition, the symptoms must cause clinically significant distress or impairment in functioning and not be due to a general medical condition or mental disorder.

It is interesting to note that cravings and the urge to smoke are not listed as part of the withdrawal syndrome by *DSM–IV*, although craving is considered a symptom of withdrawal by some (e.g., Hughes, 1992; West, 1984). A full discussion of craving–urging is provided in chapter 8. Adults and adolescents are known to exhibit the same withdrawal characteristics (Prokhorov et al., 2001), a finding which suggests that smokers of all ages may be potential candidates for nicotine-replacement treatment.

In addition to knowing the signs and symptoms of nicotine withdrawal, it is helpful to know the time course. For example, how long should withdrawal persist? This important question was studied by Hughes (1992). Hughes's study was unique in that subjects were self-quitters who were followed for 180 days postcessation. Most studies evaluating nicotine withdrawal use smokers in treatment programs, who represent only about 5% of all smokers and who typically smoke more cigarettes and score higher on dependence scales (Hughes, 1992). Most signs and symptoms of nicotine withdrawal increased for 1 to 4 days, then decreased. The majority of signs or symptoms normalized in 7 to 30 days, with the exception of hunger, heart

---

EXHIBIT 3.2
Diagnostic Criteria for Nicotine Withdrawal

1. Dysphoric or depressed mood
2. Insomnia
3. Irritability, frustration, anger
4. Anxiety
5. Difficulty concentrating
6. Restlessness
7. Decreased heart rate
8. Increased appetite, weight gain

Note. From *Diagnostic and Statistical Manual of Mental Disorders* (4th ed., pp. 244–245), by the American Psychiatric Association, 1994, Washington, DC: Author. Copyright 1994 by the American Psychiatric Association. Adapted with permission.

rate, and weight gain. Hunger appears to persist for 4 to 10 weeks and weight gain for up to 6 months. The course of heart rate changes appears more variable, so no definite pattern can be described. Craving did not spike postcessation in this study and has been found to persist for up to 6 months, or even longer. The absence of a postcessation increase of craving suggests that it may not be a reliable symptom of nicotine withdrawal. Hughes (1992) noted that overall withdrawal severity did not differ between men and women, or between heavy and light smokers, leaving open the question as to the determinants of severity of withdrawal.

NONPHARMACOLOGICAL FACTORS AND SMOKING

Smoking is a multifaceted behavior. Cigarettes are excellent products for consuming nicotine, but they are so much more. Smokers routinely include factors such as taste, aroma, and sensations in their throat and respiratory tract when they cite sources of pleasure from cigarettes. In addition, behaviors associated with smoking are central to the habit of smoking. This is not unlike the reports of addicts of other substances. For example, many intravenous (IV) heroin users have reported to me that once they were dependent, the injection of the heroin was almost anticlimactic. More pleasurable were behaviors associated with use: getting the drug, "cooking" it, handling the paraphernalia, and so forth. Research supports the validity of the importance of non-nicotine-related factors in the maintenance of smoking behavior. Pritchard, Robinson, Guy, Riley, and Stiles (1996) manipulated the nicotine levels of cigarettes and found that sensory factors such as taste, perceived draw, and chest impact were as important as nicotine levels in smoking satisfaction and reduction of desire to smoke. Similarly, Pickworth, Fant, Nelson, Rohrer, and Henningfield (1999) used denicotinized tobacco-based cigarettes that only differed from commercial cigarettes by an absence of nicotine. When subjects smoked the denicotinized cigarettes they did not show telltale signs of nicotine consumption: There was no increase in heart rate, or EEG activation. However, the denicotinized cigarettes reduced tobacco withdrawal and cigarette cravings; in addition, overall satisfaction was the same for both commercial and denicotinized cigarettes.

To further separate the pharmacological and nonpharmacological aspects of smoking, subjects were compared in their responses to IV-administered nicotine, nicotine-containing cigarettes, and denicotinized cigarettes (Rose, Behm, Westman, & Johnson, 2000). Smoking denicotinized cigarettes produced satisfaction, psychological reward, and craving reduction and increased euphoria. By contrast, IV-administered nicotine reduced craving and withdrawal but did not produce a significant positive response. The combination of IV-administered nicotine and smoking denicotinized cigarettes closely matched the rating obtained by subjects smoking their usual brand of cigarette. In this study, it can be seen that both sensory and behavioral factors and nicotine contribute independently to smoking pleasure.

Some perspective on the relative contributions of nicotine and nonnicotine factors needs to be provided. Denicotinized (and very-low-nicotine) cigarettes have been marketed to the public and have sold very poorly. Although the sensory and behavioral factors are part of what makes smoking pleasurable and maintains use, they are clearly secondary to nicotine.

SUMMARY

There is presently no doubt that nicotine is the primary active ingredient responsible for psychoactive effects of and addiction to cigarettes. Possibly because cigarettes are legal and prevalent, people tend to think of nicotine as more benign and less potent a substance than it really is. Part of establishing the credibility of treatment, and of the addiction–disease model, is to demonstrate that nicotine possesses properties like, and can be described in the same terms as, other abusable substances such as alcohol, cocaine, and heroin. Like other abusable drugs, nicotine can be classified by its effects on the CNS, effects described as biphasic because it has stimulating influences at lower levels and depressing effects at higher doses. Also, nicotine can be delivered to the individual through various routes of administration; different routes of administration result in different rates of delivery and abuse liability. Smoking happens to be one of the most efficient means of delivering nicotine, with very high addiction potential. Nicotine affects many systems of the body in addition to the CNS, including the cardiovascular, endocrine, metabolic, and musculoskeletal systems. It is important to note that nicotine is shown to stimulate the reward center of the brain; such activity is common to all substance abuse as well as other appetitive behaviors. The identification of nicotinic receptors throughout the body, to which nicotine molecules bind, provides a means to explain the release of neurotransmitters that effect changes in the systems of the body and to explain the development of tolerance and withdrawal.

Performance enhancement from nicotine turns out to be more apparent than real; most ostensible improvement in cognitive and behavioral functioning is due to the reversal of withdrawal effects. Cigarettes are an excellent method of delivery of nicotine, but it is clear that other factors are involved in the addiction to nicotine. Sensory, behavioral, and cognitive factors contribute to smoking; for treatment to be effective, it must be sufficiently broad to address these factors.

4

NICOTINE AND ADDICTION

In this chapter the current model of addiction is discussed. It is noted that the model has evolved from one of a purely physical nature characterized by the classic symptoms of tolerance and withdrawal to one that includes behavioral and psychological processes (such as loss of control and a compulsion to use a substance). Evidence is reviewed that soundly demonstrates that nicotine is addictive, like other substances of abuse, including alcohol, cocaine, and heroin. The goals of this chapter are to help the clinician (a) to understand that the fact that nicotine is addictive explains why it is so difficult to stop smoking and why treatment is too frequently unsuccessful and (b) to appreciate the need for comprehensive, sophisticated treatment to effectively assist the smoker to stop.

DISEASE CONCEPT

Whether regular nicotine consumption is representative of an addictive illness (i.e., a disease) or something else (i.e., habit, fully volitional leisure activity, etc.) is more than a matter of casual interest. This has been a hotly contested issue in the study of all substances of abuse. Therefore, it makes some sense to review the current model of addiction to determine how this general model applies (or does not apply) to nicotine. Prior to attempting to answer such questions as whether or not abuse of substances represents a disease, and whether nicotine use fits well with the broader model, one must first discuss what a disease is. Even the basic concept of disease is complex and open to scholarly debate. It would be naive to assume that the determination of what constitutes a disease is solely a medical process. Decisions about what conditions are to be considered diseases reflect cultural and political influences in addition to medical ones. It has been pointed out that significant implications follow from the conferring of disease status on a condition (Acker, 1993; Gori, 1996; Quintero & Nichter, 1996; West, 1992). For example, if certain substances are deemed addictive (i.e., they cause an addictive disease), then (a) manufacturers can be held liable for damages from use; (b) public policy regarding control of supply and use of products may be influenced; (c) treatment resources and the seeking of treatment may be greatly affected; and (d) vested interests will be aided or injured, depending on where their interests in the matter lie. For example, calling cigarette use a disease fuels the substance abuse treatment industry, researchers, and the regulatory industry and harms the tobacco industry. Because of the significant implications attendant to the determination of disease status, some (e.g., Quintero & Nichter, 1996) warn of the potential political misuse of the term "addictive disease," citing the following concerns:

1. Categorizing certain substances as addictive or not defines which substances are legitimate or illegitimate for use in the culture.
2. This process amounts to medicalization of deviance and social problems and becomes a source of control (e.g., prosecuting substance-abusing women).
3. Under the guise of public health concerns, the government is strengthened in its monitoring and control of individuals, especially in the workplace.
4. Dialogue about addiction may become a scare tactic used for political ends (e.g., the war on drugs), rather than a matter of health care.

Philosophically, there are two basic disease paradigms: the ontological model and the functional model (Acker, 1993). According to the *ontological model*, diseases are real entities with an existence independent of any particular case of illness. For example, infectious diseases are caused by living organisms that enter the body, follow a certain course, and create predictable consequences. Because disease is viewed as an entity in itself, the attributes of the host person are deemphasized, and all people are viewed as being similarly affected and are treated accordingly. Because of the generic aspects of the cause and course of illness, which require the same treatment for everyone, there tends to be a dehumanizing effect, and the individual is disregarded in such a model. Another consequence of the ontological model is the existence of a sick role, in which the person is viewed as a victim of invading illness and exempted from responsibilities to work and family, except to make efforts to return to health.

The *functional model* defines disease as the disordered functioning of a system; disease is explained as an outcome reflecting the collective influence of a person's actions, lifestyle, and relationship to the environment. The attendant sick role in this model is somewhat more stigmatizing for the affected individual; if lifestyle and behavior are involved, there is room for blaming the person. Addictions more closely adhere to this model, as do other modern illnesses such as hypertension, obesity, and Type 2 diabetes.

In light of the various meanings and motives attached to the concept of disease, it is best to keep in mind that calling addiction a disease should be understood as a metaphor or a conceptual model that can be an aid to the understanding and treatment of the condition (Shaffer, 1991). The notion of disease is a cultural construction and should not be taken literally, especially in the case of addictions.

DISEASE MODEL OF ADDICTION

The medical or disease model remains dominant in the field of addiction, although it has changed over time (Dodgen & Shea, 2000). Jellinek (1960) is credited with popularizing the disease concept of alcoholism. Despite the fact that longitudinal studies have disconfirmed some of the key elements of Jellinek's model (e.g., the idea that alcohol addiction is progressive and fatal has been found to apply only to a subset of the total population of abusive drinkers), it remains popular, although it has expanded and evolved over time and in its current incarnation exists as a biopsychosocial model. The basic elements of the disease model of addiction are as follows (Walters, 1992):

1. The disease is a primary and not a secondary symptom of psychopathology.
2. There are recognizable signs and symptoms on which a diagnosis may be made.
3. The disease has etiological agents and causes.
4. The disease has a predictable course.

The disease model has been expanded to include substances in addition to alcohol and fits the data fairly well. For example, regarding the issue of primary disorder (the first element of the disease model presented above), studies of psychiatric comorbidity support the fact that although comorbidity is alarmingly high, not all substance abusers also have other psychiatric problems. In one well-known study, 65% of people seeking treatment for drug abuse exhibited psychiatric comorbidity (Regier et al., 1990). Referring to the second element of the disease model, the existence of diagnostic criteria in the *Diagnostic and Statistical Manual of Mental Disorders* (4th ed.; *DSM–IV*; American Psychiatric Association, 1994) and the *International Classification of Diseases and Related Health Problems* (10th rev.; *ICD–10*; World Health Organization [WHO], 1992) is obvious proof that signs and symptoms of substance abuse have been described. Concerning etiology (the third element of the disease model), although clear causes are yet to be identified, the biopsychosocial model was explicitly developed to account for known contributors to substance abuse. Biologically, studies of genetic inheritance have confirmed the transmission of a predisposition to substance abuse. Psychologically, certain cognitive styles, behavior patterns, and social factors are known to contribute to the development of substance abuse. With regard to the final element of the disease model, the course of substance abuse has been well articulated by the development of models of use (discussed in Dodgen & Shea, 2000), perhaps best represented by Kandel's (1975) stage model of progression. Admittedly, stage models are imperfect because of the fact that progression of substance use can be characterized by significant variability. However, despite their imperfection, they do adequately describe a typical course of substance use.

Strengths of the disease model include the removal of social stigma and the fact that it provides clear and meaningful goals of treatment (i.e., abstinence; Walters, 1992). Drawbacks of the model are that personal responsibility is minimized and it deemphasizes psychological study, psychotherapy, and study of the problems of individuals (Bell & Khantzian, 1991) and results in generic treatment (Shaffer, 1991).

The biopsychosocial disease model is not the only model of addiction. Several other models have been conceived to understand and treat individuals who abuse substances (Quintero & Nichter, 1996); it is to be noted that the current biopsychosocial disease model is all-inclusive, accounting for the factors recognized by other proposed models of addiction. From a review of the other models, it is apparent that the biopsychosocial model captures the essence of each of a number of previously popular models of addiction, all of which represent comparatively narrow, unidimensional systems of understanding and treating the condition. The physiological model is the traditional medical model, based on the idea that addiction is ultimately physical, as evidenced by the existence of tolerance and withdrawal. The psychological model suggests that abnormal substance use is secondary to psychological dysfunction and illness. If the psychological problems are improved, the abuse of substances will automatically improve. The cultural model advances the idea that addiction is a response to many factors, including social, cultural, situational, ritualistic, developmental, psychological, and cognitive influences. That drug use results from alienation and poverty is proposed by the political economy model. The utilitarian model contends that addiction may or may not be a disease, but calling it one results in effective treatment.

NICOTINE AND THE DISEASE MODEL

Nicotine is a substance, so it would stand to reason that its use would be adequately accounted for by the general addiction model. Although it may be reasonable to assume this is the case, it is best to evaluate the specific evidence that nicotine misuse is a true addictive illness. One way to evaluate the generic model of addiction as applied to nicotine is to refer to the most widely accepted diagnostic systems: *DSM–IV* and *ICD–10*. Hughes (1993b) did exactly this in a point-by-point discussion of the diagnostic criteria of substance dependence in the then-current *Diagnostic and Statistical Manual of Mental Disorders* (3rd ed.; *DSM–III–R*; American Psychiatric Association, 1987) and *International Classification of Diseases and Related Health Problems* (9th rev.; *ICD–9*; WHO, 1990).

Starting with the classic criteria of dependence, tolerance, and withdrawal, it can easily be seen that nicotine meets these requirements. Smokers quickly develop tolerance to the toxic effects of nicotine so that after initial use nausea and dizziness are not observed. A nicotine withdrawal syndrome is accepted and exists as a diagnosable disorder in *DSM–IV*; smokers often report use of cigarettes to reverse or avoid withdrawal symptoms. Interestingly, the severity of the withdrawal experience appears quite variable, so it is difficult to know which symptoms a given individual will experience, or with what intensity. Evidence of three criteria suggestive of loss of control of substance use (substance taken in larger amounts or for longer periods of time than intended; persistent desire or unsuccessful attempts to cut down or control use; use despite negative social, psychological, or physical consequences) is seen with cigarettes. The majority of smokers have made several unsuccessful attempts to stop, and smoking despite serious medical problems is unfortunately very common.

Other behavioral criteria (great deal of time spent obtaining or recovering from use of the substance; important social, occupational, or recreational activities given up or reduced due to substance use) are observed with cigarette use. In the typical case, after tolerance develops there is little need for recovery from nicotine, and because cigarettes are widely available, less time and effort are needed to obtain them. However, smokers are known to make inconvenient trips to the store at night to assure the next day's supply, interrupt a meal to go outside for a smoke, or go out in inclement weather to take a smoking break during work. It has also been noted that in situations in which access to cigarettes has been restricted (e.g., concentration camps during World War II) efforts to obtain cigarettes can be quite significant. On a related matter, smokers also report skipping certain activities during which smoking may be disallowed. The final criterion, impairment of ability to fulfill role obligations due to intoxication or withdrawal, appears to apply only weakly to nicotine. Intoxication is not a significant problem with cigarettes because it does not cause impairment of performance (except possibly very early in use, when there may be a toxic reaction). Some impairment due to withdrawal may be seen secondary to irritable mood and diminished concentration.

Robinson and Pritchard (1995) offered some interesting arguments against the idea that cigarettes and nicotine are addictive. Among the points they attempt to make are that nicotine does not have intoxicating effects and that nicotine may enhance cognitive performance, suggesting that "true" drugs of abuse necessarily impair cognitive performance. In addition, they contend that there is no real compulsion to use cigarettes and smokers only say they want to quit because of social pressure; and they argue that there is no pharmacologically based withdrawal syndrome, simply the psychologically derived dysphoria related to the loss of a desired object. To address these points in order of presentation, I have found that intoxication does exist, as evidenced by reports of users who experience positive consequences of smoking. The fact that no impairment is usually observed does not mean that there are no intoxicating effects at typical doses of nicotine. Regarding cognitive effects, it was discussed in chapter 1 that much of the apparent benefit of smoking results from reversal of withdrawal-based cognitive deficits; the relatively minor, genuine cognitive benefits that do exist do not separate nicotine from other drugs of abuse. Stimulant drugs, for example, also enhance alertness, concentration, and mental agility. Ritalin is used for attentional problems for this reason, and cocaine users report cognitive benefits from use of the drug early on in their histories. The above discussion regarding criteria of dependence regarding loss of control clearly demonstrates that use of cigarettes is compulsive. With respect to the withdrawal syndrome, there is no doubt that a portion of the syndrome is psychologically based dysphoria related to loss of the cigarette. However, this in no way negates the fact that there is also a pharmacologically based component.

Frenk and Dar (2000) devoted an entire book to challenging the assertion that nicotine causes addiction. They proposed that nicotine use is more like a compulsion or bad habit than an addiction. They offered unconvincing challenges to key issues related to psychoactivity and withdrawal. For example, they contended that because initial use of nicotine is often unpleasant, people do not smoke to get positive effects from it. All this demonstrates is that the toxic state is unpleasant. Initial negative reactions are not uncommon with substances of abuse. For example, initial heroin use can be accompanied by a very aversive state that includes nausea and vomiting (due to a toxic reaction).

Relative to the issue of withdrawal, Frenk and Dar (2000) claimed that the symptoms observed after reduction or cessation of use of nicotine are due to the dysphoria associated with interruption of a habit. This argument is similar to that of Robinson and Pritchard (1995), discussed directly above, so no further discussion is necessary to address this point.

The surgeon general's 1988 report (USDHHS, 1988) described criteria for drug dependence that differ somewhat from those in *DSM–IV* and

ICD–10 and are also relevant to this discussion of whether or not nicotine is an addictive substance. At the time of the surgeon general's initial report (USDHEW, 1964), nicotine use was considered "habituating." That is, it was considered "only" psychologically addicting and not physically addicting. By 1988, the surgeon general's thinking on the matter had changed dramatically. The 1988 report (USDHHS, 1988) described two sets of diagnostic criteria, referred to as *primary* and *secondary* criteria of drug dependence. *Primary criteria* represent essential requirements of addiction, and *secondary criteria* are behaviors or consequences experienced by most, but not all, users of the substance. A summary of the surgeon general's findings evaluating nicotine according to their standards of addiction is presented below.

Primary Criteria of Addiction

Highly Controlled or Compulsive Use

Controlled use refers to the fact that use of nicotine is consistent and orderly and not random or capricious. Control in this sense does not imply choice or free will, but use that is routinized (controlled by the drug, not the person). Evidence that nicotine use is highly controlled is seen in the daily smoking behavior of regular smokers, which is typically patterned (e.g., person always has a cigarette after breakfast, on the car ride to work, etc.). Also, after regular use is established, smokers show very stable blood levels of nicotine. *Compulsive use* is characterized by a driven quality and the experience of strong cravings or urges for the substance. Compulsion to use nicotine is demonstrated by surveys of smokers desiring to stop while they continue to use, poor success rates for quitting, and continued smoking by some 50% of smokers recovering from surgery for smoking-related disease.

Psychoactive Effects

Psychoactivity of substances refers to the ability of a drug to induce subjective effects on mood and feeling. Several experimental methods have been used to establish the psychoactivity of nicotine (as well as other substances of abuse):

1. Discrimination testing in animals has shown that nicotine produces effects that can be discerned from nondrug states, and discrimination testing in humans has supported the findings with animals in that regardless of route of administration, human subjects were able to distinguish between nicotine and placebo and to accurately estimate dose levels of nicotine.
2. State-dependent learning in humans has been demonstrated such that cognitive performance has been enhanced for subjects consuming nicotine when the original learning took place under the influence of nicotine.

3. Conditioned place preference and conditioned aversion methods, used to determine the positive or negative subjective states induced by substances, have demonstrated that the application of nicotine can yield both preference or aversion in animals, depending on a number of factors, especially dose.
4. Conditioned taste aversion (whereby a substance is given after consumption of a distinctly flavored stimulus so that later exposure to the stimulus results in rejection) has been shown with rodents for nicotine.

Henningfield and Heishman (1995) also reported on nicotine's psychoactivity on the basis of subjective ratings of human subjects: Scores on a "drug-liking" scale were similar for nicotine, cocaine, and heroin; nicotine nasal spray yielded high scores on a "head rush" scale; and a rating of "high" was achieved by nicotine administered via smoke or nasal spray.

Drug-Reinforced Behavior

This criterion refers to whether nicotine consumption can serve as either a positive reinforcer of behavior or a punishment (evoking a negative reaction to its consumption), or whether its absence can create an aversive state generating motivation for consumption. Positive reinforcement of behavior is considered the single most important action of dependence-producing substances: Drugs serve as a reinforcing agent to strengthen the behavior of consuming them. Simply put, a drug is consumed (behavior), and a pleasurable state ensues (consequence) that serves as reinforcement of further consumption of the drug. Across many species, from rodents to humans, intravenous injections of nicotine have been found to serve as positive reinforcers; that is, the introduction of an intravenous dose of nicotine resulted in an increase in the target behavior. Nicotine's influence over behavior has also been demonstrated in the opposite direction from that of reinforcer (i.e., as a punisher to suppress behavior); for example, due to the unpleasant properties of nicotine at relatively high doses, application of nicotine at these doses has led to suppression of target behaviors in humans and animals. Finally, once tolerance is established, abstinence from nicotine results in an unpleasant withdrawal syndrome. Consumption of nicotine reliably relieves withdrawal symptoms, indicating that the absence of nicotine also influences consumption.

Secondary Criteria

Common Addictive Behaviors

Addictive behavior often involves the following: stereotypic patterns of use, use despite harmful effects, relapse following abstinence, and recurrent drug cravings. The evidence for these criteria is redundant with that cited for the primary criteria and does not warrant separate discussion.

Common Properties of Dependence-Producing Drugs

Dependence-producing drugs often result in tolerance, physical dependence (withdrawal), and pleasant (euphoriant) effects. The evidence of tolerance, withdrawal, and euphoriant effects in relation to nicotine is amply demonstrated, as discussed in the present chapter and throughout this book, so no further discussion is necessary here.

To further evaluate whether nicotine fits the generic addiction model, it was compared with other substances of abuse such as heroin, alcohol, and cocaine in the surgeon general's report (USDHHS, 1988). It was concluded that nicotine use shares many similarities with other drugs in terms of initiation of use, patterns of use, cessation and relapse, spontaneous remission, and response to both behavioral and pharmacological treatments.

Another area of commonality between nicotine and other substances of abuse is its effect on certain areas of the brain. More specifically, the consumption of nicotine results in an alteration in the mesolimbic dopamine system (Benowitz, 1999; Dani & DeBiasi, 2001; Gamberino & Gold, 1999; Picciotto, 1998; Walton, Johnstone, Munafo, Neville, & Griffiths, 2001; Watkins, Koob, & Markou, 2000). Nicotine, like alcohol, cocaine, and other drugs, results in an increase in the release of dopamine in the *nucleus accumbens*; this suggests that there is a common mechanism involved in the development of dependence on different substances. Additional evidence of the involvement of this mechanism comes from research showing that lesioning of the mesolimbic area attenuates nicotine self-administration in rats (Picciotto, 1998). Further support for the importance of this system for addiction comes from studies using drugs that block dopamine release in the *nucleus accumbens*, which show decreases in self-administration of nicotine in rats (Dani & DeBiasi, 2001) and humans (Gamberino & Gold, 1999).

The mesolimbic dopamine system is considered a brain reward center, an idea that derives from brain stimulation research (Gamberino & Gold, 1999). Not only does the abuse of drugs such as nicotine, amphetamines, cocaine, opioids, and so forth result in an increased release of dopamine in the *nucleus accumbens*, but so do the occurrence of appetitive, natural survival behaviors such as eating, drinking, and sex. It is not yet clear whether the stimulation of the dopamine pathways is pleasurable and reinforcing in and of itself, or whether stimulation of the dopamine system is necessary for associative learning that links the perception of pleasure with particular stimulation, or both (Walton et al., 2001).

If nicotine is addictive like classic substances of abuse, it should also hold true that nicotine would operate in the body like these other substances. Drugs exert their influence by modifying neurotransmission, which affects CNS functioning, ultimately affecting behavior (discussed in Dodgen & Shea, 2000; Dykstra, 1992). On a cellular level, nicotine initiates its influence by binding with nicotinic acetylcholine receptors distributed throughout the CNS (Dani & DeBiasi, 2001). The vital role of nicotinic receptors is demonstrated by research with genetically engineered mice: Mice missing a specific receptor subtype did not self-administer nicotine, and administration of nicotine did not result in an increased release of dopamine in the mesolimbic area for these mice (Perkins, 1999). There are many different subtypes of nicotinic receptors, so the stimulation of nicotinic receptors results in diverse effects via the release of neurotransmitters, as summarized in Exhibit 4.1 (Benowitz, 1999; Kellar, Davila-Garcia, & Xiao, 1999).

Nicotine is also like other substances of abuse in that the route of administration is a significant factor in abuse liability. For a drug to have any effect, it must enter the body. How a drug is introduced to the body affects the rate at which it enters the bloodstream and reaches the brain, and also affects how quickly the drug is metabolized and eliminated (Dodgen & Shea, 2000). Generally speaking, the more quickly a drug reaches the brain, the more intense the response; also, the faster it enters the bloodstream, the faster a drug is broken down and eliminated (resulting in an intense but short-lived reaction), which affects abuse liability. In order of slowest to fastest, routes of administration include (a) oral, (b) mucosa (under the tongue or in the nose), (c) inhalation, and (d) injection (Blum, 1984). Rapid delivery of nicotine via smoke inhalation is the most effective and addictive method of delivery (it is nearly as fast as intravenous delivery but perceived as much more pleasurable by smokers); the cigarette delivery system results in a high dose and a rapid rise in blood nicotine levels. Methods other than smoking that deliver nicotine more slowly are not as addictive (Benowitz, 1999; Perkins, 1999). For example, abuse liability of nicotine is highest with cigarette smoke inhalation because it results in rapid delivery of a high dose of nicotine. Next is smokeless tobacco, which allows for slower delivery

EXHIBIT 4.1
Effects of Nicotine Caused by Modification of Neurotransmitters

Neurotransmitter	Effects
Norepinephrine	stimulation, arousal, appetite suppression
Acetylcholine	memory improvement, cognitive enhancement
Glutamine	memory improvement, cognitive enhancement
Gamma-aminobutaric acid (GABA)	relaxation
Dopamine	increased pleasure, reward, appetite suppression
Beta endorphin	relaxation
Serotonin	mood improvement, appetite suppression

of a high dose of nicotine, thus carrying less risk of addiction. Nicotine replacement therapies (gum, patch) allow for even slower delivery of nicotine, at a lower dose, than smokeless tobacco and consequently have a lower potential for abuse.

An often-asked question relates to the relative addictiveness of nicotine compared with other substances. Several facts appear to suggest that nicotine is more addictive than other drugs. For example, it is noted that few smokers use cigarettes casually (Jarvik, 1995). More specifically, only 5% of smokers or fewer are chippers (i.e., smoke a maximum of five cigarettes per day) as compared with alcohol users, approximately 90% of whom are not considered dependent (Henningfield, Cohen, & Slade, 1991; Jarvik, 1995). Conversion from ever-using (i.e., having ever used the substance) to dependent status is highest for cigarettes compared with heroin, cocaine, and alcohol, respectively (Perkins, 1999). In addition, the prevalence of use is much higher for nicotine than for other substances. In terms of difficulty achieving abstinence, and relapse once abstinence is achieved, rates and patterns of relapse are similar for various substances, including nicotine, heroin, alcohol, and cocaine (Henningfield et al., 1991); however, among polysubstance abusers, nicotine is rated highest on "liking" and "need" scales. Finally, on another criterion of addictiveness, damage resulting from use, nicotine is far above the other drugs. Henningfield et al. noted that several significant nonpharmacological factors contribute to elevating the nicotine problem above those associated with other substances of abuse; these include (a) greater availability, (b) lower relative cost, (c) greater social pressure to use, (d) absence of serious legal consequences attendant on use, and (e) superior marketing by the tobacco industry. Therefore, although cigarettes are addictive, they probably are not more addictive than other drugs; the problem is of a much greater magnitude for a variety of other reasons just listed. On a similar note, Benowitz (1999) pointed out that though pharmacological factors are integral to addiction to nicotine, many factors contribute to it: (a) environmental influences; (b) nature of the tobacco product; and (c) individual vulnerability factors such as age, gender, genetic predisposition, psychiatric status, and abuse of other substances.

The existence of chippers is a further reminder that factors other than exposure to nicotine are necessary to create a dependence on the substance (Shiffman, 1989; Shiffman, Fischer, Zettler-Segal, & Benowitz, 1990). Chippers challenge the simplistic addiction model that implies it is the drug alone that is responsible for the addiction. They smoke regularly (up to five cigarettes per day) but do not develop symptoms of dependence on nicotine. They appear to smoke more for pleasure and positive reinforcement than for removal of withdrawal symptoms (which they do not experience) or to satisfy a compulsion (Shiffman, Kassel, Paty, Gnys, & Zettler-Segal, 1994). The situation with chippers is reminiscent of coping theory as discussed in chapter 2: Not only is exposure to nicotine necessary for dependence to develop, but so is the presence of a vulnerable host. What makes chippers relatively invulnerable to dependence, whether it be biological or psychological factors (or both), is still a matter of speculation.

At the start of this chapter the question of the nature of nicotine use was posed: Is it a pleasurable habit or an addictive disease? The evidence discussed throughout the remainder of the chapter has convincingly demonstrated that nicotine is addictive and causes dependence in its users. Nicotine use may be conceived of in its essence as a habitual or compulsive behavior that is supported by an exogenously administered, centrally active substance (Henningfield et al., 1993), as opposed to compulsive gambling, for example, which is habitual and driven by psychological, nonpharmacological influences. Nicotine dependence, then, can be thought of as belonging to the family of habitual or compulsive behaviors, with the additional influence of the drug; this is important to keep in mind for purposes of treatment. Multiple forces come together to motivate and support smoking behavior: (a) nicotine addiction, (b) learning factors related to positive and negative reinforcement as well as the association of smoking with many cues, and (c) the ostensible (ultimately misguided) coping benefits of smoking for managing stress and mood and increasing energy. Therefore, psychological, behavioral, and social processes must be addressed in addition to pharmacological influences to properly treat nicotine dependence. Just because a drug is involved does not negate the importance of other factors. In short, like other drug abuse, nicotine dependence is a true biopsychosocial disease and requires multifaceted treatment.

The form "Nicotine Addiction" is presented in Exhibit 4.2. This form is used to help smokers recognize symptoms of nicotine addiction. A case example showing the use of the form is discussed in Exhibit 4.3.

SOME SPECIAL ASPECTS OF NICOTINE USE

Nicotine use shares much in common with other drugs of abuse, as is discussed throughout this chapter. However, there are some special features of nicotine use that make it especially dangerous. For one thing, nicotine products are legal, and as such they are easily accessible and socially sanctioned. Their legality may help explain the high prevalence of nicotine use relative to illegal drugs such as cocaine and marijuana, but nicotine is by no means the only legal drug available for use; alcohol and prescription drugs are also legal. In contrast to other legal drugs, however, impairment from the intoxication syndrome resulting from use of nicotine is typically mild and very short-lived (usually confined to the very beginning of use). Because cigarettes and other tobacco products are legal and impairment from intoxication is almost unheard of, they may be used openly in designated areas. Compare this with other legal drugs: Smoking in public is commonplace, but

EXHIBIT 4.2
Nicotine Addiction Form

NICOTINE ADDICTION

Most everyone knows that tobacco products contain the drug nicotine. Nicotine is a naturally occurring substance in tobacco. Some people incorrectly conclude that nicotine is the substance in tobacco products responsible for the harmful effects. Actually, it is the many other chemical compounds in tobacco that do the bulk of the damage to the body. Nicotine *is* responsible for two important things, though: psychoactive effects and addiction. What is meant by psychoactive effects is that nicotine can produce changes in feelings and mood. For example, nicotine can produce feelings of relaxation, pleasure, reward, mental sharpness, contentment, relief from boredom, anxiety, and depression.

Exercise 1. Please list the psychoactive effects nicotine has on you.

_____
_____
_____
_____

Despite the fact that most researchers and therapists consider nicotine an addictive drug, there are still people who do not. Understanding that regular smoking represents an addiction to nicotine helps explain why it is so hard to stop (even when someone wants to), and why extensive treatment is sometimes necessary to successfully stop smoking. Addiction is now defined as behavior that is repeatedly engaged in despite the fact that it is harmful. Additionally, addiction is characterized by a loss of control of the behavior, a compulsion to engage in the behavior, and withdrawal symptoms. Examples of a loss of control of use of nicotine would be the inability to stop completely despite a desire to, or planning to use only several cigarettes in a day but not stopping until they were all smoked. A compulsion to use may be seen in the experience of strong cravings or urges to smoke. Withdrawal symptoms may also be experienced when cutting down or stopping the use of tobacco products. Some people experience uncomfortable feelings of nervousness, unhappiness, persistent hunger, and irritability.

Exercise 2. Please list symptoms of nicotine addiction that you have.

_____
_____
_____
_____

Note. From *Stop Smoking System*, by C. E. Dodgen, 2004, Florham Park, NJ. Unpublished manuscript. Reprinted with permission.

could you imagine open use of Xanax? Or compare smoking a cigarette on the drive to work with having an alcoholic drink. Because of intoxication, attendant functional impairments, liabilities, and legal implications, the use of other legal substances is restricted relative to tobacco products. The restrictions that are placed on smokers follow mainly from concerns about

EXHIBIT 4.3
Case Example: Alberto P.

BRIEF BACKGROUND AND SMOKING HISTORY

Alberto P. is a 26-year-old married teacher. He sought treatment services for marital problems. Both he and his wife viewed his smoking as a problem, especially since the birth of their daughter, who was 7 months old at the start of treatment. Mr. P. reported the initiation of smoking at 15 years of age, and current consumption of about one and one-half packs of cigarettes (30) per day. Three previous attempts to stop smoking indicated that he viewed smoking as a habit he should easily be able to break on his own or with minimal assistance. One attempt was a self-help method of cold-turkey cessation, one attempt was made by purchasing nicotine gum, and one final attempt was made with the nicotine patch. No counseling or formal support was ever sought. None of the attempts went beyond 3 weeks. Mr. P. felt the failures to maintain abstinence from nicotine were due to inadequate willpower. He did not recognize that nicotine dependence was a bona fide addiction requiring serious treatment.

SMOKING-CESSATION INTERVENTIONS

The completion of the "Nicotine Addiction" form, a standard part of smoking cessation treatment, was an ideal intervention for Mr. P. The psychoactive effects he identified in exercise 1 included improving concentration, alertness, and energy. In exercise 2, Mr. P. listed symptoms of addiction including withdrawal symptoms (during quit attempts he experienced dysphoria, hunger, and irritability), inability to stop despite multiple quit attempts, and the experience of strong cravings whenever he went for several hours without smoking.

COMMENTS

From the exercises came recognition of the fact that he was addicted to nicotine, and this helped Alberto understand previous failures to maintain abstinence and the need for more intensive treatment than he had sought in the past.

---

secondhand smoke and harm to others, and not about the impairment of the user, which is the primary concern attached to the use of other substances. Smokers may carry their cigarettes in their shirt pockets, coats, or purses without fear of discovery; it would be surprising to see such nonchalance about carrying a prescription pill case or container of alcoholic beverages at work, in a store, or at a recreational venue. Because of the ability to use nicotine openly, it becomes woven into the lives of users and becomes associated with many places, situations, and emotional states (i.e., its use is widely generalized). This ability to use cigarettes and tobacco products so freely, even when compared to other legal substances, makes it particularly difficult for a person to control its use.

THE FEDERAL GOVERNMENT'S ATTITUDE
TOWARD NICOTINE

Recognition that nicotine is addictive served as part of the rationale of the U.S. federal government for asserting control over tobacco products through the Food and Drug Administration in 1996 (Kessler et al., 1997). The government's attitude toward regulation of tobacco products has changed over time. At the time of the first surgeon general's report in 1964, nicotine use was seen as a habit. The goal of government at the time was to educate consumers about the risks so they could make a rational, informed choice about smoking (Gostin, Arno, & Brandt, 1997). With the recognition of nicotine as addictive, a designation endorsed by such major organizations as the American Psychological Association, American Psychiatric Association, Royal Society of Canada, World Health Organization, American Medical Association, and the Medical Research Council of the United Kingdom, the government's attitude about regulation and control of tobacco products has changed. Additional factors influential in changing the government's stance toward control of tobacco products included recognition of the harmful effects of smoke on nonsmokers, revelations of industry knowledge of addiction and health risks, and recognition of the vulnerability and purposeful exploitation of young people by tobacco companies. The government has taken a more active role in safeguarding the health of consumers by restricting the availability and marketing of tobacco products, reflecting greater awareness of the addictive and destructive powers of these products and of the need to protect people from them. Although the government is making some movement in the right direction, it is still the case, however, that cigarettes remain significantly exempt from regulation compared to other products and toxins.

SUMMARY

There are still people who do not believe that cigarette smoking is an addictive disorder (many of them are smokers themselves). It is essential to understanding the treatment process to have at least basic knowledge of the disease concept of nicotine dependence, which is provided in this chapter. The disease model provides a rational framework for understanding the compulsive use of nicotine, the difficulty of quitting smoking, and the difficulty of maintaining cessation and danger of relapse once quitting is achieved, as well as the necessity for comprehensive, intensive treatment for many smokers. One way to evaluate the question of whether or not chronic nicotine use is an addictive disorder is to use diagnostic criteria. Chronic nicotine use meets the diagnostic criteria of *DSM–IV* and *ICD–10* for substance dependence.

Another way to determine whether nicotine is an addictive substance is to compare it with other known substances of abuse. Nicotine shares many similarities with other classic drugs of abuse in terms of initiation of use, patterns of use, cessation and relapse, and response to behavioral and pharmacologic treatments. There is currently no doubt among researchers and clinicians that nicotine is an addictive substance.

5

ASSESSMENT OF NICOTINE DEPENDENCE

Proper assessment is an integral step in the development of an individualized treatment plan. This chapter presents an assessment model that includes five stages: screening, diagnosis, triage, treatment planning, and outcome monitoring (this stage is only briefly covered in the discussion to follow). Examples of techniques, both formal psychometric tools and less formal clinical methods, are provided that allow the clinician to achieve the assessment objective at each stage. The purpose of this chapter is to provide the clinician with knowledge of what information he or she needs to gather, and methods with which to obtain this information, so as to develop an effective, individualized treatment plan.

OVERVIEW

In a profession that assesses abstract and elusive concepts like self-esteem and psychological defenses and uses techniques such as projective measures, assessment of the overt behavior of smoking should be a snap. Of course, if our only interest were to determine the presence or absence of smoking behavior at a point in time, it would be that simple. However, we are more interested in the pattern of use and behaviors indicative of a dependence syndrome; in addition, for treatment purposes such things as the degree of dependence and severity of withdrawal symptoms and the status of other variables (e.g., attitudes about smoking, psychiatric history, substance abuse history) may be as important, or perhaps more important, than the simple fact of the subject's smoking or not at the time of assessment. That factors beyond those directly pertaining to smoking behavior are of vital importance to treatment is not unique to the treatment of nicotine dependence. My previous work in a hospital-based weight management program provided many examples of why the scope of assessment and treatment needed to be much broader than those behaviors directly influencing weight per se. The cornerstones of any weight management program are, essentially, diet and exercise. The ability of a given individual to learn and apply specific diet and exercise programs varied greatly, depending on many factors, including but not limited to age, medical status, psychiatric status, initial weight, intellectual functioning, substance abuse history, and weight management treatment history. For example, if a person with a history of significant depression who had diabetes and had been unsuccessful in prior attempts at treatment was not properly identified through a comprehensive assessment process, and treated accordingly, a treatment failure would be almost certain even though he or she might be given the same education on diet and exercise as other patients with different histories. Similarly, with nicotine dependence and other chronic conditions that ultimately necessitate lifestyle changes, the assessment and treatment processes must be duly comprehensive.

STAGE MODEL OF ASSESSMENT

Assessment of psychoactive substance use disorders, including nicotine, may be thought of as a multistage process with several goals (Allen & Mattson, 1993): (a) to gather information sufficient to develop an individualized treatment plan, (b) to match patients to appropriate treatment interventions, and (c) to monitor progress and effectiveness of treatment. Allen and Mattson described a five-stage model of assessment of psychoactive substance use disorders that is applicable to nicotine, and that applies to assessment of children, adolescents, and adults: (a) screening, (b) diagnosis, (c) triage, (d) treatment planning, and (e) outcome monitoring. Each stage has distinct goals that are accomplished through the use of various assessment methods and instruments. The goal of screening is to determine in a cost- and time-efficient manner if a potential problem exists and requires more intensive evaluation. The goal of the diagnosis stage is to determine if criteria for a disorder have been met in accord with a diagnostic system, such as the *Diagnostic and Statistical Manual of Mental Disorders* (4th ed.; *DSM–IV*; American Psychiatric Association, 1994) or the *International Classification of Diseases and Related Health Problems* (10th rev.; *ICD–10*; World Health

Organization, 1992). The objective of the triage stage is to decide the appropriate setting and intensity for treatment (e.g., inpatient versus outpatient treatment and treatment schedule). Treatment planning aims to establish individualized treatment goals and interventions directed to identified problem areas. Outcome monitoring addresses the patient's response to treatment and whether the patient requires further or different treatment.

The Allen and Mattson (1993) model serves as a useful organizing system for the presentation of nicotine assessment methods, which are discussed below in terms of their role in the assessment process (i.e., screening, diagnosis, etc.). It is to be noted that designation of a measure can be somewhat arbitrary and instruments are not always easily or neatly categorized, so a tool identified as a screening instrument might also function as a diagnostic tool, for example.

Screening of Nicotine Use

Interview Techniques

Screening methods vary from the straightforward asking of a patient their smoking status (e.g., current, never, or former smoker) to more formalized and extensive psychometric tools (which might be considered diagnostic tools), as well as some in between. The traditional smoking history taken by a physician consisted of three simple questions to determine if the patient was a smoker; if so, how much they smoked; and for how long (Frank & Jaen, 1993). In line with the medical tradition, the Clinical Practice Guideline for physicians (U.S. Department of Health and Human Services [USDHHS], 2000b) recommends a simple determination of smoking status by direct questioning (current, former, or never smoker) as a screening method; it also recommends assessment of other variables (e.g., motivation to quit) to guide treatment interventions.

Because of the highly addictive nature of cigarette smoking, as evidenced by the high degree of conversion from casual use to addiction, and low percentage of chippers, discussed in chapter 4, a simple, direct approach is appropriate for screening purposes. In other words, if someone is a current smoker, that is sufficient evidence that further evaluation is necessary for diagnostic purposes. This is contrasted with alcohol, for example, where admission of current use is not sufficient information to suspect dependence; many people use alcohol with no other signs or symptoms of abuse or dependence.

An example of a more formal and extensive psychometric screening tool is the Tobacco Dependence Screener (TDS; Kawakami, Takatsuka, Inaba, & Shimizu, 1999). The TDS is a 10-item questionnaire adapted from the tobacco-use section of the World Health Organization's Composite International Diagnostic Interview (CIDI; WHO, 1993). The CIDI is primarily a research scale; it is a structured interview tool designed to be administered by trained interviewers who read questions exactly as written, in a predetermined order, and record responses exactly as reported. The TDS consists of 10 questions posed in a yes–no format; an affirmative response indicates the presence of a symptom of nicotine dependence. Although this scale is referred to as a screening measure, it is brief and easy to administer; it may also be considered a diagnostic measure because it yields a diagnosis of nicotine dependence if enough symptoms are identified.

Biological Screening Methods

In addition to paper-and-pencil measures and screening via interview, biological screening is sometimes used. There is a prevalent misperception about the role of biological testing in the treatment of tobacco and other substance abuses. The opinion has been expressed that biological testing is the ultimate and definitive diagnostic method—if a substance or metabolite is found in the body through testing, this is concrete evidence of abuse. Biological testing is classified as screening, as opposed to a diagnostic method, because it can determine only if use has occurred within a certain time frame from when testing was conducted. A positive finding on a lab test indicates only that the substance in question was recently used; this information tells nothing about the pattern of use, consequences, or functional impairments of use, all of which are determined via other methods. With tobacco, the role of biological testing is relatively circumscribed and limited primarily to verifying abstinence in research and treatment programs (Cocores, 1993).

The typical clinician in independent practice may not always use biological testing in his or her office. Biochemical confirmation of abstinence is a necessity in the treatment of pregnant smokers (Hebert, 2004; Russell, Crawford, & Woodby, 2004; Society for Research on Nicotine and Tobacco [SRNT], 2002). Self-reports of pregnant smokers are notoriously inaccurate, with deception rates (i.e., underreporting) estimated at 24% to 50% (Hebert, 2004). Other populations for which deception may be a significant problem, and for whom biochemical validation is necessary, are adolescents and smokers experiencing smoking-related conditions. For research in which treatment interventions are being validated, biochemical confirmation of self-reported abstinence is absolutely required.

Tobacco use can be detected in expired air, saliva, hair, urine, and blood (Sobell, Toneatto, & Sobell, 1994). Drug and drug metabolites are most commonly measured by blood and urine analysis. Urine analysis is preferred for several reasons: It is less invasive than drawing blood, large samples are easier to collect, and because of the concentrating effects of the kidneys, relatively large concentrations of drugs and metabolites are found in urine (Council on Scientific Affairs, 1987). With urine testing of substances, it is important to monitor the collection of samples so no substitution or tampering will occurr, although with tobacco this may be less of a concern (except with the groups mentioned above: pregnant smokers, adolescents, and smokers with smoking-related illnesses); users of illegal substances are more apt to engage in such deceptive tactics in order to avoid negative consequences.

Biological testing of cigarette use involves sample analysis for the presence of carbon monoxide, thiocyanate, and cotinine (Sobell et al., 1994). Nicotine metabolites, cotinine, and thiocyanate can be found in saliva. Advantages of testing saliva are that it is not prone to tampering and the testing is relatively noninvasive (Sobell et al., 1994). Analysis of saliva is considered inferior to urinalysis because the concentration of drugs is relatively low in saliva, and they are retained for a shorter period of time. Carbon monoxide is a byproduct present in tobacco smoke measured via expired air; it has a short half-life (3–5 hours). Devices to measure carbon monoxide are commercially available and relatively inexpensive. Specificity of carbon monoxide measurement is good for heavy smoking but much less so for lower levels of smoking due to environmental sources of carbon monoxide (SRNT, 2002). Thiocyanate is a metabolite of hydrogen cyanide, a compound found in large amounts in cigarette smoke. Thiocyanate has a long half-life (approximately 2 weeks) and is present in blood, urine, and saliva. There is a high false positive rate with thiocyanate, especially with light smoking, because of the metabolite's presence in food sources. Cotinine is the major metabolite of nicotine and has a much longer half-life than nicotine (19–30 hours). Cotinine is present in blood, urine, and saliva.

Hair analysis is sometimes used for the detection of long-term substance use. Two limitations of this method are that it is a relatively expensive process and it does not detect recent use, so if someone quit using recently it would not be detectable by this technique (Sobell et al., 1994). Practically speaking, the information hair analysis yields is of limited value for tobacco treatment except for confirming abstinence over a long period of time. Hair analysis appears to be a more useful method for epidemiological research, in which it is used to test for exposure to environmental tobacco smoke (ETS, or secondhand smoke; Al-Delaimy, Crane, & Woodward, 2000; Mahoney & Al-Delaimy, 2001). The advantages of hair analysis for epidemiological studies are that nicotine and cotinine remain in hair significantly longer than in blood and urine; it is less invasive to take a hair sample (especially important when subjects are children); results are not subject to recall or report bias like questionnaires, which are often used to assess exposure to ETS; and results may be more sensitive to low exposures to ETS than questionnaires are.

Diagnosis of Nicotine Dependence

Assessment of Nicotine Dependence

Once an individual is identified in the screening process as having a potential problem, a diagnostic evaluation is indicated. For practical

purposes, if there is, or has ever been, any tobacco use, further evaluation is appropriate. To render a diagnosis, obviously a classification system
must be used. Typically, the *DSM–IV* is used for this purpose; the reader is
reminded that the *DSM–IV* and the *ICD–10* were explicitly developed to
be compatible with respect to codes and terms, so one would expect very
similar results from using either one. It is to be noted that although the
DSM–IV and the *ICD–10*, the national and international diagnostic classification systems, respectively, are the predominate classification systems for
psychiatric disorders, the Fagerstrom Tolerance Questionnaire (FTQ; Fagerstrom, 1978) is a measure designed specifically for the diagnosis of nicotine
dependence. The FTQ and updated versions are highly accepted and widely
used for clinical and research purposes (the FTQ is discussed fully later in
this chapter). Although very similar, the diagnostic criteria in the *DSM–IV*
and the *ICD–10* are not identical regarding nicotine dependence (Colby,
Tiffany, Shiffman, & Niaura, 2000b). For example, the *DSM–IV* has separate diagnostic criteria for nicotine withdrawal, which is not the case with
the *ICD–10*. It is interesting to note that the *ICD–10* refers to the term
"tobacco dependence" (rather than "nicotine dependence," found in the
DSM–IV), underscoring the fact that nicotine dependence is rare without
delivery via a tobacco product.

Three diagnostic categories relating to nicotine misuse can be found in
the *DSM–IV*: nicotine dependence, nicotine withdrawal, and a residual category of nicotine-related disorder not otherwise specified. Substance abuse
as defined by the *DSM–IV* is basically recurrent use of a substance despite
the experience of significant psychosocial consequences. As discussed in
chapter 1, psychosocial consequences do ensue from tobacco use but not in
as dramatic or obvious ways as are seen with other substances of abuse, so
a diagnostic category for nicotine abuse does not currently exist. This absence of a separate diagnosis for abuse of nicotine might also reflect the fact
that, due to the nature of nicotine addiction, there is not likely to be abuse
without dependence (Colby et al., 2000b). It is also the case that there is
no diagnostic category of nicotine intoxication; this should not be taken to
mean that there is no intoxication with nicotine. Rather, intoxication with
tobacco does not usually pose significant problems. The diagnostic criteria of
the *DSM–IV* for generic substance dependence have been discussed in chapter 4 with respect to nicotine addiction and are presented in Exhibit 5.1.

Clinicians should be familiar with the criteria so they are able to render
a diagnosis. In order for a diagnosis of nicotine dependence to be made, three
or more of the criteria must be present, occurring at any time in the same 12-
month period, and should result in clinically significant impairment.

Diagnostic specifiers exist relating to the presence or absence of physiological dependence, as do specifiers concerning the course (states of remission) and presence of agonist therapy; the reader is referred to the *DSM–IV*
for a review of these categories.

EXHIBIT 5.1
Diagnostic Criteria for Substance Dependence

1. Tolerance
2. Withdrawal
3. Substance taken in larger amounts or over longer period than intended
4. Persistent desire or unsuccessful attempts to reduce or control use
5. Great deal of time spent obtaining, using, or recovering from use
6. Important social, occupational, or recreational activities are given up or reduced because of substance use
7. Substance use despite knowledge of physical or psychological problems

Note. From *Diagnostic and Statistical Manual of Mental Disorders* (4th ed., pp. 244–245), American Psychiatric Association, 1994, Washington, DC: Author. Copyright 1994 by American Psychiatric Association. Adapted with permission.

The information necessary to make a diagnosis of nicotine use disorder can be gathered from a typical diagnostic interview (i.e., an unstructured or semistructured interview conducted by a clinician) as long as the clinician is familiar with the diagnostic criteria; or, the information can be apprehended through more formal means. Formal interview schedules such as the CIDI and the Diagnostic Interview Schedule (DIS; Robins, Helzer, Cottler, & Golding, 1989) may be impractical for most clinicians; they may be of use for researchers employing nonclinicians, or for clinicians employing technicians to perform some aspects of the diagnostic phase of treatment. The Structured Clinical Interview for the *DSM–III–R—Clinical Version* (SCID–CV; Spitzer et al., 1992) is a tool for use by clinicians. The CIDI, DIS, and SCID–CV yield not just diagnoses for tobacco use but other psychiatric diagnoses and so may be helpful in overall treatment planning (e.g., identification of psychiatric conditions that require addressing in treatment, in addition to nicotine dependence), although an experienced and skilled clinician should assess for the presence of such conditions in the diagnostic interview.

Various methods have been attempted to measure nicotine dependence (Payne, Smith, McCracken, McSherry, & Antony, 1994): (a) biochemical assessment, discussed earlier in this chapter, is primarily useful only for verification of abstinence; (b) physiological assessment (e.g., changes in functioning, such as heart rate) can be useful in the same way as biochemical methods; (c) reporting of history can provide important information and is the basis of diagnostic interviews; and (d) self-report measures have been developed with the rationale of gathering information on aspects of smoking thought to reflect the influence of dependence. The most popular self-report measure is the FTQ, which is considered the "gold standard" for measurement of nicotine dependence. It is a paper-and-pencil self-report measure that consists of eight items and was originally conceived to assess degree of physical dependence on nicotine. The eight questions on the FTQ and the scoring criteria are shown in Exhibit 5.2.

EXHIBIT 5.2
The Fagerstrom Tolerance Questionnaire

Question	Scoring criteria
1. How many cigarettes a day do you smoke?	0 = 1–15 cigarettes 1 = 16–25 cigarettes 2 = 26+ cigarettes
2. What brand do you smoke?	0 = low nicotine 1 = medium nicotine 2 = high nicotine
3. Do you inhale?	0 = no 1 = sometimes 2 = always
4. Do you smoke more in the morning than during the rest of the day?	0 = no 1 = yes
5. How soon after you wake up do you smoke your first cigarette?	0 = >30 min. 1 = ≤30 min.
6. Which cigarette would you hate most to give up?	0 = not first 1 = first of day
7. Do you find it difficult to refrain from smoking in places where it is forbidden, for example, in church, at the library, in the cinema?	0 = no 1 = yes
8. Do you smoke if you are so ill that you are in bed most of the day?	0 = no 1 = yes

Total scores range from 0 to 11. Higher scores on the FTQ indicate more severe nicotine dependence.

Note. From "Measuring Degree of Physical Dependence to Tobacco Smoking With Reference to Individualization of Treatment," by K. O. Fagerstrom, 1978, *Addictive Behaviors, 3*, p. 236. Copyright 1978 by Elsevier Science. Reprinted with permission.

Self-report methods such as the FTQ have the considerable advantage of being noninvasive to the person being assessed. Another strength of the FTQ (Colby et al., 2000b) is its ease of administration. In addition, its widespread use allows for comparison with many studies and clinical reports, and its reporting of scores as a single continuous variable, not a categorical diagnosis such as that yielded by the *DSM–IV*, may better reflect the nature of addiction as a continuous, rather than dichotomous, variable. Fagerstrom (1978) noted that in the design of the questionnaire the distinction between physical and psychological dependence did not imply that physical dependence was worse, just different and possibly requiring different treatment. The FTQ has been extensively researched and has been found to be effective as designed: It has successfully predicted the best candidates for nicotine replacement therapy (NRT) and the best dose of nicotine replacement (i.e., more dependent subjects, as measured by FTQ score, required a higher dose for replacement; Fagerstrom, 1991). The FTQ has also effectively predicted success in smoking cessation programs and distinguished between light and heavy smokers (Pomerleau, Carton, Lutzke, Flessland, & Pomerleau, 1994). In addition, FTQ scores have been found to correlate with biochemical markers such as expired carbon monoxide and levels of nicotine and cotinine in the body (Becona & Garcia, 1995; Heatherton, Kozlowski, Frecker, & Fagerstrom, 1991).

Psychometric limitations of the FTQ are that it appears to have a multifactorial structure (although it originally purported not to); poor item selection with some items adding nothing but error variance; and relatively low internal consistency (Heatherton et al., 1991; Tate & Schmitz, 1993). Because of the psychometric weaknesses that were identified, revisions of the FTQ have been made. Two of the revised scales most commonly encountered in the literature are the Fagerstrom Test for Nicotine Dependence (FTND) and the Heaviness of Smoking Index (HSI; Heatherton et al., 1991). The FTND consists of six questions instead of the original eight. In addition to dropping two items, the scoring systems of two other items were altered. The two items eliminated from the FTQ were numbers 2 (nicotine yield) and 3 (inhalation). These two items were dropped because they were thought to add little to the utility of the scale for distinguishing between levels of dependence, because compensatory smoking renders standard tar and nicotine yields of cigarettes almost irrelevant, and almost all smokers inhale. The items whose scoring was changed were numbers 1 (cigarettes per day) and 5 (time to first cigarette). For each item an extra scoring category was added. Revised scoring for item number 1 is as follows for the FTND: (a) 0 = 10 cigarettes or less, (b) 1 = 11 to 20 cigarettes, (c) 2 = 21 to 30 cigarettes, and (d) 3 = 31+ cigarettes. Scoring for item number 5 is as follows in the FTND: (a) 0 = >60 minutes, (b) 1 = 31 to 60 minutes, (c) 2 = 6 to 30 minutes, and (d) 3 = 5 minutes or less. Scores on the FTND may range from 0 to 10. Although there is no universally used qualitative classification system for the FTND, Moolchan et al. (2002) suggested the following as a gauge of severity of nicotine dependence:

1. Scores of 1–2 = very low dependence
2. Scores of 3–4 = low dependence
3. Score of 5 = medium dependence
4. Scores of 6–7 = high dependence
5. Scores of 8–10 = very high dependence

Although the FTND may represent an improvement over the FTQ in terms of internal consistency and account for more variance (Payne et al., 1994; Tate & Schmitz, 1993), it has its limitations as well. For example, the FTND may not be good at assessing smoking behavior of relatively light smokers (Etter, Duc, & Perneger, 1999). The applicability of the FTQ and FTND to assessment of the adolescent and young adult populations has been questioned. Because most smoking begins in adolescence, this is a large and significant population. Prokhorov, Koehly, Pallonen, and Hudmon (1998) found that with slight modifications the FTQ was applicable to adolescent smokers. Others (e.g., Haddock, Lando, Klesges, Talcott, & Renaud, 1999) have noted that the FTND without modifications may not apply well to younger, less experienced smokers. Neither the FTQ nor the FTND assesses some key aspects of the dependence syndrome described by the *DSM–IV*, such as withdrawal symptoms, desire to stop smoking, and unsuccessful quit attempts. In a study comparing dependent smokers assessed by the FTND to those identified via the *Diagnostic and Statistical Manual of Mental Disorders* (3rd ed., rev.; *DSM–III–R*; American Psychiatric Association, 1987), little agreement was found (Moolchan et al., 2002). Each method appears to identify different aspects of nicotine dependence, reflecting differing concepts of dependence. The FTND emphasizes morning smoking, heaviness of smoking, and liking for tobacco—relating to physical dependence; the *DSM–III–R* puts more emphasis on adverse consequences, desire to stop and failed quitting, and withdrawal symptoms—that is, on awareness of dependence and psychological symptoms (Moolchan et al., 2002). These findings suggest that nicotine dependence may be multifactorial and that no one instrument or method of assessment will perfectly capture all elements.

The HSI (Heatherton et al., 1991) is simply an abridged version of the FTND consisting of two items (numbers 5 [time to first cigarette] and 1 [cigarettes per day]), which are scored using the revised systems of the FTND. The HSI is psychometrically adequate but due to its brevity provides few insights into smoking behavior that would be helpful for treatment planning purposes. An even shorter measure, the first item of the HSI (latency to first cigarette of the day) is sometimes used as a very brief assessment of nicotine dependence.

Assessment of Nicotine Withdrawal

The assessment of nicotine withdrawal is important for a number of reasons (Patten & Martin, 1996; Welsch et al., 1999): The presence of a withdrawal syndrome in response to declining levels of nicotine in the body is evidence of physical dependence and so has diagnostic implications; aversive withdrawal symptoms provide obstacles to quit attempts; and smokers who have quit often attribute relapse to the experience of negative withdrawal symptoms. For the clinician who is experienced or who prefers the semistructured clinical interview, awareness of the *DSM–IV* criteria for nicotine withdrawal serves to guide questioning. *DSM–IV* diagnostic criteria for nicotine withdrawal are presented in Exhibit 3.2 and briefly summarized here:

1. Daily use of nicotine for at least several weeks.
2. At least four of the following of sufficient severity to cause significant distress or impairment in functioning within 24 hours

following cessation or reduction of nicotine use: (a) dysphoria; (b) insomnia; (c) irritability, frustration, anger; (d) anxiety; (e) difficulty concentrating; (f) restlessness; (g) decreased heart rate; (h) appetite increase or weight gain.

To get a quick estimate of the severity of withdrawal discomfort, a simple, face-valid item may be used; that is, the smoker may be asked to rate withdrawal discomfort experienced in previous quit attempts or after a reduction of nicotine intake on a scale from 1 to 10 (1 being the *least discomfort* and 10 the *most discomfort*).

When evaluating for the presence of nicotine withdrawal for research purposes, or in other circumstances in which a formal diagnostic tool is desired, self-report measures are commonly used. Several alternative questionnaires exist with various strengths and weaknesses (see Patten & Martin, 1996, for a review of three measures). A frequently used measure is the Minnesota Nicotine Withdrawal Scale (MNWS; Hughes & Hatsukami, 1986). The MNWS is a questionnaire that may be conceived as consisting of three parts, including subjective items, physiological indicators, and behavioral ratings (described and discussed in Patten & Martin, 1996). Subjective items inquire about the presence of symptoms of nicotine withdrawal that parallel those listed in the *DSM–IV*, with the exception that an item on craving is included on this scale (Welsch et al., 1999). Individual items are rated on a 4- or 5-point scale (depending on original or updated version of the scale, respectively) with 0 representing the absence of the symptom and 4 (or 5) the most intense; individual item scores are added together to yield a total withdrawal discomfort score. The MNWS total score is considered satisfactory for predicting cessation of nicotine use and the need for pharmacotherapy; however, when information regarding individual items is necessary, it is limited (Welsch et al., 1999). Physiological assessment includes measurement of weight and heart rate by the subject or by the treatment or research staff. Behavioral ratings of observable signs of withdrawal are provided by the subject and an observer (e.g., spouse, coworker, friend); evaluators are asked to rate only some signs of withdrawal, including irritability, anger and frustration, anxiety and nervousness, impatience and restlessness, and depression.

The MNWS is straightforward and easy to use, making it popular in clinical and research contexts. However, it, like other nicotine withdrawal scales, does suffer from psychometric deficiencies. Nicotine withdrawal scales evaluated by Patten and Martin (1996), including the MNWS, were characterized generally as assessing symptoms with single items possessing only face-validity and being deficient with respect to reliability and validity. A more recently developed scale, the Wisconsin Smoking Withdrawal Scale (WSWS; Welsch et al., 1999), purports to incorporate and improve on pre-existing scales, most notably the MNWS. The most significant improvement appears to be the provision of multiple items to assess the major symptom elements of the nicotine withdrawal syndrome, which allows for the establishment of reliable subscales.

Triage Stage

The triage process of assigning patients to the appropriate treatment setting and intensity is less critical for the treatment of nicotine dependence than for other substance use disorders. The reason is that there are fewer options to weigh. Treatment of nicotine dependence is conducted almost exclusively on an outpatient basis and does not require consideration of the list of residential options (e.g., inpatient treatment in a medical facility, halfway house, medical detoxification) that are relevant to the treatment of some substance use disorders; inpatient programs do exist (e.g., as discussed in Hoffman, Blackburn, & Cullari, 2001), but the vast majority of treatment occurs on an outpatient basis. The most important triage decision to be made is that regarding treatment intensity (Abrams et al., 2003). Smokers who are less nicotine dependent, do not have comorbid psychiatric or substance use disorders, and have a supportive social or family environment are appropriate candidates for less intensive treatment options (all others should receive more intensive treatment). Treatment history is also relevant in determining intensity of treatment. Smokers with a lifetime quit attempt of at least 1 year's duration, and with a most recent quit attempt of at least 5 to 14 days of abstinence, may be appropriate for less intensive treatment. If there is no past history of attempts at cessation, in the absence of other indicators of the need for intensive treatment, less intensive treatment may be considered. Smokers not currently ready for a quit attempt should still receive treatment, with the intermediate goal of moving them toward readiness to change. Outpatient treatment options usually available include formal quit programs, hypnosis, acupuncture, traditional psychotherapy and individual counseling, 12-step programs, pharmacotherapy, bibliotherapy (self-help), and brief counseling by a medical practitioner, in no particular order. The range of outpatient options will be discussed fully in chapters 6 and 7. Of course, selection of treatment intensity and interventions, like all other aspects of treatment, is best when it is a shared process between patient and clinician.

Treatment Planning

It was stated at the outset of this chapter that all substance use disorders require a comprehensive assessment for effective treatment. The diagnosis of nicotine dependence, if it exists, is only a step toward a treatment plan. Because any two individuals with nicotine dependence may be very different in other important ways, diverse treatment needs can exist. Some factors that may reasonably be expected to affect treatment response, and therefore require assessment, are attitudes, outcome expectancies, stages of change, intellectual functioning, medical history, psychiatric status, treatment history, presence of a learning disability, and substance use history.

Attitudes, outcome expectancies, and stages of change are similar concepts. They are, of course, distinct areas of interest, each occupying its own niche in the literature. However, one important commonality that allows them to be grouped and discussed together is that they refer to primarily cognitive, evaluative processes that relate to decisions and behavior (in this instance about smoking). Assessing the status of cognitive factors such as these can guide treatment interventions and aid in the understanding of treatment success and failure. Abstinence as an outcome measure reveals only so much information; if there is treatment success (continued abstinence) or failure (relapse), we gain little insight from these facts alone about what was helpful in the treatment, and what was not. It can be beneficial to study such things as changes in a smoker's thoughts and behavior before quitting, prior to relapse (Etter, Humair, Bergman, & Perneger, 2000; Rustin & Tate, 1993), or in any other circumstances where a decision is made regarding smoking behavior.

Attitudes, referring to the favorable or unfavorable appraisal or evaluation of some behavior (Etter et al., 2000), are known to relate to behavior. For example, if a smoker reports predominately positive thoughts about smoking, it would follow that this person is less likely to make a quit attempt at that time. In support of this point, attitudes have shown a strong association with stages of change such that, for example, precontemplators (those not thinking of giving up smoking) rate negative aspects of smoking lower, and positive aspects higher, than contemplators (smokers considering quitting; Etter et al., 2000).

Outcome expectancies are probability ratings of consequences of specific behaviors; scales exist for assessment of expectancies for alcohol, drugs, and tobacco. The Smoking Consequences Questionnaire (SCQ; Brandon & Baker, 1991) and the Smoking Consequences Questionnaire—Adult (SCQ–Adult; Copeland, Brandon, & Quinn, 1995) are scales designed to assess outcome expectancies of adolescents and adults, respectively, regarding smoking. The SCQ and SCQ–Adult are self-administered, paper-and-pencil questionnaires. Items are statements that derive from 10 scales, and respondents are required to rate the likelihood of occurrence on a scale from 0 (*least likely*) to 9 (*most likely*). The scales are Negative Affect Reduction, Stimulation/State Enhancement, Health Risk, Taste/Sensorimotor Manipulation, Social Facilitation, Weight Control, Craving/Addiction, Negative Physical Feelings, Boredom Reduction, and Negative Social Impression. The SCQ–Adult (Copeland et al., 1995) is presented in Exhibit 5.3.

With the SCQ–Adult, ex-smokers were found to have fewer positive expectancies and more negative expectancies about smoking than smokers

EXHIBIT 5.3
The Smoking Consequences Questionnaire—Adult

Scale	Items
Negative affect reduction	When I'm angry, a cigarette can calm me down. Smoking calms me down when I feel nervous. If I'm feeling irritable, a smoke will help me relax. Cigarettes help me deal with anger. When I'm upset with someone, a cigarette helps me cope. Cigarettes help me reduce or handle tension. If I'm tense, a cigarette helps me to relax. Cigarettes help me deal with anxiety or worry. When I am worrying about something, a cigarette is helpful.
Stimulation/state enhancement	Smoking a cigarette energizes me. Cigarettes can really make me feel good. A cigarette can give me energy when I'm bored and tired. I feel better physically after having a cigarette. When I'm feeling happy, smoking helps keep that feeling. I feel like I do a better job when I am smoking. I like the way a cigarette makes me feel physically.
Health risk	Smoking is taking years off my life. The more I smoke, the more I risk my health. By smoking I risk heart disease and lung cancer. Smoking is hazardous to my health.
Taste/ sensorimotor manipulation	I enjoy the taste sensations while smoking. When I smoke, the taste is pleasant. I will enjoy the flavor of a cigarette. I enjoy feeling the smoke hit my mouth and the back of my throat. Cigarettes taste good. I will enjoy feeling a cigarette on my tongue and lips. I enjoy the steps I take to light up. Just handling a cigarette is pleasurable. I like to watch the smoke from my cigarette.
Social facilitation	I feel more at ease with other people if I have a cigarette. I feel like part of a group when I'm around other smokers. Smoking helps me enjoy people more. Conversations seem more special if we are all smoking. I enjoy parties more when I am smoking.
Weight control	Smoking keeps my weight down. Cigarettes keep me from eating more than I should. Smoking helps me control my weight. Cigarettes keep me from overeating. Smoking controls my appetite.
Craving/addiction	Nicotine "fits" can be controlled by smoking. Smoking will satisfy my nicotine cravings. Smoking temporarily reduces those repeated urges for cigarettes. A cigarette can satisfy my urge to smoke. I will become more dependent on nicotine if I continue smoking. I become more addicted the more I smoke.

continues

EXHIBIT 5.3 *(Continued)*

Negative physical feelings	Cigarettes make my lungs hurt. Smoking irritates my mouth and throat. My throat burns after smoking.
Boredom reduction	If I have nothing to do, a smoke can help kill time. When I'm alone, a cigarette can help me pass the time. Cigarettes are good for dealing with boredom. When I feel bored and tired, a cigarette can really help.
Negative social impression	I look ridiculous while smoking. People think less of me if they see me smoking. Smoking makes me seem less attractive.

Note. From "The Smoking Consequences Questionnaire—Adult: Measurement of Smoking Outcome Expectancies of Experienced Smokers," by A. L. Copeland, T. H. Brandon, and E. P. Quinn, 1995, *Psychological Assessment, 7*, pp. 493–494. Copyright 1995 by the American Psychological Association.

attempting to quit and current smokers with no intentions to quit (Copeland et al., 1995).

The SCQ and SCQ–Adult also allow for the assessment of desirability of outcome in addition to probability. However, the authors concluded that the inclusion of desirability scores did not add to the strength of the scales but did add time to administration and scoring, so use of the additional scores is not recommended (Copeland et al., 1995). It is preferable to use the SCQ–Adult without formal scoring as a way to stimulate thinking and discussion about the function(s) of smoking for that individual. If a patient is having difficulty identifying motives for smoking while completing the "What I Like About Smoking" form (presented in Exhibit 5.4), share a copy of the SCQ–Adult with him or her to assist in completing the assignment. Please see the Appendix for discussion of the role of this form in the assessment and treatment of nicotine dependence. In Exhibit 5.5, a case example illustrating the use of the "What I Like About Smoking" form is presented.

The Stages of Change Model, also known as the Transtheoretical Model, is a model describing five stages of change and the processes involved in movement from stage to stage for smokers and users of other substances (Prochaska & DiClemente, 1983; Prochaska & Goldstein, 1991). The stages of change are

1. *Precontemplation*. Smokers are not thinking about stopping and have no interest in changing in the next 6 months. They avoid information about smoking, exaggerate benefits and minimize risks, and do not like to talk or think about smoking.

WHAT I LIKE ABOUT SMOKING

People are often reluctant to give up smoking. Their reluctance to stop smoking partially stems from the fact that they feel they get some benefits from smoking. Smokers frequently feel that cigarettes can help them to feel better, look better, feel rewarded, think more clearly, and be more successful socially. These apparent benefits may serve as roadblocks to cessation efforts.

Exercise 1. Please list the three things you like most about smoking.

1. _____
2. _____
3. _____

In order to help lessen the grip nicotine has on you, it may be helpful to identify other ways to get what you enjoy from cigarettes. For example, if you smoke cigarettes to calm your nerves, it can be helpful to identify and practice other methods of relaxation.

Exercise 2. Please list at least one alternative method to smoking for achieving the desired effects listed above.

1. _____
2. _____
3. _____

Note. From *Stop Smoking System*, by C. E. Dodgen, 2004, Florham Park, NJ. Unpublished manuscript. Reprinted with permission.

2. *Contemplation*. Smokers are aware there is a problem, are considering a change, but have no firm plan; they are considering changing within the next 6 months. Contemplators see the positives and negatives of smoking as almost equal, with the cons a little higher.
3. *Preparation* (sometimes referred to as *determination*). Smokers have made a definite decision to stop smoking, but have not yet taken action; they intend to stop in the next month. In addition, smokers in the preparation stage have tried to stop smoking at least once in the past year.
4. *Action*. Smokers have actually stopped at this stage, but have quit for less than 6 months.
5. *Maintenance*. (Former) smokers have achieved successful change and are maintaining abstinence from smoking for more than 6 months. If resumption of smoking occurs, the relapse results in the smoker reentering the cycle once again at an earlier stage.

EXHIBIT 5.5
Case Example: Donald M.

BRIEF BACKGROUND AND SMOKING HISTORY

Donald M. is a married police officer. He is 39 years old with two teenage children. His wife of 17 years encouraged him to seek treatment. Mr. M. presented with symptoms of mild to moderate depression. He experienced these symptoms for years but never previously sought treatment. His wife thought that their arguing and his eruptions of anger at home were occurring more frequently, which was the reason she was pressing Mr. M. to seek treatment. Mr. M. was identified as a smoker in the initial evaluation. He had smoked regularly since he was 16 years old and currently smoked about a pack of cigarettes (20) per day. He is very active at work, and used to enjoy sports and physical exercise in his leisure time. Being previously into health and fitness, he recognized that smoking was not good for him and quit several times. He ultimately resumed smoking after each quit attempt. The longest stretch of abstinence from cigarettes was about 4 months, approximately 10 years prior to coming to treatment.

SMOKING-CESSATION INTERVENTIONS

Mr. M. immediately accepted the offer of assistance to stop smoking but did not feel ready to actually attempt cessation until about 10 months into treatment. In completing the "What I Like About Smoking" form, he reported in Exercise 1 that smoking helped to "relax, calm me down." He also reported feeling that cigarettes provided a break or escape when he felt overwhelmed at home or work. Mr. M. additionally felt that smoking provided a little reward; it was his way of treating himself to something he likes and desires. For Exercise 2 of the form, Mr. M. identified physical exercise as an alternative means of achieving relaxation. He suggested the taking of a walk or water break as escapes from overwhelming situations at work and home and identified his favorite dessert (ice-cream sundae) as a reward he could give himself. After discussion of his responses, it was agreed that Mr. M. might benefit from relaxation methods that he could use quickly, and at almost any time or place. Therefore, in addition to physical exercise that he would engage in 3 to 4 days per week after work, he would practice and use deep breathing exercises to calm himself down. He chose this method of relaxation from a book purchased at a local bookstore. It was also decided together that although an ice-cream sundae was undoubtedly rewarding, it could be problematic as an exclusive means of treating himself because of the obvious negative implications for his weight and health. Mr. M. thought that other methods to reward himself could include the establishment of nightly "down time" consisting of a half hour to do as he pleases, such as watch a favorite television show, listen to music, or take a hot bath.

COMMENTS

If smokers feel as though they are getting some benefit from smoking (as most smokers do), one is almost asking the impossible by requesting they quit without also providing them with alternative means to get what they feel they are deriving from smoking. Through this collaborative intervention, smokers attempting to quit are taught that there are other, healthier ways to achieve the desired outcomes provided by smoking, and that they are capable of learning and using them.

Smokers do not typically proceed in a linear movement from Stages 1 to 5. Rather, a cyclical pattern is noted with relapses to smoking once abstinence is achieved, and with the smoker reentering at an earlier stage after relapse, usually contemplation (Prochaska & Goldstein, 1991). Upwards of three to six cycles may be necessary, on average, before successful maintenance is achieved.

Stage of change at the start of treatment has been found to be significantly related to outcome: Progressively more successful quitters were found from among those identified as precontemplators, contemplators, and those prepared for change (Stages 1, 2, and 3, respectively). It appears that most smokers are in the precontemplation stage (60%), with fewer in the contemplation stage (30%), and fewer still in the preparation stage (10%) (Prochaska & Goldstein, 1991). This finding is especially unfortunate given that most treatment programs are geared to people ready for behavior change. The implication from the study of stages of change is that the level of readiness needs to be assessed for each individual and treatment matched to the smoker's current stage. For smokers in the first two stages, the goal should be to move them to the next stages, rather than to attempt behavior change immediately. Such an approach has the potential to enhance motivation for smokers who are poorly motivated to change, ultimately increasing treatment effectiveness and empowering treatment professional and patient alike.

A major strength of the Stages of Change Model is that it provides a system to describe, understand, and, ideally, influence motivation for change. Motivation for change is seen as a dynamic state open to alteration, not a static trait (Sobell et al., 1994). A prevalent attitude in the treatment of substance abuse is to simply conclude that a given individual is "not ready" for treatment if he or she shows any resistance to treatment recommendations. The clinician can then only wait for the patient's motivation to change (e.g., by "hitting bottom"). With this model, the patient's motivation can be assessed and specific interventions can be applied in an attempt to actively affect the patient's motivation for change. The Stages of Change Model is closely associated with a client-centered approach to treatment, also referred to as motivational interviewing. *Motivational interviewing* is a treatment approach that strongly contrasts with traditional substance abuse treatment models (Bell & Rollnick, 1996). The style of the therapist and goals of intervention are very different in motivational interviewing and traditional treatment. Rather than aggressively challenge and attempt to directly convince the patient to change behavior, in motivational interviewing the therapist attempts to collaborate with patients, to engage them at their own internal level of motivation, and to enhance their internal desire to change behavior. The client-centered style of treatment is thought to maximize patient involvement in treatment and to minimize attrition (Dodgen & Shea, 2000).

Central to the discussion of motivation for change are the 10 processes of change that may be used in an effort to alter (improve) motivation (discussed in Sutton, 1996):

1. *Consciousness raising:* the gathering of information about oneself and the problem (smoking); a key element of most therapies.
2. *Self-liberation:* belief in one's ability to change (reminiscent of the concept of self-efficacy).
3. *Dramatic relief:* the smoker's awareness of his or her feelings about smoking, quitting, and treatment, and expression of these feelings.
4. *Environmental reevaluation:* gauging the effect of one's behavior on the environment; for smokers, the impact of second-hand smoke is relevant.
5. *Helping relationships:* seeking the assistance of trusted friends and family, or supportive relationships with treatment professionals.
6. *Stimulus control:* avoidance of stimuli associated with smoking (a staple of recovery from all substances).
7. *Counterconditioning:* substitution of healthier alternatives for smoking behavior (e.g., walking when feeling stressed rather than smoking).
8. *Social liberation:* expanding the range of nonproblem behaviors (combating reliance on the tried-and-true behavior of smoking).
9. *Self-reevaluation:* self-image, especially with respect to being a smoker versus nonsmoker.
10. *Reinforcement management:* reward of self or by others for quitting smoking (refers to the importance of positive reinforcement for making changes).

Processes of change do not appear to be randomly used by smokers attempting cessation; that is, a relationship appears to exist between stage of change and processes of change used by the quitter. Smokers in the precontemplation stage use the fewest change processes overall, as expected. Contemplators use cognitive and evaluative processes (i.e., consciousness raising and self-reevaluation) much more than precontemplators because they are open to information about smoking and thinking about the problem. Smokers in the preparation stage use behavioral and social processes (e.g., helping relationships) more than contemplators. Smokers in the action stage tend to use processes such as counterconditioning, stimulus control, reinforcement management, and helping relationships. Processes of change have been broadly classified as experiential (consisting of cognitive or emotional activity, or both) and behavioral; those in the former category are consciousness raising, dramatic relief, self-reevaluation, environmental reevaluation, and social liberation; the remaining processes are in the latter category. Generally speaking, smokers in the contemplation and preparation stages tend to use the experiential processes; those in the action stage use the behavioral processes. Explicit in this approach is the idea that cessation of smoking behavior is largely dependent on the individual's deciding to stop or not (Davidson, 1996), so the smoker's intrinsic level of motivation must be identified, respected, and taken into account in the treatment process.

There are several instruments designed to measure stages of change. One measure is the URICA (University of Rhode Island Change Assessment scale; McConnaughy, Prochaska, & Velicer, 1983). The URICA is a 32-item scale assessing a subject's attitude toward change that allows for classification of the respondent's stage of change. One particularly appealing method for assessing progress toward abstinence or relapse is the Contemplation Ladder (Rustin & Tate, 1993). The Contemplation Ladder is conceptually based on the Stages of Change Model of Prochaska and DiClemente (1983) and the presentation format of Biener and Abrams (1989). The ladder is described as a visual-analog scale on which smokers identify their stage of change based on their agreement with statements occupying different rungs on a ladder. With the Rustin and Tate method, there are six separate ladders, each with 11 statements, one to a rung; at the bottom rung of each ladder (score = 0) are statements showing the least progress, and at the top (score = 10), the most progress toward abstinence. The first ladder is the Precontemplation/Contemplation Ladder, which measures willingness to stop smoking with the bottom statement "I do not have a problem with smoking and I do not intend to cut down or quit" and the top statement "I have decided to quit smoking." The other ladders are presented in the same manner as the Precontemplation/Contemplation Ladder and correspond to stages of change including, in order, Determination Ladder, Action Ladder, Abstinence Ladder, Maintenance Ladder, and Relapse Ladder.

Assessment of stage of change can also be achieved by asking the smoker a series of questions (Prochaska & Goldstein, 1991) as shown in Exhibit 5.6.

Clear acknowledgment of the need to assess the smoker's motivation to quit is made in the Clinical Practice Guideline (USDHHS, 2000b). The recommendation is for physicians to ask directly if the smoking patient is now willing to quit and, if so, for physicians to provide appropriate treatment. If the smoker is not interested in quitting, the physician is advised to actively promote motivation to quit through the use of the "5 Rs": (a) Relevance (identifying how and why quitting is personally relevant for the patient), (b) Risks (identifying possible negative consequences of smoking), (c) Rewards (identifying possible positive consequences of quitting), (d) Roadblocks (identifying and overcoming barriers to quitting), and (e) Repetition (repeating motivational intervention in every subsequent contact).

EXHIBIT 5.6
Questions to Assess Stage of Change

1. Are you intending to quit smoking in the next 6 months? If no, the patient is in the precontemplation stage; if yes, proceed to the next question.
2. Are you intending to stop smoking in the next month? If no, the smoker is in the contemplation stage; if yes, proceed to the next question.
3. Did you try to quit smoking in the past year? If no, the smoker is in the contemplation stage. If yes, the smoker is in the preparation stage.
4. If the smoker has already quit, ask them how long ago they stopped smoking. If less than 6 months ago, they are in the action stage; if more than 6 months, maintenance stage.

Note. From "Process of Smoking Cessation: Implications for Clinicians," by J. O. Prochaska and M. G. Goldstein, 1991, *Clinics in Chest Medicine, 12*(4), p. 730.

Nicotine dependence treatment history was mentioned above in the triage section as a means to assess treatment intensity that may be required for a given individual. Treatment history may also provide other information for treatment planning purposes by determining what was and was not helpful in prior quit attempts (if there were any). In general, it is advisable not to replicate treatment that has already proven ineffective for someone. Careful attention must be paid to details, however. For example, I have had smokers inform me that they had tried NRT in the past and did not find it helpful. When they were questioned about it, it became clear that they had used the medication inappropriately or had had unrealistic expectations, so the treatment was not given a fair trial.

A new assessment tool that has been developed and is currently being evaluated in validity studies is the Wisconsin Inventory of Smoking Dependence Motives (WISDM–68; Piper et al., 2004). The WSDM–68 is a 68-item scale based on the idea that tobacco dependence is multidimensional and determined by diverse motives. Dependence is thought to be related to 13 motives for drug use, which form the subscales of the inventory: Affiliative Attachment, Automaticity, Behavioral Choice (melioration), Cognitive Enhancement, Craving, Cue Exposure (associative processes), Loss of Control, Negative Reinforcement, Positive Reinforcement, Social (environmental goads), Taste and Memory Properties, Tolerance, and Weight Control.

Evaluation of the remaining factors (intellectual functioning, medical history, psychiatric history, learning disability, and substance use history) for treatment planning may be achieved by conducting a standard psychosocial, diagnostic interview. A copy of an assessment form that I use in my practice is presented in Exhibit 5.7. The psychosocial assessment form is the product of my training and experience. The areas of functioning assessed on the form derive from mental health clinic and psychiatric hospital intake forms, standard mental status questions, and questions to assess for potential substance abuse.

EXHIBIT 5.7
Psychosocial Assessment Form

Name_____

Date: _____

Age: _____

DOB: _____

S.S. #: _____

Address: _____

Phone Numbers: _____

Chief Complaint: _____

_____

_____

_____

_____

History of Present Illness: _____

_____

_____

_____

_____

_____

Educational History: _____

_____

_____

_____

Vocational History: _____

_____

_____

_____

Developmental History: _____

_____

_____

_____

Social/Interpersonal History: _____

_____

_____

Sexual History: _____

_____

_____

Family of Origin: _____

_____

_____

_____

continues

EXHIBIT 5.7 *(Continued)*

Current Family: _____
_____
_____
_____
_____

Psychiatric/Psychological Treatment History: _____
_____
_____

Family Psychiatric/Psychological Treatment History: _____
_____
_____

Major Medical History: _____
_____
_____

Head Injury/Accidents: _____
_____
_____

Substance Use:

    List all substances used (including nicotine): _____
_____

    Age of first use for each substance: _____
_____

    Routes of administration for each substance: _____
_____

    Age of peak use, and amount used, for each substance: _____
_____

    Number of days of current use of each substance per week: _____
_____

    Amount of each substance used on a typical day of use: _____
_____

    Date of last use of each substance: _____
_____

    Negative consequences (problems with family, marriage, friends, work, the law, physical health, mental health, finances, or religion/spirituality): _____
_____

Dangerous Behavior: _____
_____
_____

Presence of Symptoms of Severe Disturbance
(hallucinations/delusions/bizarre behavior):
_____
_____

continues

EXHIBIT 5.7 *(Continued)*

Obsessive–Compulsive Rituals; Tic Behaviors: _____

_____

_____

Mood: _____

_____

_____

Anxiety: _____

_____

Significant Losses: _____

_____

Memory: _____

_____

Orientation: _____

Judgment: _____

Observations:

    Level of Consciousness: _____

    Affect: _____

    Appearance and Behavior: _____

    _____

    _____

    Content and Form of Thought: _____

    _____

    _____

    Language: _____

    _____

Initial Diagnostic Impression: _____

_____

_____

_____

Initial Treatment Plan: _____

_____

_____

_____

_____

_____

_____

Signature and Date

Note. From *Substance Use Disorders: Assessment and Treatment* (pp. 87–89), by C. E. Dodgen and W. M. Shea, 2000, San Diego, CA: Academic Press. Copyright 2000 by Academic Press. Reprinted with permission.

It is my impression that some clinicians may know which areas of functioning they need to assess (especially if they have a form in front of them) but be uncertain why they need to assess those areas or what questions to ask to make the assessment. For this reason, Exhibit 5.8 presents examples of questions that can be asked to obtain the desired information, as well as rationales for inclusion of items on the form.

SUMMARY

With nicotine dependence, as with any other disorder, assessment drives treatment. A stage model may be used to describe the assessment process. Stages of assessment include screening, diagnosis, triage, and treatment planning. Screening may be achieved through formal psychometric tools or with a clinical interview; biological testing is sometimes used for screening purposes, mainly to monitor compliance with treatment.

Diagnosis of nicotine dependence and nicotine withdrawal can be achieved with the use of the *DSM–IV* (by interview), with psychometric interview schedules, or with paper-and-pencil tests (using the FTQ or one of its derivatives). The triage phase is less relevant to the treatment of nicotine dependence than dependence on other abusable drugs because almost all treatment is rendered on an outpatient basis. However, it is still important to identify the proper intensity of treatment, and this is accomplished in the triage phase. For the treatment planning phase of assessment, a complete evaluation must be made to develop an appropriate, individualized treatment plan. Assessment of many variables is necessary (essentially requiring a full psychodiagnostic evaluation); some variables of particular interest are medical history, psychiatric and substance use history, nicotine dependence treatment history, and stage of change. If the individual is experiencing current medical problems from smoking, these consequences would be an important source of motivation for treatment. A positive psychiatric or substance abuse history complicates the treatment picture, as will be discussed fully in chapter 9. Previous treatment history gives some idea of how to improve on past attempts. Stage of change is a crucially important concept in the treatment of nicotine dependence. The Stages of Change Model is an explicit reminder of the need to work with the patient at his or her level of motivation. If the patient is not highly motivated, intermediate goals can help move the smoker ahead on the continuum of behavior change, making a cessation attempt more likely at a later date. In this model there are reasons to be in treatment and for the clinician to pursue smoking cessation before, during, and after a cessation attempt. Such a mindset gets away from the acute-care model that leads to such unproductive notions as someone being untreatable or "a failure" if abstinence is not attempted, achieved, and maintained, and the ensuing hopelessness and

EXHIBIT 5.8
Sample Questions and Rationales for Inclusion of Items on the Psychosocial Assessment Form

1. Categories 1 through 7 allow for the recording of basic identifying information.

2. Chief complaint
   a. Example of a question to ask
      (1) What brings you here?
   b. Rationales for assessment of this item
      (1) Obtain description of the problem as perceived by the patient.
      (2) Assessment of insight. The person who recognizes he or she is experiencing problems and can identify probable causes will be better able to cooperatively engage in the treatment process.

3. History of present illness
   a. Examples of questions
      (1) How long have you experienced these problems?
      (2) What have you done (currently and in the past) to resolve these difficulties?
   b. Rationales for assessment of this item
      (1) A longitudinal perspective is necessary in order to accurately assess psychoactive substance use as well as other psychiatric disorders. For example, someone may present as severely depressed on evaluation; a review of their history is necessary to determine whether their current presentation is representative of bipolar disorder, unipolar depression, or a symptom of amphetamine withdrawal, to name several possible causes.
      (2) Efforts made to resolve difficulties give some idea of coping skills and motivation to help self, or to seek assistance for problems.

4. Educational History
   a. Examples of questions
      (1) How far did you go in school?
      (2) What kind of a student are/were you?
      (3) Any history of child study team involvement or receipt of special services or placement?
      (4) Any behavior problems in school? Ever suspended? Expelled?
   b. Rationale for assessment of this item
      (1) A major demand of childhood is to attend and perform at school. Difficulties adequately meeting academic demands can indicate learning disability, intellectual deficiency, attentional problems, emotional or behavioral problems. Generally speaking, a good educational history is associated with positive adjustment and is a prognostically favorable sign.

5. Vocational History
   a. Examples of questions
      (1) Are you currently working? If so, what kind of work do you do? If not, how do you support yourself?
      (2) Do you like your work?
      (3) Have you ever been terminated from a job or experienced significant problems? If so, what kinds of problems did you experience?
      (4) Have you ever experienced extensive periods of unemployment or underemployment?
      (5) Have you ever received disability benefits? If so, what for?

continues

EXHIBIT 5.8 *(Continued)*

---

    b. Rationales for assessment of this item

        (1) A major demand of adulthood is to work. Similar to educational history, a solid work history is prognostically favorable and an indicator of a person's general adjustment to life. For example, someone who is currently employed and has been so continuously for the past 5 years is functioning more effectively than someone receiving disability benefits for the past year.

        (2) Current employment status has significant implications for scheduling of treatment as well as ability to pay for treatment.

6. Developmental History

    a. Examples of questions

        (1) Are you aware of having experienced any significant delays or abnormalities in terms of achievement of developmental milestones: Sitting up? Crawling? Standing? Walking? Talking? Toilet Training? Separation for school?

    b. Rationale for assessment of this item

        (1) Significant developmental delays are associated with developmental disorders and behavioral, intellectual, emotional, and neurological problems.

7. Social/Interpersonal History

    a. Examples of questions

        (1) Are you currently socially active? If so, what kinds of things do you do with friends? If not, have you ever been socially active?

        (2) Do you have any close friends that you can discuss almost any topic with?

        (3) Growing up, did you like other children? Did they like you?

        (4) Are you able to form and maintain long-term relationships?

    b. Rationales for assessment of this item

        (1) Inability to engage in satisfying, healthy, and long-lasting relationships is a sign of serious maladjustment.

        (2) A solid social network is a very significant aid to treatment of mental and physical maladies. If a supportive social network is lacking, it often must be provided in treatment. For example, someone with an advanced psychoactive substance use disorder who has alienated family and friends requires the considerable social support offered in group-based treatment and/or NA/AA networks.

8. Sexual History

    a. Examples of questions

        (1) What is your sexual orientation?

        (2) How old were you when you began dating?

        (3) Are you sexually active? If so, do you practice safe sex regarding disease protection? Pregnancy? How old were you at the time of first sexual intercourse?

        (4) Describe your longest continuous relationship.

        (5) Have you ever been a victim of sexual abuse?

        (6) Have you ever experienced any sexual difficulties?

        (7) Do you engage in any unusual sexual behaviors?

    b. Rationales for assessment of this item

        (1) Sexual behavior is often disturbed by substance abuse. More specifically, with frequent substance use, sex drive usually diminishes.

        (2) Disease transmission among substance abusers is a serious health risk.

continues

EXHIBIT 5.8 *(Continued)*

    (3) Victims of sexual abuse are at elevated risk for various forms of psychopathology.

    (4) The ability to engage in long-term sexual relationships is a developmental challenge starting in adolescence. How successful one is in negotiating this developmental challenge offers another gauge of overall developmental progress/adaptation.

    (5) Sexual perversions can be a source of shame and discomfort. Direct questioning allows for a rare opportunity to discuss these very private matters that may otherwise not be reported.

9. Family of Origin
  a. Examples of questions
    (1) Do you have any siblings? If so, what are their names and ages? How do you get along with them? If any are deceased, what did they die of?
    (2) Are your parents alive? If not, when and what did they die of? If alive, how old are they? Describe your mother to me; your father.
  b. Rationales for assessment of this item
    (1) Positive family relationships are correlated with good physical and mental health, and are an asset to recovery for someone with psychosocial difficulties.
    (2) If family members are deceased, cause of death provides information about risk factors for illness for the individual being assessed.

10. Current Family
  a. Examples of questions
    (1) What is your marital status? If married, how long are you married? How would you characterize the marital relationship? If divorced, what factor(s) contributed to the divorce?
    (2) Do you have any children?
    (3) Has there ever been any violence in the home?
  b. Rationales for assessment of this item
    (1) Makeup and quality of current family life provides an indicator of a person's ability to establish and maintain a satisfying heterosexual relationship in marriage, parenting ability, and responsibility toward his or her family. Especially in cases of substance abuse, deterioration in marital and family relationships is observed.
    (2) Inquiries about violent behavior are directly made to assess for the presence of potentially dangerous behavior and the risk of its occurrence.

11. Psychiatric/Psychological Treatment History
  a. Examples of questions
    (1) Have you ever received mental health or substance abuse treatment services by a psychiatrist, psychologist, social worker, physician, or some other type of counselor? If so, what were you treated for? What kind of services did you receive? Was medication prescribed? Did you find the treatment helpful? How did you decide to stop treatment if it is not currently under way?
  b. Rationale for assessment of this item
    (1) Treatment history offers diagnostic and prognostic information, as well as information relevant to treatment planning. Diagnostically, if someone presenting for treatment previously received treatment for a psychiatric or substance use disorder, the evaluating clinician should be particularly alert for the reoccurrence of the same condition(s). Prognostically,

continues

EXHIBIT 5.8 *(Continued)*

previous response to treatment will give the clinician some expectation of the current response to treatment. Finally, the current treatment plan should be guided in part by the past response to treatment. That is, those elements helpful in previous treatment should be employed in current treatment; those not helpful should be altered in the current treatment. Changes should be considered with respect to modality of treatment (e.g., individual, group, family), type of therapy (e.g., cognitive–behavioral, psychodynamic), intensity of services (number of hours of contact per week), and type of program (e.g., NA/AA, outpatient substance abuse program, partial hospitalization program).

12. Family Psychiatric/Psychological Treatment History
    a. Examples of questions
        (1) Has anyone in your family ever received mental health or substance abuse services by a psychiatrist, psychologist, social worker, physician, or any other type of counselor? If so, what were they treated for and what type of treatment did they receive?
    b. Rationale for assessment of this item
        (1) Since most, if not all, psychiatric conditions have some genetic underpinnings, the clinician is attempting to establish risk for specific psychiatric/substance use disorders.

13. Major Medical History
    a. Examples of questions
        (1) Are you currently receiving medical treatment? If so, what is the nature of the illness and the treatment?
        (2) Have you experienced any significant health problems due to illness or injury?
    b. Rationales for assessment of this item
        (1) Medical conditions may be a consequence of substance abuse (e.g., respiratory infection from smoking cigarettes or marijuana).
        (2) Some medical conditions may present as psychiatric conditions. For example, diabetes and thyroid dysfunction may present as depressive disorders.
        (3) Medical conditions, especially chronic and/or severe illnesses, may create secondary psychiatric disorders.
        (4) Medications for the treatment of physical conditions may significantly alter cognitive, behavioral, and/or emotional functioning and may create psychiatric symptoms. For example, hormone replacement therapy (for menopausal women) has been observed to contribute to the experience of symptoms of depression and anxiety.

14. Head Injury/Accidents
    a. Examples of questions
        (1) Have you ever lost consciousness due to an accident (e.g., sporting, industrial, automobile)? If so, were there any residual changes in your thinking, emotional functioning, or behavior?
    b. Rationale for assessment of this item
        (1) A head injury with lingering effects may be the cause of psychiatric symptoms and/or may be a factor complicating treatment.

15. Substance Use
    a. Examples of questions
        (1) The questions listed on the form are self-explanatory.

continues

EXHIBIT 5.8 *(Continued)*

   b. Rationales for assessment of this item
     (1) The questions on the form are standard ones employed to assess patterns of use and the experience of negative psychosocial consequences.

16. Dangerous Behavior
   a. Examples of questions
     (1) Are you currently experiencing any thoughts or feelings about hurting or killing yourself? If yes, do you have any plans or have you engaged in any behavior? If not currently experiencing such thoughts or feelings, have you ever? Have you ever made plans or engaged in any such behavior?
     (2) Are you currently experiencing any thoughts or feelings about hurting or killing anyone else? If yes, do you have any plans or have you engaged in any behavior? If not currently experiencing such thoughts or feelings, have you ever? Have you ever made plans or engaged in any such behavior?
   b. Rationales for assessment of this item
     (1) Assessment for risk of suicide is necessary to determine whether steps will be necessary to protect the individual from self-harm.
     (2) Presence of risk of self-harm conveys diagnostic information, often being associated with depressive conditions and character pathology.
     (3) Assessment of risk of danger to others is necessary to determine whether steps will be necessary to protect someone from the individual being assessed.

17. Presence of Symptoms of Severe Disturbance
   a. Examples of questions
     (1) Have you ever heard voices when nobody was with you?
     (2) Have you ever seen visions of people or things that were not really present?
     (3) Have you ever felt you had special powers or abilities?
     (4) Have you ever felt people were out to get you or hurt you?
     (5) Have you ever engaged in behavior you or others would consider bizarre?
   b. Rationale for assessment of this item
     (1) Hallucinations and delusions are symptoms of severe disturbance associated with psychotic disorders and substance-related disorders.

18. Obsessive–Compulsive Rituals; Tic Behaviors
   a. Examples of questions
     (1) Have you ever experienced any involuntary muscle movements or vocalizations?
     (2) Have you ever experienced any intrusive thoughts, impulses, or images that interfere with your ability to function?
     (3) Have you ever engaged in any rituals designed to alleviate anxiety and that interfered with your ability to function?
   b. Rationale for assessment of this item
     (1) The above questions are posed to directly inquire about the possible presence of symptoms of tic disorders and obsessive–compulsive disorder.

19. Mood
   a. Examples of questions
     (1) How would you describe your mood?

continues

EXHIBIT 5.8 *(Continued)*

(2) How is your energy level?

(3) Are you experiencing any difficulty concentrating while doing work or reading? Are your thoughts racing?

(4) Are you experiencing any difficulty making decisions?

(5) Are you experiencing guilt?

(6) Would you say that you experience low self-esteem or an inflated sense of your self?

(7) Do you feel helpless/hopeless?

(8) How is your sleep?

(9) Are you experiencing any changes in appetite or weight?

(10) Are you experiencing any changes in your motivation or interest in doing things?

(11) Are you experiencing any thoughts or feelings of hurting or killing yourself?

  b. Rationale for assessment of this item

(1) The above are standard questions to assess for depressive and bipolar disorders.

20. Anxiety

  a. Examples of questions

(1) Have you ever experienced anxiety characterized by sweating, palpitations, feeling lightheaded, fear of dying, or numbness/tingling?

(2) Do you experience discomfort doing things out of the home?

(3) Do you find it difficult to be around people?

(4) Do you experience fear of animals or situations like being in high places or tight quarters?

  b. Rationale for assessment of this item

(1) The above questions are employed to assess for anxiety disorders such as panic and phobic disorders.

21. Significant Losses

  a. Example of a question

(1) Have you ever experienced a loss of anybody or anything that had a significant effect on you?

  b. Rationale for assessment of this item

(1) Poorly resolved loss has been associated with depressive disorders as well as anxiety disorders.

22. Memory

  a. Examples of questions

(1) Can you repeat these three words now and in a minute or so from now when I ask you? (Offer respondent three words and ask for them again in one minute.)

(2) Can you tell me what you had for breakfast today? Lunch?

(3) Can you tell me my name?

(4) Can you tell me today's date?

(5) Can you tell me the name of the town you grew up in?

(6) What is your mother's maiden name?

(7) Who was the first president of the U.S.?

  b. Rationale for assessment of this item

(1) Questions are posed to assess immediate memory (1), recent memory (2, 3, 4), and long-term memory (5, 6, 7). Memory disturbance is associated with dementing disorders, mood disorders, and disturbances of attention.

continues

EXHIBIT 5.8 *(Continued)*

23. Orientation
    a. Examples of questions
        (1) Can you tell me today's date?
        (2) Can you tell me your name?
        (3) Can you tell me where you are right now?
    a. Rationale for assessment of this item
        (1) Disorientation or confusion is indicative of serious mental dysfunction associated with psychotic disorders, dementing disorders, or substance-related disorders.

24. Judgment
    a. Examples of questions
        (1) Questions from the WAIS–R (Wechsler, 1981) Comprehension subtest are commonly employed—for example, "What should you do if while in the movies you are the first person to see smoke and fire?" (p. 129).
    b. Rationale for assessment of this item
        (1) Impairment of judgment is associated with severe psychiatric disturbance, dementing disorders, and poor impulse control.

25. Information gleaned from direct observation
    a. Level of consciousness
        (1) The examiner observes to see if the respondent is alert and able to relate to the examiner and to the environment in general. Lethargy or more severe disturbances in consciousness (obtundation or coma) not only impair the ability to conduct an interview but are indicative of organic pathology and/or intoxication.
    b. Affect
        (1) Affect refers to the outward expression of emotion. Affect is usually observed in tone of voice, attitude, facial expression, and body language. Affective expression is related to mood and is particularly helpful in the assessment of mood disorders, although alterations in affective functioning may also be associated with substance abuse and schizophrenia.
    c. Appearance and behavior
        (1) The examiner observes for general appearance, appearance for age, gender, cleanliness, style of dress, eye contact, general attitude toward interviewer, and for unusual behavior. Appearance and behavior may relate to psychiatric and organic impairment. For example, a slovenly appearance may indicate depression, or neglect due to a cerebrovascular accident (CVA) or substance abuse. Bizarre behavior may indicate acute intoxication, dementia, or a psychotic disorder.
    d. Content and form of thought
        (1) The interviewer should observe to determine that the respondent's speech is logical, goal-directed, and coherent. Additionally, content should be free from bizarre ideas or preoccupations suggestive of delusions. Disturbances of thought are often observed with psychotic disorders, dementing disorders, and in cases of acute intoxication.
    e. Language
        (1) The examiner is interested in assessing the respondent's ability to comprehend spoken language and ability to express himself or herself effectively. Disturbances in basic language functioning usually indicate organic impairment (e.g., CVA), or acute intoxication.

continues

EXHIBIT 5.8 *(Continued)*

26. Initial Diagnostic Impression
    a. The items included on this assessment form have been chosen in order to gather information necessary to diagnose most major categories of psychiatric and substance use disorders, according to the *DSM–IV*.

27. Initial Treatment Plan
    a. The identification of problem areas and the rendering of a diagnosis usually serve as the basis of a preliminary treatment plan.

helplessness felt by patients and providers. Outcome monitoring in smoking cessation treatment is typically accomplished by self-report. In certain high risk cases where self-report may not be reliable (e.g., pregnant smokers), and in smoking cessation research, biochemical confirmation is needed to validate self-reported abstinence.

6

INTERVENTION STRATEGIES

The growing awareness of harm caused by cigarette smoking has resulted in increased interest in stopping it. Many different types of treatment interventions have been attempted over the past several decades. This chapter provides a comprehensive list of treatment interventions used for smoking cessation that have had a significant presence in the professional literature. Interventions are described, and at least one representative study is included to illustrate the application of each method. A broad overview of the treatment landscape can aid in the appreciation and understanding of what methods are effective; for this reason some interventions are included that are rarely used today (e.g., electric shock) as well as some that are used but do not have much empirical support (e.g., silver acetate). On a practical level, a reader may be interested in learning about a particular intervention, and, if it is not found in the book, may be uncertain as to the reason for the omission. He or she may wonder if the intervention was not included in the discussion because it was thought to be ineffective, for theoretical reasons, or due to an oversight. Furthermore, a clinician or researcher may want to know about the strengths and weaknesses of some interventions even if they are not currently up to standard, to evaluate the possibility of alteration and improvement. This chapter is devoted to the description of counseling and pharmacological interventions for the treatment of nicotine dependence. Discussion of the empirical and clinical evidence associated with the use of all techniques presented in this chapter is deferred to chapter 7 (please see Tables 7.1 and 7.2 for meta-analytic efficacy findings for counseling and pharmacological interventions, respectively).

Methods of treating nicotine dependence may be divided into two broad categories: counseling and pharmacological. Counseling interventions include the clinical application of classical (Pavlovian) and operant (Skinnerian) conditioning principles, cognitive interventions, skill building to manage stress and improve coping, and enhancement of the social support network of the smoker. Pharmacological agents have been developed and used to control and ultimately eliminate nicotine intake through different nicotine replacement systems, to alter the emotional status of the smoker (i.e., reduce anxiety and depression), and to modify neurotransmitter levels to soften the withdrawal experience and reduce cravings with non-nicotine products.

COUNSELING INTERVENTIONS

I have very deliberately chosen the term *counseling* instead of *psychotherapy* to describe the treatment of nicotine dependence. The behavioral and cognitive–behavioral treatment interventions discussed below are designed to address nicotine dependence. Treatment of nicotine dependence can aptly be described as a treatment specialty. This specialized treatment reflects reasoning such as the following, which is prevalent today (Hajek, 1994):

1. Smokers do not exhibit the obvious psychosocial impairment that abusers of other substances do.
2. There is assumed to be less underlying psychopathology for the smoker than the abuser of other substances.
3. With smoking, there is an emphasis on pharmacology and conditioned reactions.
4. The psychopathology, general psychology, and life problems of the smoker are deemphasized.
5. Therefore, it is assumed that a specific treatment technology may be used and more general psychotherapeutic treatments are not required.

Treatment interventions are not aimed at broad personality change; goals are specific (to stop smoking) and do not address the general functioning of the smoker. Of course, as noted in chapter 1, with smoking there is more psychosocial damage than meets the eye, a fact that becomes more evident with extended use, so longer use histories will generally reflect greater damage, which may necessitate psychotherapeutic treatment in addition to "standard" smoking-cessation treatment. Obviously, if the initial assessment process identifies problems coexistent with nicotine dependence, other treatment interventions would be indicated. It also merits mention that if psychotherapy is already under way when nicotine dependence is identified as a problem, psychotherapy need not be interrupted; both psychotherapeutic treatment and nicotine dependence treatment may proceed simultaneously. This practice of simultaneous treatment is commonly done with certain problems for which specialized treatment exists, for example, weight management and substance abuse treatment. The fact that there is separate, specialized treatment for nicotine dependence is in no way an indictment of traditional psychotherapies. It is common practice in all professions to have specialized services, whether in medicine, law, or mechanics, and this does not diminish the generalist.

Treatment methods for nicotine dependence have been developed, by and large, in university clinics and hospitals and have filtered their way into other settings over time (Klesges, Ward, & DeBon, 1996). Interventions are discussed separately below. However, it should be noted that treatment programs typically use multiple treatment procedures together (referred to as *multicomponent treatment*) in an attempt to maximize effectiveness (Lando, 1993; U.S. Department of Health and Human Services [USDHHS], 1988). The fact that no single treatment intervention has emerged as so superior as to obviate the need for other interventions reflects the multidetermined nature of smoking behavior with its psychological, social, pharmacological, learning, and cognitive facets (Lando, 1993).

Strategies Derived From Learning Paradigms

The theoretical basis for using interventions derived from learning or conditioning principles, established in chapter 4, is very sound. In that chapter the validity of the addiction model of nicotine dependence was discussed; an extension of the model as a rationale for treatment can be summarized as follows (Tiffany & Cepeda-Benito, 1994):

1. Chronic cigarette smoking is an addictive disorder like use of other classic drugs of abuse such as alcohol and heroin.
2. Nicotine is the pharmacological substance responsible for addiction to cigarettes and has been demonstrated to promote self-administration in animals, including humans.
3. Both positive reinforcement (by delivery of pleasure) and negative reinforcement (through removal of aversive withdrawal symptoms) are involved in the acquisition and maintenance of cigarette smoking behavior.
4. Therefore, treatments that address the learning components of addiction can be effective.

Interventions based on learning principles may be further divided into aversive and nonaversive techniques. Specific treatment techniques are discussed immediately below; the methodology of a specific study is described for each technique for illustrative purposes.

Aversive Techniques

Aversive techniques all have in common the fact that they use an aversive (i.e., unpleasant) unconditioned stimulus (US), which is paired with smoking behavior. Theoretically, it is not clear whether aversive conditioning is effective through reduction of the pleasure of smoking or the increase of unpleasantness of smoking with the net result of enhancing motivation to quit smoking (Lando, 1993). Because of the nature of these treatments, the most highly motivated participants are typically selected for aversive treatment methods.

Electric Shock. The use of electric shock as a US is straightforward operant conditioning. Electric shock is paired with smoking behavior to build a strong association between the behavior of smoking and the unpleasant experience of being shocked. Some weaknesses of procedures that use shock are that they require specialized equipment, patient acceptance and therapist acceptance can be obstacles, and they require medical screening. A study by Levine (1974) used electric shock as the US in a smoking-cessation procedure. The experiment was designed to determine if the contingent delivery of electric shock would attenuate smoking behavior. Using college-student smokers, Levine divided them into three groups: a no-treatment control group, a contingent-shock group, and a noncontingent-shock group. Subjects in the contingent-shock group were seen individually for four 15-minute sessions (two sessions per week, for 2 weeks). The sessions started with subjects being hooked up to the electric shock device, which delivered a shock of 110 V with a 50 mA current applied through two metal electroencephalogram (EEG) electrodes to opposite sides of the subject's left wrist. Subjects were instructed to inhale a lit cigarette, then place it in an ashtray for five beats of a metronome (present before them) before picking it back up to inhale again. Immediately following inhalation, the subject was given a 1-second electric shock. After 15 inhalation trials, subjects were instructed to light a second cigarette and repeat for another 15 inhalations. By the end of 2 weeks' treatment, subjects had received a total of 120 paired associations between smoke inhalation and electric shock. Subjects in the noncontingent-shock group received the same instructions and procedure as those in the contingent-shock group, except they received shock when the cigarette was in the ashtray; they received the same total of 120 shocks.

It is evident from the Levine (1974) study that the design is relatively simple and not time-consuming or lengthy, requiring only a few cigarettes and a device that delivers controlled electric shock. Concerns about acceptance are underscored by the author's statement that several subjects dropped out after they were informed that electric shock would be used on them.

Satiation and Rapid Smoking. Two stop-smoking techniques use cigarette smoking procedures in ways that make the smoking experience itself aversive. With satiation methods, smokers are asked to significantly increase their smoking. Typically, they increase smoking to two to three times their normal consumption for a specified period of time before cessation is attempted.

With rapid-smoking procedures, the emphasis is on the consumption of the individual cigarette: Smokers are asked to significantly increase their rate of inhaling from a cigarette, typically to the point where illness would result if they continued (due to toxicity). Often, the smoker is asked to puff every 6 seconds to the point of illness, and to do this for six to eight sessions before attempting cessation.

Limitations of both procedures relate to medical risks, especially with rapid smoking, because increased heart rate, elevated blood pressure, and electrocardiogram (EKG) abnormalities have been observed during such procedures. Therefore, screening and close medical monitoring are necessary in treatment. Rapid smoking is considered safe for healthy adults screened for conditions such as cardiovascular disease, diabetes, COPD, seizure disorder, and hypertension. The procedure may be used with at-risk populations if under close medical supervision (USDHHS, 1988).

In a study by Best, Owen, and Trentadue (1978), satiation and rapid-smoking techniques were compared. Prior to being assigned to one of three treatment groups (satiation alone, rapid smoking alone, or satiation plus rapid smoking), subjects were medically screened for symptoms affected by smoking (e.g., high blood pressure, respiratory ailments, cardiac arrhythmia). The subjects in the satiation group were instructed to smoke as many cigarettes as possible on each of 3 days with a target of at least double their baseline rate of smoking. Subjects were told that the most important objective was to achieve subjective discomfort from the excessive smoking, and they were required to complete a symptom rating form nightly to rate the unpleasantness of the experience. Subjects were instructed to stop smoking on the morning after the 3 days of increased smoking. Subjects met with an experimenter on the quit date, and coping responses designed to maintain abstinence were discussed during this and two subsequent sessions.

Subjects in the rapid-smoking group were instructed to smoke cigarettes, starting on their quit date, in the following manner on prescribed days: take a puff, inhaling normally, every 5 to 6 seconds until you cannot tolerate it anymore, lighting new cigarettes as necessary to continue; when the limit is reached, verbalize the aversiveness of the experience, explicitly focusing attention on the most salient unpleasant reactions; then repeat this procedure until no more trials can be tolerated. When done for the day, subjects completed a rating scale to assess the aversiveness of the experience. After the initial trial in a lab, subjects in the rapid-smoking group were instructed to conduct smoking trials at home on the

2nd, 3rd, 5th, 7th, 10th, and 13th days following the quit date. Subjects in the rapid-smoking group also received several follow-up sessions with the experimenter to discuss coping strategies, the same as given to the satiation group.

By comparing the two procedures, it can be seen that both endeavor to use smoking to generate a negative experience for the smoker by greatly increasing cigarette consumption. The satiation procedure was done before the quit date, and individual cigarettes were smoked normally but in significantly increased number. With rapid smoking, discrete trials of intense, rapid smoking were used; rapid-smoking trials started on the quit date. Because of the increased intake of nicotine, both procedures require medical screening. The only "equipment" needed is cigarettes, and both procedures may be conducted at home or in an office setting.

Reduced Aversion Techniques. These methods include focused smoking, smoke holding, and rapid puffing. In response to concerns about acceptance and safety of aversive techniques, alternative methods have been used. Focused smoking is a procedure in which the person smokes in a regulated fashion. For example, the smoker is asked to smoke for a sustained period of time but at a slow or normal rate, and to focus on the negative sensations. Unlike both rapid smoking and satiation techniques, there is no increase in smoking behavior or nicotine consumption. Rather, there is essentially normal smoking behavior with a conscious emphasis on negative sensations that may be experienced during the process (USDHHS, 1988).

Smoke holding involves requesting that the person hold smoke in his or her throat and mouth while also breathing through the nose. Becona and Garcia (1993) used a smoke-holding technique in their study as part of an investigation of the effectiveness of several different multicomponent treatment packages for smoking cessation. Subjects were recruited by radio and print advertisement and randomly assigned to one of five treatment groups, four of which included the technique of smoke holding as one element of the multicomponent package. Subjects receiving smoke-holding training were instructed to (a) draw smoke into their mouths from a lit cigarette; (b) hold the smoke there for 30 seconds while breathing normally through their noses; (c) consciously focus on the unpleasant sensations caused by the process; (d) repeat this procedure five to six times on each of three trials, with 5-minute rest intervals between each of the three trials, and 30-second rest intervals between each 30-second mouthful.

Rapid puffing is similar to rapid smoking except that the smoke is not inhaled. The advantages of rapid puffing over rapid smoking are that it is not as aversive (so there may be less chance of rejection of the technique) or medically risky. Erickson, Tiffany, Martin, and Baker (1983) conducted an investigation comparing the effectiveness of rapid-smoking and rapid-puffing interventions on cessation of smoking. Subjects were obtained by radio, local newspaper advertisements, and bulletin boards and were randomly assigned to one of three treatment groups (rapid smoking and behavioral counseling, rapid puffing and behavioral counseling, behavioral counseling only). Smokers in the rapid-puffing group received six 90-minute sessions (45 minutes of rapid puffing, 45 minutes of behavioral counseling) over a 2-week period, with three sessions on the first 3 days, then sessions on the 5th, 8th, and 11th days of treatment; they were asked to stop smoking on the 1st day of treatment. To enhance the effectiveness of the treatment, subjects were asked to not eat or drink anything for several hours prior to the session so that there would be no taste interference with the smoking-induced malaise; and they were also requested to not smoke (if they had not stopped completely) just prior to a treatment session to not increase nicotine tolerance, which would reduce the potency of the treatment cigarette as a US. As with rapid smoking, the rapid-puffing method focuses on the smoking of the individual cigarette. In treatment sessions subjects were required to (a) take a puff of a lit cigarette every time a tone sounded (every 6 seconds in this procedure, a puff being explicitly contrasted with the inhalation used in rapid smoking; with a puff, the smoke is taken into the mouth, held there momentarily, then blown out); (b) concentrate on the unpleasant sensations of the process; (c) continue smoking in this manner until it could no longer be tolerated or until they had finished three cigarettes, whichever came first; (d) stop when tolerance was reached and complete a questionnaire assessing which sensations were experienced and rating their aversiveness; and (e) repeat the procedure two more times per treatment day.

Covert Sensitization. *Covert sensitization* is a procedure whereby the US that is used is an unpleasant mental representation (i.e., image, thought, or memory). With covert sensitization, the mental image of smoking is paired with thoughts and images of negative correlates of smoking (e.g., nausea, dizziness, health consequences). A covert sensitization procedure was used as part of a study by Lowe, Green, Kurtz, Ashenberg, and Fisher (1980). Subjects for the study were recruited from the community through local newspaper advertisements and randomly assigned to one of two treatment scenarios: self-control training only (i.e., learning cognitive and behavioral coping skills to assist the individual to choose abstinence over smoking) or self-control training plus covert sensitization. Covert sensitization training consisted of having subjects: (a) imagine themselves smoking or experiencing an urge to smoke; (b) with the first image, also imagine themselves either coughing and choking, or nauseated and vomiting; (c) then, following the negative imagery, imagine putting the cigarette out or ignoring the urge to smoke; and (d) imagine feeling fresh and relaxed. Subjects received six covert sensitization trials per meeting, over a total of 12 meetings, spanning from prior to their quit date to 90 days after the quit date. For half the covert sensitization trials, subjects were encouraged to individualize the process by imagining circumstances in which they were more likely to smoke and to practice using individually chosen consequences they found most aversive.

Advantages of this method are that it does not require any equipment, can be practiced anywhere, and is not medically risky.

Silver Acetate. Silver acetate products are pharmaceutical preparations that may be found in several forms, including gum, lozenge, and spray (Hymowitz & Eckholdt, 1996). Silver acetate is available as a nonprescription aid to smoking cessation and has been used primarily in Europe. When silver acetate interacts with the sulfides in tobacco smoke, an unpleasant, metallic taste results (Jarvik & Henningfield, 1988) that serves as an aversive US. The use of silver acetate as a deterrent to smoking is often analogized to the use of disulfiram (Antabuse) as a deterrent to the use of alcohol (Lando, 1993). Silver acetate is conceived of as a daily aid in initial cessation, and then as a product to be used on an as-needed basis for relapse prevention (Hymowitz & Eckholdt, 1996).

Some advantages of using silver acetate are that the products have the potential to be used by a wide-reaching self-help audience and, in contrast to nicotine replacement therapy, there is no concern about developing tolerance or withdrawal from the products (Malcolm, Currey, Mitchell, & Keil, 1986). There are some significant limitations of silver acetate use. The different preparations have varying lengths of duration of effectiveness but generally last only for a few hours (Jarvik & Henningfield, 1988), requiring users to take them repeatedly throughout the day and creating problems with compliance. In addition, the combination of aversive treatment and self-administration can equate to compliance problems (Morrow, Nepps, & McIntosh, 1993); when faced with the choice of stopping smoking or the deterrent, some may choose to stop the silver acetate. Some investigators (e.g., Morrow et al., 1993) have found they can improve compliance by use of an instructional video, monitoring, and frequent follow-up contact with product users. A particular problem with the gum preparation of silver acetate is seen for denture wearers. In addition, some side effects are noted with silver acetate use in terms of gastrointestinal functioning, yielding symptoms of nausea, heartburn, and abdominal cramps (Malcolm et al., 1986). Users of the products must therefore be screened for gastrointestinal disease as well as silver allergy. A rare but potentially serious complication is a condition known as *argyrism*, a permanent discoloration of tissues, including skin (which turns a blue-gray color) (Hymowitz & Eckholdt, 1996; Morrow et al., 1993). Argyrism is the result of excessive silver consumption beyond a level at which the body can safely eliminate it. Cases of argyrism are rare and have been documented only when doses consumed were extraordinarily large or over a much longer time period than recommended (e.g., when continued for more than 2 years), so use as recommended is thought safe.

The 1986 study by Malcolm et al. nicely illustrates some key elements in the use of the gum preparation of silver acetate. In this double-blind study, all subjects were screened for, among other things, pregnancy and allergy to silver; during the treatment, inspections of skin and oral mucosa were performed. Subjects in both experimental and control groups (i.e., those receiving gum containing 6 mg of silver acetate and placebo gum, respectively) were instructed on the use of the gum: chew the gum six times per day for 30-minute intervals for a time period lasting 3 weeks. Subjects were additionally required to smoke cigarettes for the first week of gum use and to pick a quit date between days 8 and 17. The summary of the study by Malcolm et al. illustrates important aspects of silver acetate use: the need to do medical screening before and during treatment; frequent daily use of the gum; use of the gum during the initial part of the cessation process and in a time-limited (3-week) manner; and use of the silver acetate product while still smoking, prior to the quit date (so the smoker will actually experience the aversive US).

Non-Aversive Techniques

Two treatment procedures that derive from the Pavlovian conditioning paradigm are stimulus control and cue exposure; contingency management (operant conditioning), nicotine fading, and cognitive procedures will also be discussed.

Stimulus Control. In Pavlovian conditioning, cues signal the presence of a US, thereby creating an expectancy. One of the well-known problems with cigarette smoking is that because nicotine use is legal, it becomes associated with many different cues. The cues then become signals that create an expectancy to smoke. A standard piece of advice in drug recovery is to avoid "people, places, and things" associated with their drug use, as a way to limit temptation triggered by the expectancy of drug use in the presence of the cues. With stimulus control, recommendations are made to avoid cues of nicotine use and reduce the threat of urges to use (by limiting pro-smoking stimulation from external sources). Stimulus control is typically used as a preparation strategy prior to a quit attempt. Different methods to reduce environmental stimuli to smoke have been tried (Lando, 1993): for example, restricting when and where the person may smoke and smoking at predetermined times regardless of the individual's desire to smoke (to detach internal cues from smoking behavior). Recommendations may include avoiding associates who smoke; avoiding the use of other substances such as alcohol and coffee; removing extra cigarettes from home as well as paraphernalia like matches, lighters, and ashtrays; and avoiding certain places such as bars, smoking sections of restaurants, and smoking areas at work. Becona and Garcia (1993) used stimulus control procedures as part of their study consisting of a recommendation to restrict subjects' smoking by eliminating it in a number of situations that act as stimuli: making telephone calls, reading, studying, watching television, driving, working, having coffee, after breakfast, while in a bar. It can be seen that the goal of stimulus control interventions is to attempt to narrow down the range of cues that are associated with smoking prior to the quit attempt. When this is done, the opportunities to experience cue-induced cravings to smoke during the quit attempt should be diminished. Otherwise, the person may potentially feel bombarded by the temptation to smoke, evoked by cues from practically everywhere.

A form that I use to educate patients about the principles of stimulus control, "Reducing Temptation," is presented in Exhibit 6.1. A related case example is provided in Exhibit 6.2.

Cue Exposure. Stimulus control interventions are used as strategies to avoid environmental sources of stimulation and minimize their ability to evoke an association with smoking (and generate urges), which may lead to use of cigarettes. Cue exposure procedures are a more active process of extinction, achieved through purposeful exposure to cues and response prevention (Dodgen & Shea, 2000; Laberg, 1990). Niaura et al. (1999) tested cue exposure training for smoking relapse prevention. Subjects were recruited from local newspaper advertisements and were randomly assigned to one of four treatment groups, two of which received cue exposure training. All subjects had one meeting prior to their quit date, devoted to assessment and brief cessation counseling and to establishing a quit date; a part of the session was devoted to completing a Smoking Triggers Interview (STI). The STI is a questionnaire that assesses personal high-risk situations characterized by the combination of strong urges to smoke and low self-efficacy in resisting the urge. Subjects were encouraged to provide details of high-risk situations, including salient visual, olfactory, and taste cues. The STI responses are rank-ordered from highest- to lowest-risk situations.

Subjects received five cue exposure sessions, lasting approximately 75 minutes each, after the quit date (two the same week as the quit day, three the following week). For cue exposure training, the information gathered through the STI (the high-risk situations and the accompanying detailed reports of the smokers) was used. To start the treatment, the highest-ranked risk situation was chosen first. Subjects were requested to focus on the high-risk situation, attempting to recall as vividly as possible all accompanying cues, internal and external, and to build the urge to smoke to the highest degree; to facilitate the process, the therapist supplied descriptions reported by the smoker from the STI. Subjects were encouraged to pretend to see, handle, smell, and smoke a cigarette to enhance the experience. They were then instructed to monitor the intensity of the urge to smoke until it peaked and began to diminish, to inform the therapist when the urge was about half as strong as it was at its peak, and to rate the intensity of the urge at its peak as well as their self-efficacy not to smoke. Subjects were asked how they might cope with the situation, with the therapist suggesting different cognitive–behavioral strategies and reinforcing any that were reported spontaneously by the individual. This procedure was repeated until the end of the session for the next several high-risk scenarios. Subjects were advised to practice the cue exposure exercises at least once per day at home between sessions and to

EXHIBIT 6.1
Reducing Temptation Form

REDUCING TEMPTATION

You may be familiar with the famous experiments of the Russian psychologist Ivan Pavlov. Many years ago Pavlov found that by pairing environmental stimuli (for example, sounds or lights) with the presentation of food, dogs began to react to the sounds or lights even when the food was not presented. If you ever owned a cat you could see this same process at home. Cats come to associate the sound of the can opener with getting their food. So anytime the can opener is operated, they come running. What happens is an association is formed between certain sounds, sights, or smells and the occurrence of some important event (for example, being fed). We know that humans learn associations in the same way as dogs, cats, and other animals. This kind of learning takes place with the use of tobacco products. Take smoking, for example. After some experience with smoking, just the sight of the cigarette pack can activate an association and craving to smoke. Likewise with the many other stimuli that are present when smoking: lighters, matches, ashtrays, certain people, beverages, foods, places (for example, the car, or the home of a friend who smokes), certain activities (for example, when watching television, reading, on the computer, on the telephone, etc.), certain times of day (for example, always first thing in the morning), or moods (for example, always when bored, or angry, or nervous).

You might wonder how the discussion of Pavlovian or associative learning is relevant to the cessation of use of tobacco products. To answer this, consider the following question: Would it be easier to stop smoking in a home with cigarettes, lighters, and ashtrays in every room, or in one where there was only one pack of cigarettes, one lighter, and one ashtray kept in only one room? Obviously, in the first situation the person would be confronted with reminders of smoking everywhere he or she went in the home, and this would make it much more difficult to stop smoking. This is the whole idea behind controlling stimuli associated with smoking. You want to avoid things associated with smoking so that the association is not activated. Some things associated with the use of tobacco products cannot be avoided or directly controlled. For example, feelings or moods; time of day and day of week cannot be controlled either. However, what can be controlled is your response to these stimuli. For things that cannot be avoided, the key is to wait as long as possible to smoke so as to break the automatic association of the stimuli with smoking. For example, if you routinely smoke whenever you feel angry, definitely do not smoke until several minutes after the feeling is experienced. Remember, avoidance of temptation is an activity used in preparation of a quit attempt, so at this stage in the process smoking still occurs. The goal is to break the strength of association between smoking and other stimuli. The following are recommended:

1. Do not possess any more than a single pack of cigarettes at any time.
2. Avoid people, places, and things associated with cigarette use.
3. If some circumstances associated with smoking cannot be avoided, be sure not to smoke when you normally would have. Wait at least several minutes before lighting up.

Exercise. Please identify stimuli associated with smoking for you and ways to avoid those situations, or manage them if unavoidable.

1. People_____
_____
_____

continues

INTERVENTION STRATEGIES   125

EXHIBIT 6.1 *(Continued)*

2. Places_____

_____

_____

3. Things (including feelings, moods) _____

_____

_____

Note. From *Stop Smoking System*, by C. E. Dodgen, 2004, Florham Park, NJ. Unpublished manuscript. Reprinted with permission.

practice coping responses identified as helpful during the cue exposure training. Subsequent sessions were begun by reordering the high-risk situations in case circumstances had changed to alter the relevancy of a given situation, and the most powerful situations were addressed in each session.

With cue exposure treatment there are no significant health risks, and the exercises can be practiced at home without any special equipment or room requirements.

Contingency Contracting (Contingency Management). Contingency contracting, or *contingency management*, as it is also referred to, is based on operant learning principles. It involves the incentivizing of desired behaviors through positive reinforcement and the discouraging of undesired behaviors by removing positive reinforcement (Dodgen & Shea, 2000). Contingency contracting is thought to increase commitment and motivation for treatment (Lando, 1993) and is used to support outcomes (e.g., abstinence) or intermediate goals (e.g., adherence to a prescribed treatment regimen). An example of the latter for substance abuse treatment was described by Kadden and Mauriello (1991), who used these principles in an attempt to enhance treatment compliance on an inpatient substance abuse treatment unit. Patients in the study received rewards (e.g., access to preferred activities) for performing target behaviors such as attendance in group therapy and compliance with program rules. In a smoking-cessation study, Lando (1976) incentivized abstinence by requiring subjects to put up a cash deposit they could earn back by remaining abstinent for a specified period of time; in addition, subjects shared in the deposits lost by nonabstinent subjects in the study.

Nicotine Fading. This is a procedure in which the clinician attempts to wean the smoker from nicotine dependence by progressively lowering nicotine intake prior to stopping altogether (Foxx & Brown, 1979; Lando, 1993). The rationale for this method is that when nicotine intake is tapered, withdrawal discomfort can be minimized, allowing for a less unpleasant cessation experience; withdrawal discomfort is often reported by smokers as a deterrent to quitting. Fading is used as a preparation strategy to quitting, not as a long-term strategy. The dosage of nicotine is typically reduced by a process of substitution of cigarettes lower in tar and nicotine,

EXHIBIT 6.2
Case Example: Nicole B.

BRIEF BACKGROUND AND SMOKING HISTORY

Nicole B., an 18-year-old high school student, presented for treatment because of depression. Depressive symptoms had developed and were intensifying over the course of her senior year in high school. She reported starting smoking over the past year but is not a daily smoker. She smokes about 3 days per week, and approximately five to seven cigarettes on a day of use. She reported a desire to stop smoking but was unable to with several attempts. The cessation efforts consisted of her deciding she was quitting, picking a quit date, and trying not to smoke anymore. Attempts lasted only a couple of days at most.

SMOKING-CESSATION INTERVENTIONS

As part of the smoking-cessation treatment, Ms. B. completed the form "Reducing Temptation." She identified two friends in particular with whom she liked to smoke. There were two places she most strongly associated with smoking, her car and a coffee shop. In terms of "things" associated with smoking, she noted that smoking was at times related to feeling down; she felt that it gave her an emotional lift when she felt low.

With respect to managing temptation evoked by her friends, Ms. B. decided that she would not socialize with them except in situations where smoking was not allowed (e.g., in school), or unless accompanied by another friend whom she identified as a smoking-cessation support person. She informed her two close friends of her intentions to stop smoking and reassured them of a desire to remain friends, just without smoking.

The temptation of smoking associated with the coffee shop was relatively easy to deal with. Ms. B. committed to getting coffee at a convenience store, and if she wanted to socialize (the other function of the coffeehouse), she planned to do that in a smoke-free environment (a local bookstore and a diner were chosen).

Handling urges to smoke evoked by driving in her car was a little more complicated: A car cannot just be discarded or avoided. However, some steps could still be implemented to diminish the association of driving and smoking. Ms. B. agreed not to smoke in the car. She took the ashtray out of the car and had the car cleaned to rid it of the smell of smoke. If she felt an irresistible urge to smoke, she agreed to get out of the car to smoke.

Breaking the link between feeling down and smoking was difficult, as is often the case with feeling states. Obviously, an internal experience like a feeling state cannot be easily changed or avoided, so interventions are aimed at expanding the time frame from when the feeling is consciously experienced, when the urge is identified, and when the cigarette is smoked. Ms. B. felt as though she could commit to waiting 10 minutes after the experience of a feeling-related urge before smoking.

COMMENTS

Reduction of temptation (stimulus control) is a strategy used in preparation for a quit attempt. The fewer cues an individual must encounter, the less opportunity there will be for a craving to smoke to be evoked. For cues that are encountered, the goal is to put off the smoking of the cigarette as long as possible so that the automaticity of smoking in response to the urge will be disrupted.

and sometimes by reducing the number of cigarettes smoked. A nicotine fading procedure was used by Foxx and Brown. Subjects were recruited from the university and local community via radio, newspaper, and poster advertisements and were randomly assigned to one of four groups, two of which used nicotine fading. Subjects undergoing the fading procedure received the following treatment: The rationale for nicotine fading was explained, and in conjunction with consulting a government publication listing levels of tar and nicotine in cigarette brands, subjects were instructed to change their brand of cigarette to brands containing progressively less tar and nicotine according to a predetermined schedule. The schedule was as follows: Week 1—regular brand, Week 2—30% nicotine reduction from the regular brand, Week 3—60% nicotine reduction from the regular brand, Week 4—90% reduction from the regular brand, Week 5—quit smoking. Subjects were told to quit at this point in the process because the nicotine intake had been reduced so much that a significant withdrawal reaction would not be expected. Subjects were required to smoke only those cigarettes designated for a given week, but they were allowed to smoke as many as desired. Subjects met for five consecutive 1-hour weekly group meetings; no specific treatment was offered, and only group support was provided. With nicotine fading, all that is needed is easily acquired information on the tar and nicotine content by brand, and cigarettes. No medical screening is required, the treatment is not aversive, and some suggest that self-efficacy is enhanced prior to quitting, as smokers are aware that they are successfully reducing their nicotine intake (Foxx & Brown, 1979). A potential problem with nicotine fading is that compensatory smoking behavior may result in less of a reduction in nicotine than would be expected based on measured tar and nicotine levels of cigarette brands.

Cognitive Procedures: Pledging, Norm-Setting, and Values Clarification. These interventions are grouped together because they are all intended to enhance motivation for smoking cessation by cognitive methods. The reason behind having the smoker make a pledge to stop smoking is to increase personal responsibility and commitment to abstain from the use of nicotine (Hansen, 1992). Typically, a smoker is asked to sign a statement declaring his or her intentions to stop smoking. Norm-setting can be helpful because smokers tend to dramatically overestimate the prevalence and acceptability of smoking. Because they tend to socialize with other smokers and to congregate in areas that allow smoking, they entertain distorted views of smoking. A norm-setting intervention involves discussion of the prevalence statistics that demonstrate that smokers are in the minority (roughly one fifth to one fourth of American adults are regular smokers, including about one fourth to one third of American adolescents), and that they are very negatively evaluated by the nonsmoking majority (see the discussion in chap. 1 on this topic). Values clarification is another brief, simple procedure intended to demonstrate to individuals that smoking is incompatible with their personal values. For example, smokers may be asked to list the five things that are most important to them (sometimes choosing from a preprinted list of values); invariably, values involving health and family are listed, as well as other values that are obviously at odds with smoking behavior. Discussion would ensue about how their smoking behavior is inconsistent with their core values. The "Personal Values" form, used to assist with values clarification, is shown in Exhibit 6.3. An accompanying case example is provided in Exhibit 6.4.

Coping Skills

"Coping skills" is an umbrella term for various interventions such as strategies for coping with high-risk situations and urges to smoke (part of

---

EXHIBIT 6.3
Personal Values Form

PERSONAL VALUES

Instructions: Below is a list of values, or things that are important to people. Please review the list, then complete the two exercises. If there are values you think of that are not on the list, feel free to add them.

Exercise 1. Please list the five most important values you use to guide your behavior. Please list them in order starting with the most important first.

1. _____
2. _____
3. _____
4. _____
5. _____

Exercise 2. For each value you listed above, please indicate whether you think using tobacco is consistent or inconsistent with the value.

1. _____
2. _____
3. _____
4. _____
5. _____

VALUES

1. Achievement	6. Friendship	11. Courage	16. Hard work
2. Wealth	7. Wisdom	12. Responsibility	17. Appearance
3. Family	8. Independence	13. Respect	18. Feeling good
4. Health	9. Cleanliness	14. Equality	19. Faith/religion
5. Happiness	10. Honesty	15. Education	

Note. From *Stop Smoking System*, by C. E. Dodgen, 2004, Florham Park, NJ. Unpublished manuscript. Reprinted with permission.

EXHIBIT 6.4
Case Example: Sara H.

BRIEF BACKGROUND AND SMOKING HISTORY

Sara H. is a 42-year-old married mother of four children. She presented for psychotherapy treatment with symptoms of anxiety and appeared to be a generally "high-strung" person. She is a stay-at-home mother with children ranging in age from 7 to 15 years old. During the initial evaluation, Mrs. H. reported that she had smoked since she was 14 years old. Currently, she smokes about 10–12 cigarettes per day. She was surprised to learn that nicotine intake may affect anxiety and tension and so was open to the recommendation that she consider stopping smoking.

SMOKING-CESSATION INTERVENTIONS

As part of the smoking-cessation program, Mrs. H. completed the "Personal Values" form. For Exercise 1, she listed the three values most important to her, in order: family, health, and faith/religion. For Exercise 2, she determined that health was inconsistent with smoking, but for family and faith/religion she responded with an answer of "not sure." Regarding family, she felt that because she never smoked in the home she was not harming the family through exposure to secondhand smoke. However, she was encouraged to think about ways the family might be affected other than by smoke in the home. She admitted that she was concerned about the idea of modeling smoking to her children. In addition, she recalled that at many different times her husband and children had been upset by her smoking and requested she stop; clearly they were upset about the possibility of her being harmed by smoking.

Mrs. H. also felt that because she was a regular attendee at church services and lived a life in general accord with her religious beliefs, smoking might be irrelevant to this personal value. I encouraged Mrs. H. to talk with her minister to get an opinion about smoking as it squared with the practice of her religion. In talking to her minister she was informed that cigarette smoking, or any other behavior known to harm the body, was not considered desirable behavior.

COMMENTS

Values clarification is similar to the use of negative consequences. That is, it is done to create dissonance and mental discomfort that can generate motivation to change smoking behavior, or strengthen already existing motivation. Reminding smokers of their stated values at times of ambivalence about quitting can help make the decision-making process conscious, deliberate, and thoughtful, as opposed to the more risky impulsive response to a craving. Anything that can be done to delay the behavior of smoking, such as thinking of the inconsistency of smoking with important personal values, provides an opportunity for more rational processes to take over and for more effective coping to take place.

---

relapse prevention training), problem-solving, resistance skills training, and relapse prevention training. Which particular interventions are applied in any individual case is determined by the clinician and the needs of that individual. The rationale behind coping skills training is to develop alternative, healthy responses to the urge to smoke and, through healthier means, get what smoking provides—comfort, pleasure, satisfaction, and reward. Examples of behavioral responses that are taught to help individuals cope with urges to smoke include eating and chewing (e.g., hard candy, gum); distracting activities (e.g., reading, crossword puzzles); leaving a stressful situation; relaxation training; self-management (e.g., reward of self for abstinence for a designated period of time); and physical exercise (Lando, 1993; USDHHS, 1988). Cognitive responses that are taught to help cope with urges to smoke include actively and deliberately thinking of the benefits of quitting and the negative consequences of smoking; mentally pushing thoughts of smoking aside, or thought stopping; not considering smoking an option; using positive self-talk that says "you can do it"; using positive, relaxing mental images; and mentally anticipating high-risk situations and accompanying responses before the situations occur. Smokers are taught to use coping responses to address urges and situations that evoke urges.

Erickson et al. (1983) included a behavioral counseling (coping skills) group in the study discussed above in which a rapid puffing procedure was used. Subjects in the behavioral counseling group received six 45-minute training sessions over a 2-week period; the first three sessions occurred on consecutive days, with subsequent sessions on the 5th, 8th, and 11th days of treatment. Subjects were required to complete smoking record forms (recording the number of cigarettes smoked each day) and urge-rating forms (recording the time, intensity, context, and affective state accompanying the urge to smoke) for each day during treatment. Coping skills training consisted of identifying high-risk smoking situations and coping responses that could be used at these times. High-risk situations were identified for each smoker by noting patterns in his or her smoking records (e.g., always smokes in the car), and urge-rating forms for patterns (e.g., urge to smoke is highest in the morning), and by soliciting the subject's self-reports of anticipated difficult situations. As part of the training, subjects were initially given a general list of coping strategies for how to respond to the identified high-risk situations. Strategies included behavioral responses such as physical exercise, withdrawal from the situation, use of gum or mints, and cognitive–behavioral strategies such as relaxation exercises. Subjects in this group also signed abstinence contracts to enhance motivation and, in addition, received education about withdrawal symptoms underscoring their transient, time-limited nature.

Problem-solving skills can be helpful by equipping smokers to make rational decisions and to apply rational procedures when dealing with problem situations (Hansen, 1992). Smokers trying to quit encounter many obstacles to the achievement and maintenance of abstinence from tobacco products; having a general formula to address problems can be of great assistance. Problem-solving is usually taught as a step procedure. For example, Johnson (1997) described the following steps for problem-solving: (a) acknowledgement and identification of the problem, (b) analysis of the problem, including identification of the needs of those who will be affected, (c) brainstorming to generate possible solutions, (d) evaluating the pros and cons of each option, (e) implementing the option selected, and (f) evaluating the outcome.

Resistance skills training is designed to help smokers identify sources of pressure to smoke (typically peers, family, and tobacco advertisements and sponsorships) and to resist that pressure. Self-efficacy for resisting urges and pressure to smoke is increased by learning to effectively manage the temptation to smoke (Hansen, 1992). Smokers are usually requested to identify sources of pressure to smoke that are specific to them and are assisted to develop comfortable responses.

Social Support

There probably is not a condition for which social support of some kind would not help. My observations in a nursing home where I provide psychotherapeutic services fully support this point. Residents of the nursing home usually have a variety of physical ailments resulting in different degrees of disability that necessitate their being there. All things being equal, those residents who receive regular, supportive contact from family, friends, other residents, or staff members generally tolerate their conditions better and are psychologically healthier. That social support would be beneficial to the smoker attempting to stop should be self-evident. Research supports this claim, as supportive behaviors have been found to positively correlate with treatment outcomes (Collins, Emont, & Zywiak, 1990). To fully appreciate the value of social support, one need only consider the opposite situation, a nonsupportive social environment. For example, imagine the difficulties posed in a situation with a smoking spouse who does not quit or control cigarette use around the quitter, or a spouse who is unsupportive for other reasons and complains about the quitter's mood or weight gain while he or she is attempting to quit. Indeed, negative behavior from family and friends has been identified as a significant contributing factor to relapse (Collins et al., 1990).

If positive and negative social behavior is influential in the success or failure of smoking cessation, then it makes sense for attempts to be made in treatment to strengthen social support. Such efforts have been made to improve the natural support system of smokers through education and training of friends and family, as well as worksite "buddies" (Lando, 1993; USDHHS, 1988). For those smokers with a weak support system, support can be provided by treatment either in group or individual therapy, or in a mutual-help format like Nicotine Anonymous. In recognition of the salience of social support, the Clinical Practice Guideline (USDHHS, 2000b) recommends use of intra- and extra-treatment social support for smoking cessation. *Intra-treatment support* is formal treatment rendered by the clinician or program in the forms of individual and group counseling. *Extra-treatment support* is that provided outside the treatment program from the home and social environment or from self-help support programs.

Pirie and associates (Pirie, Rooney, Pechacek, Lando, & Schmid, 1997) incorporated a social support component into a communitywide smoking-cessation contest. Smokers were given an option to participate in the contest alone, or with a support person whom they selected. Both the participant and support person were incentivized with eligibility for prizes if the smoker remained abstinent throughout the contest. The support persons were requested to sign a contract pledging to be supportive of their friends' efforts to quit by remaining positive, understanding, and helpful. Note the attention to positive support and lack of specific instruction or technique; the emphasis is on the provision of emotional support, and an attempt is not made to turn the support person into a treatment professional. Abrams et al. (2003) recommended that the smoker identify people in his or her environment who can provide support for a quit attempt and have them sign a "buddy contract." In the contract the buddy agrees to be supportive in ways specifically requested by the smoker (help with problem solving, emotional support, help with specific tasks like household chores or child care, information and resources about coping from someone who has been through the quitting process). To effectively assist the individual in treatment, it is also helpful to identify, together with the clinician, the kind of support he or she would find most beneficial from the clinician. A copy of the "Support Agreement" form used is presented in Exhibit 6.5, and a case example illustrating the form's application is discussed in Exhibit 6.6.

Referral Considerations

Some smoking-cessation procedures are not directly provided by psychotherapists but may be valuable to the therapist as resources for referral; it is therefore useful for clinicians to have some awareness of services such as Nicotine Anonymous, brief physician advice, acupuncture, hypnosis (provided by some therapists), and self-help. Also available for referral, if needed, are programs sponsored by voluntary organizations and commercial interests.

Nicotine Anonymous

The original 12-step recovery program is Alcoholics Anonymous (AA), which serves as a prototype for all other 12-step programs (Lichtenstein, 1999). AA has spawned more than 100 types of 12-step programs, addressing problem behaviors such as drug abuse and other destructively compulsive behaviors, including gambling, sex, and overeating. AA and other 12-step programs used to be poorly accepted by the professional community but now

EXHIBIT 6.5
Support Agreement Form

SUPPORT AGREEMENT

I am planning to stop the use of all tobacco products on _____.
I realize that it is difficult to stop smoking, and support from friends and family can help me achieve this important goal. I have identified you as a support person in my attempt to stop smoking. A support person is not meant to be a "police officer" or professional therapist. Rather, he or she provides assistance by always being positive about my cessation of smoking, supporting my efforts to remain in treatment, and encouraging my continuation of healthy practices after treatment ends. I want to be clear that while I am seeking your assistance, I maintain responsibility for my behavior relating to treatment and smoking behavior.

For my part, I agree to

1. Attend all scheduled treatment meetings.
2. Earnestly comply with all treatment recommendations during and after treatment. Where I have difficulties with compliance, I will discuss and attempt to resolve them with the counselor.
3. Accept full responsibility for decisions and behavior concerning smoking, and for participation in smoking cessation treatment.

Ways that you may be able to help me stop smoking include

1. Being positive about this good thing that I am doing.
2. Being understanding and tolerant of negative moods, feelings, or thoughts that I have during this difficult process.
3. Being open to listening to me if I need help/support.
4. Not smoking in front of me or offering me cigarettes if you are a smoker.
5. Assisting me to engage in behaviors consistent with treatment recommendations (for example, providing transportation to treatment if needed; allowing me time to exercise or engage in other healthy behaviors; etc.).
6. Helping me to contact my counselor if I am struggling with temptation to smoke, or if I have resumed smoking.

Things that a support person definitely should not do are

1. Lecture or nag me about my behavior.
2. Punish or verbally put me down.
3. Take any responsibility for my behavior.

_____   _____
             Signature   Signature of Support Person

Note. From *Stop Smoking System*, by C. E. Dodgen, 2004, Florham Park, NJ. Unpublished manuscript. Reprinted with permission.

appear welcomed as bona fide treatment options serving typically as components of comprehensive treatment or, in some cases, as stand-alone treatment. AA is explicitly based on the original disease model (Alcoholics Anonymous, 1952), with the belief that alcoholism is a progressive, ultimately fatal illness unless total abstinence is maintained; the disease is partially perpetuated by

EXHIBIT 6.6
Case Example: Evan F.

BRIEF BACKGROUND AND SMOKING HISTORY

Evan F. is a 16-year-old, only child living with his parents. His is in many ways a typical adolescent case. He was brought to treatment by his parents due to concerns about perceived underachievement in high school and a "poor attitude" in general (for example, he is verbally disrespectful to his parents, has to be pressed to give any assistance in the home or to do schoolwork). In addition, Evan smoked about three to five cigarettes per day and his parents wanted him to stop. Although originally compelled to seek treatment by his parents, he admitted to having concerns about his behavior, including smoking, and how it might negatively affect his future. He agreed to smoking-cessation treatment.

SMOKING-CESSATION INTERVENTIONS

As part of the treatment to stop smoking, Evan reviewed the "Support Agreement" form and wondered whom he might designate as support persons. He was concerned that several of his good friends were regular smokers, and his mother smoked as well. His mother also wondered if she had a right to expect Evan to stop smoking. It was explained to Evan and his parents that they had every right to challenge Evan's smoking on legal as well as health grounds. Just as with alcohol, Evan was not of legal age to smoke and therefore was in no position to make the choice for himself. Being a smoker herself does not eliminate his mother as a support person. The role of support person is to be understanding, to reinforce nonsmoking behavior, and to assist the quitter to engage in treatment and other healthy behaviors; these things can be done whether the support person smokes or not, especially if the person is a parent.

Evan identified both parents, his girlfriend, and a teacher at school with whom he had a particularly positive relationship, and all were willing to sign an agreement to be a support person for him. His parents were able to assist Evan by transporting him to treatment meetings, tolerating his irritable behavior at home, and verbalizing support for his efforts to stop smoking. At school, his teacher provided positive verbal reinforcement, as did his nonsmoking girlfriend.

COMMENTS

Signing the support agreements serves a couple of functions. First, it places Evan on public record with his intention to stop smoking, providing some incentive to follow through with cessation and a barrier to resuming smoking. Second, having explicitly identified a support team, he can more easily call for their assistance when needed.

---

the psychological defense of denial that must be confronted and cracked before the help process can begin. In the model, alcoholism is never cured; the only alternative possibility is recovery, which is an active state requiring lifelong attention. The road to abstinence and recovery from the unhealthy addiction is through the 12 steps of AA. The 12 steps, which provide a model to guide the recovery process, encompass cognitive, behavioral, and spiritual realms of functioning. AA is the quintessential mutual-help program; its mainstay is group meetings whose participants are other individuals recovering from the same problem and providing support, encouragement, and coping tips. Strengths of AA include low cost, wide availability, and social support (meetings are available worldwide, and the social network can be accessed 24 hours a day through a sponsor and other members).

Nicotine Anonymous is one of the 12-step programs based on AA. Nicotine Anonymous was started relatively recently (in the early 1980s); this reflects the late acceptance of nicotine as an addictive drug. The national office and clearinghouse (Nicotine Anonymous World Services) is located in San Francisco, California. Information about nicotine addiction and recovery and about meetings can be obtained by contacting the national office. Nicotine Anonymous may be a particularly attractive treatment option for smokers with other addictions who are familiar with 12-step programs (Lichtenstein, 1999).

Brief Physician Advice

Being skilled in the treatment of addictive disorders, and with over-the-counter availability of some pharmaceutical aids to smoking cessation, psychologists are not dependent on physicians for the treatment of nicotine addiction. This, however, does not mean that physicians cannot or do not continue to serve a valuable role in the treatment process. First of all, there are still some pharmaceutical products that require a physician's prescription. Second, the support of a physician can be a positive adjunct to the treatment offered by the psychotherapist. Physicians do not typically schedule appointments in a strictly timed manner like therapists do; they allow for less time and are intervention focused, which dissuades extensive or in-depth discussion. Physicians may still be able to be positively persuasive in their relatively brief patient encounters, and because of this potential influence, therapists ought to consider linkage with a patient's physician, or helping patients who do not have a physician to get one, as a part of smoking-cessation treatment.

There is no single description of physician advice in the literature, and methods vary from informal encounters to very formal protocols, but they have in common that they are brief in duration (usually 3–5 minutes). For example, on the informal side would be a single intervention of physician advice that might consist of the doctor advising the patient to quit smoking, establishing a quit date, discussing prior quit attempts, and dispensing literature on cessation (Law & Tang, 1995). More formal physician encounters that make use of assessment and intervention strategies are suggested and described in the Clinical Practice Guideline (USDHHS, 2000b). The guideline suggests physicians in primary care settings intervene according to the "5 As" that are presented here:

1. Ask about tobacco use.
2. Advise those who are using tobacco to quit in a clear, strong, and personalized manner.
3. Assess the willingness to make a current quit attempt. If the smoker is unwilling to stop, provide a motivational intervention stressing personally relevant reasons why cessation is important for him or her, acknowledging the negative consequences of smoking, the benefits of quitting, and barriers to stopping. These interventions should be repeated at every patient encounter.
4. Assist those interested in a quit attempt by establishing a quit date, encouraging the smoker to tell family, friends, and coworkers about the quit attempt, discussing challenges (such as withdrawal), providing supportive literature, and providing pharmacotherapy.
5. Arrange follow-up contact for shortly after the quit date with a second meeting (within the first month after the quit date). In these meetings provide support, identify problems, and refer the patient for more intensive treatment, if necessary.

Acupuncture

Acupuncture, considered an ancient Chinese form of therapy, is a technique that involves the stimulation of specific points in the body. Stimulation is applied through the insertion of needles or staples, electrically or with the application of heat or pressure, to the acupuncture points. Stimulation at the specified sites is said to allow for the even flow of energy through the body, which is necessary for healthy functioning. Acupuncture has been used in the treatment of many types of substance abuse, including abuse of tobacco, opioids, cocaine, and alcohol, primarily in the detoxification phase of treatment (Brewington, Smith, & Lipton, 1994; Dodgen & Shea, 2000).

In the treatment of nicotine dependence, acupuncture is usually conducted through the use of needles or staples in the ear lobe (Lando, 1993; USDHHS, 1988). The mechanism of action for the softening of withdrawal symptoms from substance abuse appears to be the release of endogenous opiates (Brewington et al., 1994). MacHovec and Man (1978) used an acupuncture procedure with subjects recruited from the community by poster advertisements. Subjects were placed in one of five groups, of which one was a correct-site acupuncture group. Those subjects in the acupuncture group had a small plastic bead sutured to one ear lobe and were instructed to touch or press the site when they felt a strong urge to smoke.

More recently, Bier, Wilson, Studt, and Shakleton (2002) conducted a study of acupuncture for smoking cessation using acupuncture needles. Subjects were placed in one of three groups, one being a correct-site acupuncture group and another a sham acupuncture group. Subjects in the acupuncture group received acupuncture bilaterally at five correct ear points. Subjects in the sham group also received five bilateral needle treatments in their ears, but not at the correct sites. Acupuncture treatments lasted for 4 weeks.

Concerns about medical risks of acupuncture are not observed in the literature, the procedures are not aversive, and subjects undergoing acupuncture treatment are relatively passive, which has some appeal.

Hypnosis

Hypnosis is "an altered state of consciousness in which a person is able to bypass certain aspects of reality, tolerate logical inconsistency, experience distortions of perception and memory as real, and feel a compulsion to follow cues from an outside source" (Covino & Bottari, 2001, p. 340). It is a procedure used to alter the thoughts, feelings, and behavior of an individual through the use of suggestion, focused attention, and the influence of the therapy relationship. Hypnosis has been applied to smoking cessation as a means to weaken the desire to smoke, enhance motivation to stop, and to improve focus and commitment to treatment (Abbot, Stead, White, Barnes, & Ernst, 2001; Lando, 1993). There is no single hypnotherapy technique, but for smoking cessation the most frequently used approach is that of Spiegel (1970). Referred to as a one-session, three-point approach, Spiegel's method is based on the assumption that motivation is a key to smoking cessation, and concentrating on the protection of one's body and life are strong incentives to stop smoking (Covino & Bottari, 2001). The three suggestions of the Spiegel method are (a) smoking is a poison to your body, (b) you need your body to live, and (c) you owe your body respect and protection. Spiegel also teaches self-hypnosis to be practiced at home. Other clinicians also use hypnotic suggestions relating to the aversive aspects of smoking, problem-solving skills, and desensitization to environmental cues (Lando, 1993).

In the MacHovec and Man (1978) study, discussed above in the section on acupuncture, a hypnosis group was also evaluated. The hypnotherapy procedure consisted of three 30-minute sessions, with a focus on aversive suggestions relating to taste, odor, expense, health consequences, and infantile orality. Subjects in this group were also trained to relax and instructed to pair a deep breath with the aversive message whenever an urge to smoke was experienced.

Self-Help

Self-help with respect to nicotine dependence treatment may be described as programs or materials used to aid smokers in cessation efforts without the assistance of a therapist (Lancaster & Stead, 2003). The content of self-help information may vary widely from relatively brief motivational pamphlets (e.g., American Cancer Society, 1982) to relatively intense, self-administered programs which are basically clinical programs presented in such a manner that they can be learned and applied at home (Lando & Gritz, 1996; Orleans et al., 1991). Thus, the more extensive programs may serve as a bridge between the clinic and public health. An example of a more comprehensive manual is published by the American Lung Association (American Lung Association [ALA], 1984). In addition to the cessation manual (entitled *Freedom From Smoking in 20 Days*), the ALA also publishes a maintenance manual for ex-smokers (*A Lifetime of Freedom from Smoking: A Maintenance Program for Ex-Smokers*; ALA, 1986). The ALA cessation manual endeavors to have the smoker abstinent by the 16th day of a 20-day schedule, or sooner if desired (Davis, Faust, & Ordentlich, 1984). The program involves written exercises, record-keeping (number of cigarettes smoked), identification of smoking cues, and effective responses to urges, as well as the signing of a contract to quit smoking. In addition, relaxation exercises are discussed, as well as weight control information to address two known obstacles to abstinence (i.e., tension and weight gain, respectively). The maintenance manual is a relapse-prevention program with an emphasis on identification of high-risk situations and coping responses.

Self-help information can be found in various forms, including written matrials (the most common form), audiotapes, videotapes, and computer programs. Self-help interventions hold great promise. Research reveals that most smokers prefer to quit on their own rather than through formal treatment (Lancaster & Stead, 2003), and approximately 90% of Americans who have quit have done so on their own (Orleans et al., 1991). A method that could help the otherwise unassisted smoker attempting to quit would benefit a large proportion of smokers. Self-help interventions can reach far more smokers than formal treatment programs, and they are much less costly. Self-help materials have been combined with other treatment interventions such as nicotine replacement therapy and supportive telephone calls (Lando & Gritz, 1996). Efforts have been made to tailor self-help material for specific subpopulations to maximize effectiveness (Curry, 1993). For example, tailored self-help manuals are available for smokers who are Hispanic, African American, pregnant, older, and young mothers, as well as smokers at a particular stage of change (Lancaster & Stead, 2003).

Other Referrals

For mental health clinicians not providing smoking-cessation services at all who wish to refer the smoker out for treatment of nicotine dependence, there are several options available in addition to physicians and other mental health clinicians providing such services—programs offered by voluntary health organizations and commercial programs (reviewed in Lando, 1993). Examples of programs offered by voluntary health organizations are those sponsored by the American Cancer Society, American Lung Association, and Seventh-Day Adventist Church. Examples of commercial programs are Smokenders, Smokeless, SmokeStoppers, and Schick Smoking Centers.

All of these programs, although different in certain ways, use combinations of the same techniques described above, such as education, cognitive and behavioral coping skills, social support, interventions from learning theory, and maintenance strategies, so they do not warrant separate discussion here. Before making referrals, clinicians should advise patients to be wary of exaggerated claims and questionable, unconventional methods. It would be best if the clinician assisted the patient to evaluate programs before initiating treatment.

PHARMACOLOGICAL INTERVENTIONS

In the Clinical Practice Guideline (USDHHS, 2000b), reference is made to first- and second-line medications for the treatment of nicotine dependence. As implied by the name, first-line medications should be considered first in treating nicotine dependence except when contraindicating factors are present. First-line medications are approved by the U.S. Food and Drug Administration for use in the treatment of nicotine dependence and have an empirically based record of efficacy and safety. Second-line medications, by contrast, are medications with evidence of efficacy in the treatment of nicotine dependence but which are not approved by the Food and Drug Administration for this treatment, and for which there are more serious concerns about potential side effects than for first-line medications. Second-line medications are to be considered on an individual basis only after first-line treatments have been used or considered. Of the medications reviewed below, the nicotine replacement therapies and bupropion sustained release (SR) are classified as first-line; second-line medications discussed below are nortriptyline and clonidine.

Nicotine Replacement Therapy (NRT)

The rationale for NRT is fourfold (Brown, Larkin, & Davis, 2000; Glover & Glover, 2001; Hughes, 1993a; Jarvik & Henningfield, 1988):

1. To replace nicotine obtained by smoking with nicotine supplied in a form that is safer (i.e., free of the toxins and many other chemical compounds found in cigarettes in addition to nicotine) and more manageable. Supplying nicotine in an alternative form blocks initial withdrawal and allows for control of the nicotine dose, and eventual tapering of the dose with the goals of ceasing nicotine intake while minimizing withdrawal discomfort. Suppression of withdrawal symptoms allows the patient to focus on behavior change and psychological factors and not on acute discomfort associated with early nicotine abstinence.

2. To reduce craving.
3. To diminish the reinforcing effects of smoking cigarettes. The empirical basis for this aspect of NRT comes from studies that demonstrate that pretreatment with nicotine in any form that raises nicotine levels in the bloodstream decreases smoking. For example, nicotine administered intravenously, orally (in capsule form), buccally (with gum), transdermally (with a patch), by the nasal route (nasal spray method), and even by the rectum (with suppositories) has resulted in reduced smoking.
4. To decondition nicotine by making its intake separate from smoking behaviors and cues. The act of smoking is reinforced many times throughout the day, and many cues become associated with smoking as well. Having nicotine intake independent of the behavioral rituals and smoking cues may help with some of the learned aspects of smoking.

Nicotine as a therapeutic agent is currently available in the United States in five pharmaceutical preparations: gum, patch, inhaler, nasal spray, and lozenge. Despite the fact that they all deliver the same active ingredient, nicotine, to the user, they are not identical, and each has its own associated advantages and disadvantages. For example, only some forms are available as over-the-counter, nonprescription products; in addition, because of the different routes of nicotine delivery, side effect profiles vary. Although NRT in all forms is considered safe, some restrictions on usage are noted. Before any of these products is used, the insert information that accompanies the products should be read closely for use instructions, potential side effects (also referred to as *adverse reactions*), and contraindicating factors of use; also, it is prudent to have the smoker gain physician approval before recommending any of the pharmacological products, prescription and over-the-counter alike. Contraindicating factors that are common to all forms of NRT include the experience of a myocardial infarction within the preceding 2 weeks, existence of a serious cardiac arrhythmia, worsening angina pectoris, and pregnancy or nursing (Kotlyar & Hatsukami, 2002).

Several unfounded myths (Brown et al., 2000) exist about NRT; they are discussed in Table 6.1. Concerns are sometimes expressed in treatment about possible long-term dependence on NRT, the worry being that the smoker will replace one addiction (to cigarettes) with another (the nicotine replacement product). Although this is a reasonable fear, it turns out that long-term dependence on NRT is not common, and use of some form of NRT is still preferable to smoking (USDHHS, 2000b).

The significant characteristics of the five forms of NRT are summarized in Exhibit 6.7 (Benowitz, 1997; Brown et al., 2000; Kotlyar & Hatsukami, 2002; Lando & Gritz, 1996; Mallin, 2002; Rustin, 2001; Sutherland, 2002).

TABLE 6.1
Unfounded Myths About Nicotine Replacement Therapy

Myth	Comment
1. Health benefits from smoking cessation do not accrue until the NRT program is completed.	1. Damage to the cardiovascular and respiratory systems, as well as risks of cancer, results from exposure to compounds and toxins in cigarettes other than nicotine; NRT does not cause damage to the body, so health benefits from cessation are initiated when smoking ceases.
2. NRT should not be recommended to any patient who may continue to smoke during treatment.	2. First, if this were the case, almost nobody would be appropriate for NRT. Second, although smoking during NRT is strongly discouraged, the level of safety appears acceptable even with high nicotine levels.
3. NRT is expensive, which is a possible deterrent to its use.	3. Cost studies demonstrate that the average monthly cost of any of the forms of NRT is approximately equal to the monthly cost of smoking between one and two packs of cigarettes per day. Not only is the cost of NRT in the short term not significantly different from the cost of continued smoking, but future savings from smoking cessation and reduced health expenses over time make the treatments extremely cost-effective.

Brand names of products are mentioned for illustrative purposes only and should not be construed as specific product endorsement, as a comprehensive commercial product evaluation is not the aim of this discussion.

In addition to the use of single NRTs, combination NRTs have been investigated (Fagerstrom, 1994; USDHHS, 2000b). Conceived of to address the common problem of underdosing of nicotine with replacement therapies, it usually involves use of the patch system with one other form of NRT (e.g., patch and gum; patch and nasal spray). The reasoning is that the patch can provide a stable baseline level of nicotine in the body and the second form of NRT can be used for craving control and self-titration of nicotine levels. Combining NRTs may be particularly helpful with highly nicotine-dependent individuals. Combination NRT is classified as a second-line medication treatment for nicotine dependence due to the existence of insufficient safety data and because of concerns about possible nicotine overdose; combination NRT should be considered only after failure with a single form of NRT.

Non-Nicotine Pharmacological Therapies

An assortment of non-nicotine pharmacological products have been investigated to assist in the treatment of nicotine dependence, drawing from

EXHIBIT 6.7
Significant Characteristics of Various Forms of Nicotine Replacement Therapy for Treatment of Nicotine Dependence

1. Nicotine Gum
   a. *Prescription status.* Nicotine gum was the first available form of nicotine replacement and is currently available as an over-the-counter, nonprescription product. The gum is available in regular, orange, and mint flavors.
   b. *Use instructions.* Users should stop smoking completely. The gum is a resin to which nicotine is bound; nicotine in the gum is released by chewing and dissolves in saliva. Proper use of nicotine gum is not as easily achieved as one might think. It is not to be used like regular chewing gum. The nicotine gum should be chewed intermittently, then placed between the cheek and gum for absorption. The Nicorette brand nicotine gum instructions recommend that each piece of gum be chewed in the following manner: After the user places the gum in his or her mouth, it should be chewed slowly and deliberately until a "peppery" taste and slight tingle are noted (indicating the release of nicotine from the gum); the gum should then be parked between the cheek and gum until the peppery taste and tingle fade (which takes about a minute), at which time the chewing and parking processes should be repeated. The chewing and parking cycle should be continued until the gum is exhausted (indicated by an absence of the taste and tingle when chewed), which usually takes about 30 minutes per piece. Food and drink restrictions while using the gum are necessitated by the fact that absorption of nicotine is significantly affected by the acidity of the mouth; anything that raises the acidity impairs absorption, so consumption of all food and beverages (except water) is to be avoided for at least 15 minutes before and during chewing.
   c. *Dosage information.* Nicotine gum is available in two doses, 2 mg and 4 mg. The higher-dose preparation is recommended for the more heavily dependent smoker. The manufacturer of Nicorette gum recommends that smokers of 25 or more cigarettes a day choose the 4-mg gum, and smokers of 24 or fewer cigarettes a day use the 2-mg gum. Other methods may also be used to determine degree of nicotine dependence for the purpose of deciding which dose of medication to use. For example, the Fagerstrom Tobacco Questionnaire (Fagerstrom, 1978; see chap. 5) has also been used for this purpose. A score of 7 to 11 on the FTQ is recommended to identify highly dependent smokers (Herrera et al., 1995).
   d. *Absorption characteristics.* With nicotine gum, peak levels of nicotine are attained in approximately 30 minutes by absorption through the oral mucosa. Nicotine delivered by this method differs significantly from nicotine delivered by cigarette smoke, which reaches the brain in under 10 seconds.
   e. *Duration and schedule of treatment.* Nicotine gum use is recommended for 12 weeks. The manufacturers of Nicorette gum recommend the following tapered schedule of use: (a) one piece of gum every 1 to 2 hours for Weeks 1 through 6 of treatment, (b) one piece of gum every 2 to 4 hours for Weeks 7 through 9, (c) one piece of gum every 4 to 8 hours for Weeks 10 through 12. No more than 24 pieces of gum per day should be used.
   f. *Advantages of nicotine gum preparation.* Nicotine gum is easily obtained and familiar to people owing to its status as the oldest method of NRT (which may help with both patient and therapist acceptance). Nicotine gum has been shown to delay (but not prevent) postcessation weight gain, a problem often cited as a barrier to maintenance of abstinence. The delay in weight gain can be helpful to support abstinence and allow time for other coping skills to establish maintenance and weight control, rather than having to deal

continues

EXHIBIT 6.7 *(Continued)*

with weight gain early in treatment. Additional advantages of gum use are that it enables the user to control titration of nicotine and control cravings (i.e., the gum can be used when desired to combat urges), and it provides some oral substitution for smoking.

g. *Weaknesses of nicotine gum preparation.* Common side effects of the use of nicotine gum include throat and mouth irritation, mouth sores, jaw soreness, hiccups, nausea, indigestion, and dental problems (loose and cracked teeth, pulling out of fillings and bridges, sticking to dentures). However, side effects of gum use are usually described as minor. Concerns about improper use of the gum are significant and include chewing too rapidly and swallowing too much nicotine in saliva (resulting in the adverse reactions of hiccups, nausea, and indigestion); also, social acceptance is sometimes cited as a barrier to use because the chewing of the gum is not a totally private matter. Failure to achieve sufficient blood levels of nicotine due to improper use or underutilization is another problem with the gum; the latter may reflect the burden of frequent use of the gum or the fact that many users find the taste of the gum aversive.

2. Nicotine Transdermal Patch

a. *Prescription status.* The nicotine patch is available as an over-the-counter, nonprescription product.

b. *Use instructions.* Smoking should be completely stopped. The nicotine patch should be applied once daily in a clean, dry, relatively hairless location on the body to allow good skin contact; the upper arm is suggested. The site of placement of the patch should be rotated with each application. The patch is considered to be the easiest to use of all methods of NRT.

c. *Dosage information.* The nicotine patch comes in two versions: 16-hour and 24-hour patches. The 16-hour patch should be applied in the morning and removed at bedtime; the 24-hour patch, of course, is meant to be worn until replaced by a new one the following day. The 24-hour patch is recommended for those individuals who have strong morning urges to smoke. The nicotine patch also comes in varying doses, with initial recommended dose depending on degree of nicotine dependence (discussed below in section e).

d. *Absorption characteristics.* With the patch, nicotine is delivered from a reservoir in an adhesive patch that functions as a rate-controlling membrane. The patch system delivers a steady dose of nicotine throughout the day, with no rapid spike in the blood level of nicotine, in contrast to the effects of smoking.

e. *Duration and schedule of treatment.* The recommended treatment duration for the nicotine patch is 8 to 12 weeks, depending on the particular brand or system and the degree of initial nicotine dependence. For example, with the NicoDerm CQ system, there are 10-week and 8-week programs for heavier and lighter smokers, respectively. NicoDerm CQ patches come in three doses: 21 mg, 14 mg, and 7 mg. It is recommended that users who smoke more than 10 cigarettes per day follow the following schedule: Step 1 (21-mg patch) for 6 weeks, Step 2 (14-mg patch) for 2 weeks, Step 3 (7 mg) for 2 weeks. If users smoke 10 cigarettes or fewer per day, it is recommended that they start with Step 2 (14-mg patch) for 6 weeks, then Step 3 (7-mg patch) for 2 weeks.

f. *Advantages of the nicotine patch.* Its unobtrusive nature, ease of use, and related patient acceptability are the strengths of this method of NRT; users have to make only one medication decision a day. Because of the way the nicotine is delivered with this method, a more reliable blood level of nicotine is achieved, resulting in effective nicotine replacement. Because a

continues

EXHIBIT 6.7 *(Continued)*

more or less steady level of nicotine is obtained with the patch, the risk of dependence is minimal and prevention of withdrawal is achieved without the reinforcing effects of nicotine delivered in a more rapid, episodic manner that more closely resembles smoking.

    g. *Weaknesses of the nicotine patch.* The most commonly reported side effect of the nicotine patch is local skin irritation, which is usually described as minor and easily treatable with lotions and by rotating the patch site. Provision of a steady level of nicotine means that the individual cannot regulate the nicotine level or apply on demand for craving control. Smoking while using the patch can be particularly problematic, resulting in significant discomfort from high nicotine levels and increasing the chances of discontinuation of treatment and relapse. With the 24-hour patch, insomnia can be a problem; the 16-hour patch may then be used, or some 24-hour patches may be removed at bedtime if insomnia occurs.

3. Nicotine Inhaler

    a. *Prescription status.* The nicotine inhaler is available only as a prescription medication.

    b. *Use instructions.* Users should stop smoking completely. The nicotine inhaler is explicitly designed to be used in a way that closely mimics the behavior of smoking. For example, the Nicotrol Inhaler is a nicotine inhalation system that consists of a mouthpiece and nicotine cartridge that is inserted into the mouthpiece. It is fashioned in the shape of a cigarette and has a light menthol taste. Users are instructed to use their own technique to draw on the mouthpiece, so they may inhale deeply on the mouthpiece into the back of the throat, or with short puffs. The nicotine in the cartridge is vaporized as it is inhaled through the mouthpiece. The mouthpiece is reusable and should be cleaned regularly. It is recommended that the user puff for 20 minutes at a time when the inhaler is used.

    c. *Dosage information.* Users of the Nicotrol Inhaler are advised to use at least 6 cartridges a day to ensure adequate dosing of nicotine, and not to exceed a maximum of 16 cartridges per day. One cartridge contains the same amount of nicotine found in two cigarettes; the nicotine in a cartridge is used up after about 20 minutes of puffing.

    d. *Absorption characteristics.* Despite the fact that the nicotine is inhaled, absorption takes place mainly in the mucosa of the mouth and upper respiratory tract.

    e. *Duration and schedule of treatment.* Nicotine inhalation therapy can be used for up to 6 months. A tapered schedule of use is recommended. For example, with the Nicotrol Inhaler, 6 to 16 cartridges are recommended for up to 12 weeks, with a gradual reduction in the number of cartridges used per day suggested for the next 6 to 12 weeks (the tapering schedule is less precise than those for other NRT systems).

    f. *Advantages of the nicotine inhaler.* The nicotine inhaler has the potential advantage of coming the closest to mimicking the behavioral aspects of smoking. The user can also titrate the level of nicotine he or she receives and can use the inhaler on demand for craving control.

    g. *Weaknesses of the nicotine inhaler.* Common side effects of use of the inhaler system include irritation of the mouth and throat, coughing, and rhinitis; side effects are described as minor. Because absorption takes place primarily in the mouth, as with the nicotine gum, restrictions on eating and drinking must be observed (no eating or drinking except water for 15 minutes before and during use). The need to use the product frequently and the fact that it is an observable procedure may be additional obstacles to the use of this method.

continues

EXHIBIT 6.7 *(Continued)*

4. Nicotine Nasal Spray
   a. *Prescription status.* Nicotine nasal spray is available only as a prescription product.
   b. *Use instructions.* Users should stop smoking completely. Nicotine nasal spray is used like other nasal sprays that people are generally familiar with. Users of Nicotrol NS nasal spray are instructed to start by clearing the nasal passages (by blowing if necessary), then tilt the head back slightly, place the tip of the bottle in the nostril, breathe through the mouth, and spray the mist into the nostril, without sniffing, swallowing, or inhaling while spraying. Then they repeat the process for the other nostril. If the nose runs, they are to gently sniff to keep the nasal spray in the nose and wait 2 minutes before blowing the nose.
   c. *Dosage information.* Nicotrol NS comes in a 10 ml bottle that contains 100 mg of nicotine, about enough for 200 sprays. One spray in each nostril is considered one dose; one dose delivers 1 mg of nicotine to the body.
   d. *Absorption characteristics.* Nicotine nasal spray is a solution of nicotine in water. Nicotine is absorbed in the richly vascularized nasal membranes and has a relatively fast onset of action (approximately 4–15 minutes for most of the nicotine to enter the bloodstream). This method of NRT delivers the quickest dose of nicotine.
   e. *Duration and schedule of treatment.* The manufacturer of Nicotrol NS recommends a course of treatment of 12 weeks; a gradual tapering strategy is suggested but not specifically described. The minimum recommendation is 8 doses per day to ensure a sufficient supply of nicotine, with a maximum of 40 doses per day.
   f. *Advantages of nicotine nasal spray.* Because of the speed with which nicotine nasal spray delivers nicotine to the system, it relieves cravings more rapidly than other forms of NRT. The nasal spray is easy to use. This method of NRT may more effectively assist the more highly dependent smokers.
   g. *Weaknesses of nicotine nasal spray.* Nicotine nasal spray has the highest occurrence of side effects of all the forms of NRT, including runny nose, throat irritation, coughing, changes in smell and taste, and nausea; all of the side effects may diminish with time but may not entirely go away. Another concern with the nasal spray is that because of the relatively rapid delivery of nicotine, this method has the highest addiction potential.
5. Nicotine Lozenge
   a. *Prescription status.* The nicotine lozenge is available as an over-the-counter product.
   b. *Use instructions.* The user should stop smoking completely. Instructions for the Commit nicotine lozenge are as follows: The lozenge should be placed in the mouth and allowed to dissolve slowly for approximately 20 to 30 minutes. It is important not to chew or swallow the lozenge, and to keep swallowing of saliva to a minimum. A warm, tingling sensation may be noted from the lozenge, and it is helpful to move the lozenge from one side of the mouth to the other until it is completely dissolved. Lozenges should be used one at a time and should not be used continuously, one after another.
   c. *Dosage information.* The Commit nicotine lozenge is available in two doses, 4 mg and 2 mg; the 4-mg dose is recommended for the more heavily dependent smoker. Time to first cigarette is the method used by the manufacturer to determine degree of nicotine dependence: If the first cigarette of the day is usually smoked within 30 minutes of waking up, the 4-mg nicotine lozenge is suggested; if the first cigarette of the day is smoked more than 30 minutes after awakening, the 2-mg nicotine lozenge

continues

EXHIBIT 6.7 *(Continued)*

is suggested as the initial dose. To ensure adequate dosing, users should consume at least 9 lozenges per day initially; no more than 5 should be used in 6 hours, with the maximum suggested as 20 per day.

d. *Absorption characteristics.* Nicotine from the lozenge is absorbed in the mucosa of the mouth. The lozenge works in a manner similar to nicotine gum but is easier to use, and this method delivers significantly more nicotine per comparable dose of nicotine gum.

e. *Duration and schedule of treatment.* The manufacturer of the Commit nicotine lozenge recommends a 12-week course of treatment with a tapered schedule: (a) Weeks 1 through 6, one lozenge every 1 to 2 hours; (b) Weeks 7 to 9, one lozenge every 2 to 4 hours; (c) Weeks 10 through 12, one lozenge every 4 to 8 hours.

f. *Advantages of the nicotine lozenge.* The lozenge is relatively easy to use and delivers nicotine more effectively than a comparable dose of nicotine gum.

g. *Weaknesses of the nicotine lozenge.* Commonly reported side effects of using the nicotine lozenge are mouth and throat irritation and indigestion. Side effects are usually described as mild. There is a need for frequent use, which can be an obstacle to compliance. Dietary restrictions must also be observed, as with other methods in which nicotine is absorbed buccally; that is, other than water, there should be no eating or drinking for 15 minutes before and during use of the nicotine lozenge.

---

a variety of drug classes. For example, antidepressant and antianxiety medications have been used, as well as drugs used to treat hypertension and drugs that are chemically similar agonists to nicotine. As a complete review of all medications investigated in the treatment of nicotine dependence is beyond the scope of this book, only those medications that receive significant attention in the literature will be reviewed below. All of the medications presented below are prescription products; they are discussed for educational purposes only. The discussion that follows is not a substitute for medical advice. A physician must be contacted to obtain a prescription and to assure full understanding before using these products.

Antidepressant Medications

The rationale for using antidepressant medications for smoking cessation is based on several observations (Hughes, Stead, & Lancaster, 2003b): The incidence of depression is higher among smokers than nonsmokers, smoking cessation and consequent nicotine withdrawal can result in depressive symptoms, and nicotine may have antidepressant effects. These observations, in conjunction with the fact that antidepressant medications may be a more suitable method of reversing depression than nicotine, leads to the interest in antidepressants for treating nicotine dependence. A large number of medications from several classes of antidepressant medications have been tried to alter smoking behavior: tricyclics (e.g., nortriptyline), monoamine oxidase inhibitors (MAOIs; e.g., moclobemide), selective serotonin reuptake inhibitors (SSRIs; e.g., fluoxetine), and atypical antidepressants (e.g., bupropion). The two antidepressant medications that have received the most interest and support for efficacy in smoking cessation are bupropion sustained release (bupropion SR) and nortriptyline; the present discussion is restricted to these medications.

Bupropion SR. Bupropion SR (brand name Zyban) is described as an atypical antidepressant medication; it is marketed as an antidepressant medication under a different brand name (Wellbutrin). It was the first non-nicotine pharmacological treatment approved by the Food and Drug Administration for the purpose of smoking-cessation treatment (Glover & Glover, 2001; Jorenby, 2002) and is recommended as a first-line medication for this purpose. Bupropion SR is thought to operate by acting as both a norepinephrine and dopamine reuptake inhibitor, enhancing dopaminergic activity in the mesolimbic system and *nucleus accumbens* (the pleasure and reward centers of the brain). Ironically, this mechanism is not the same one thought to be involved in alleviating depression, which is supposedly related to serotonergic pathways in the brain, so the effect on smoking cessation for bupropion SR may be independent of its antidepressant effects. It has been shown to relieve nicotine withdrawal symptoms and craving, as well as to delay postcessation weight gain. Information salient to the use of bupropion SR is discussed in Exhibit 6.8.

Nortriptyline. Nortriptyline is a tricyclic antidepressant. The purported mechanism of action is by inhibiting reuptake of norepinephrine and serotonin (with the primary effect on norepinephrine). Information relevant for evaluating its use is shown in Exhibit 6.8.

Anxiolytic Medications

The rationale for the possible use of antianxiety medication in the treatment of nicotine dependence is convincing (Hughes, Stead, & Lancaster, 2003a): Anxiety is a symptom of nicotine withdrawal, and smoking can provide relief from anxiety; therefore, antianxiety medication can potentially soften this withdrawal symptom and replace an ostensibly positive function of nicotine (i.e., anxiety reduction). Unfortunately, there is insufficient evidence to justify the use of anxiolytic medications for smoking cessation purposes, especially when side effect profiles (e.g., risk of abuse and dependence on the medication) are considered, so no specific medications will be discussed here.

The use of antidepressant and anxiolytic medications in the service of smoking cessation therapy is based on the commonsense assumption that as depression and anxiety are symptoms of nicotine withdrawal, smoking-cessation efforts can be aided by treating these symptoms with medication. Interestingly, the pattern of results does not support the conclusion that

EXHIBIT 6.8
Significant Characteristics of Non-Nicotine Pharmacological Therapies
for Treatment of Nicotine Dependence

1. Bupropion SR
   a. *Prescription status.* Bupropion SR is available as a prescription pharmaceutical product only.
   b. *Use instructions.* Bupropion SR comes in pill form and is to be taken orally. Tablets should be taken whole, not chewed, divided, or crushed, and may be taken with or without food. There are significant restrictions and contraindications; bupropion SR should not be taken if any of the following conditions exist: (a) already taking Wellbutrin pills or any other medication containing buproprion; (b) history of seizure disorder; (c) history of eating disorder; (d) currently or recently taking an MAOI; (e) pregnant or breast-feeding; (f) allergic to bupropion; (g) have abruptly discontinued alcohol or other sedative. It is advised to not drink alcohol at all or very little while taking bupropion SR; some people experience lower alcohol tolerance while taking the medication, and people who drink a lot of alcohol and suddenly stop may experience increased seizure risk.
   c. *Dosage information.* Bupropion SR is available in 150-mg tablets and has a recommended target dosage of 300 mg per day.
   d. *Absorption characteristics.* Taken orally, the medication is absorbed into the bloodstream through the stomach.
   e. *Duration and schedule of treatment.* Bupropion SR is taken precessation as compared to NRT, which usually begins on the quit date. Bupropion SR is typically taken 1 to 2 weeks before the quit date because it takes time to establish a therapeutic dose. It is recommended that smoking stop on the quit date, not for safety reasons but because if smoking is not stopped on the target date, chances of cessation in the long term are seriously diminished. The recommended starting dosage is 150 mg once daily (in the morning) for 3 days, increasing to 150 mg twice daily (one in the morning, one in the early evening at least 8 hours after the morning dose—totaling 300 mg per day) for the remainder of treatment. Treatment duration is typically 7 to 12 weeks.
   f. *Advantages of bupropion SR treatment.* Bupropion SR is a non-nicotine product, so it is free of concerns about protracted dependence on nicotine and about abuse of the medication itself. The requirement of taking a pill twice per day is not onerous, so compliance is not a significant problem (Corelli & Hudman, 2002; Jorenby, 2002). The delay of weight gain while taking the medication is helpful in deferring an initial barrier to smoking cessation. The cost of bupropion SR should not be a barrier. The manufacturer reports that the cost of 7 weeks of treatment with the medication approximately equals the cost of one pack of cigarettes per day; additional savings are incurred from prevention of future medical costs and expenditure on cigarettes. Finally, bupropion SR may be used with NRT and may also be useful for treating smokers with coexisting depression.
   g. *Weaknesses of bupropion SR treatment.* Bupropion SR is reported to be generally well tolerated, but side effects that are identified include anxiety, headache, rash, shakiness, lowered seizure threshold, dry mouth, and insomnia (the latter two being the most common side effects). The side effects tend to be transient or can be managed by a reduction in dose, if necessary. Although this is not reported in the literature, some patients have expressed concern to me about taking a "psychiatric medication" to stop smoking, which is perhaps why the manufacturer has given the same medication a different name when used to treat depression.

continues

EXHIBIT 6.8 *(Continued)*

2. Nortriptyline
   a. *Prescription status.* Nortriptyline (brand name Pamelor) is available as a prescription product.
   b. *Use instructions.* The information reported on nortriptyline is provided by the manufacturer. Nortriptyline is available in two forms meant to be taken orally: tablet and liquid. Nortriptyline may be taken with or without food. There are significant precautions and dangers related to the use of this medication. Overdose may be fatal; use of nortriptyline and an MAOI together may be fatal as well. Nortriptyline can intensify the effects of alcohol, so use of alcohol should be avoided. Driving motor vehicles or operating machinery can be hazardous due to sedation. Nortriptyline interacts with many medications, affecting their performance, so a physician should be advised of all medications taken before prescribing nortriptyline. In addition, the medication should be used cautiously by those with the following conditions: cardiovascular disease, glaucoma, diabetes, seizure disorder, thyroid dysfunction, and kidney or liver disease; patients taking other antidepressant medications are also cautioned to get physician approval.
   c. *Dosage information.* The recommended target dose is in the range of 75 mg to 100 mg per day; tablets are available in a 25-mg dose.
   d. *Absorption characteristics.* As a medication taken orally, nortriptyline is absorbed through the stomach.
   e. *Duration and schedule of treatment.* Nortriptyline is usually started at 25 mg per day and increased gradually to the target dose. The medication is usually started 10 to 28 days before quit date to allow enough time for a therapeutic level to be achieved. Treatment is typically for 12 weeks.
   f. *Advantages of nortriptyline treatment.* As a non-nicotine medication, like bupropion SR, it is free from concerns about prolonged nicotine dependence, and there is no concern about abuse liability of the medication.
   g. *Weaknesses of nortriptyline treatment.* The most common side effects of nortriptyline use are sedation, dry mouth, blurred vision, urinary retention, lightheadedness, and shaky hands. Side effects may also be caused by abrupt cessation or rapid decrease after long-term use, including headache, nausea, and vague body discomfort.
3. Clonidine
   a. *Prescription status.* Clonidine (brand name Catapres) is available as a prescription product.
   b. *Use instructions.* Clonidine comes in two forms: transdermal patch and tablet form. The patch (available in 0.1-mg, 0.2-mg, and 0.3-mg preparations) is to be applied to a clean, dry, relatively hairless area of the body every 7 days. The tablet (available in 0.1-mg, 0.2-mg, and 0.3-mg preparations) is to be taken orally, several times per day (depending on the prescribed dosage) at evenly spaced intervals.
   c. *Dosage information.* It appears that no standard dose has been established for clonidine for smoking cessation; doses in clinical trials range from 0.15 mg to 0.75 mg per day of oral medication, and 0.1 mg to 0.2 mg per day delivered transdermally.
   d. *Absorption characteristics.* The oral preparation is absorbed through the stomach, and the patch system allows for absorption of the medication through the skin.
   e. *Duration and schedule of treatment.* As with dosing, other treatment parameters are not clearly defined. Initial dosing is typically 0.1 mg twice a day of the oral preparation, increasing by 0.1 mg per day per week, if necessary; or 0.10 mg per day transdermally, increasing by 0.10 mg per day

continues

EXHIBIT 6.8 *(Continued)*

per week. Duration of treatment with clonidine ranges from 3 to 10 weeks. Clonidine use is usually initiated shortly before the quit date (e.g., 3 days prior to quit date).

f. *Advantages of clonidine treatment.* As a non-nicotine replacement medication, like bupropion SR and nortriptyline, it is free from concerns about prolonged nicotine dependence, and there is no concern about abuse liability of the medication. The transdermal patch is designed so that a medication decision has only to be made once per week, which can help with compliance.

g. *Weaknesses of clonidine treatment.* The most common side effects of clonidine use are fatigue, dry mouth, headache, sedation, dizziness, and constipation. Rebound hypertension may result from abrupt cessation, with symptoms of increased blood pressure, agitation, confusion, and tremor; clonidine should be reduced gradually over 2 to 4 days. In addition, the medication should be used only with great caution if pregnant or nursing. Side effects of the patch system are local skin reactions. Compliance problems may be seen with the oral tablets because they must be taken several times per day.

treating withdrawal symptomatically is effective for smoking cessation. Some antidepressant medications (i.e., bupropion SR and nortriptyline) are effective in curtailing smoking behavior; others are not (e.g., SSRIs). In addition, bupropion SR and nortriptyline were purposely tested on nondepressed smokers to rule out the amelioration of depression as a mechanism of effectiveness. Anxiolytic medications are effective in quelling anxiety associated with nicotine withdrawal but are not useful in altering smoking behavior. It appears, then, that alteration of specific neurotransmitter levels may be as important as, or even more important than, the modification of withdrawal symptoms of anxiety and depression. It has been suggested that bupropion SR and nortriptyline are effective in smoking cessation not only because of their attenuation of withdrawal severity and cravings (due to their activity in the *locus coeruleus* by the neurotransmitter norepinephrine), but also because of their modulating effects on dopamine, which substitutes for the reinforcing effects of nicotine in the mesolimbic system of the brain (Kotlyar, Golding, Hatsukami, & Jamerson, 2001; Zwar & Richmond, 2002).

Other Medications

Two pharmaceutical products from disparate classes of medication that have received some research interest for treatment of nicotine dependence are lobeline and clonidine. Evaluations of lobeline, a partial nicotine agonist, have not produced sufficient empirical support for the use of this medication. Clonidine, on the other hand, has received support for use in smoking cessation treatment.

Clonidine is a drug with antihypertensive qualities (hypertension being the main indicator for its use) that has also been used in the treatment of opioid withdrawal (Miller & Cocores, 1991). Withdrawal states from drugs of abuse such as alcohol, opioids, and nicotine are characterized by overactivity of the sympathetic nervous system. Clonidine's mechanism of action is thought to result from the reversal of sympathetic hyperactivity, with resultant softening of nicotine withdrawal symptoms (Kotlyar et al., 2001). Factors relevant to the use of clonidine are discussed in Exhibit 6.8.

SUMMARY

The treatment of nicotine dependence is a specialized treatment consisting of counseling interventions. Goals of treatment are generally more circumscribed than for traditional psychotherapy, unless indications of the need to broaden treatment are identified in the assessment process. Interventions derived from learning paradigms may be divided into aversive techniques (electric shock; satiation and rapid smoking; reduced aversion techniques of focused smoking, smoke holding, and rapid puffing; covert sensitization; silver acetate) and nonaversive techniques (stimulus control, cue exposure, contingency contracting, nicotine fading, cognitive procedures). Other treatment methods assist in stress management and coping behavior or enhance social support. Coping skills involve the teaching of healthy alternatives to handling urges to smoke and include cognitive and behavioral strategies. Interventions dealing with the support system of the smoker attempt to either bolster the natural support system or provide support directly in the treatment by individual or group counseling. For clinicians not interested in directly providing any or all services to patients desiring smoking-cessation treatment, referrals are necessary. It is therefore helpful to the clinician to be aware of services provided by physicians, Nicotine Anonymous, voluntary health organizations, and commercial programs, as well as methods such as acupuncture, hypnosis, and self-help.

Pharmacological interventions are now available as options in the treatment of nicotine dependence. Pharmacological treatments can be used alone or in conjunction with counseling interventions. They consist of both nicotine replacement therapies, which are available in five different forms (some of which can be obtained without a prescription) and non-nicotine replacement therapies. Strengths and weaknesses, prescription status, use instructions, dosage information, and treatment schedules need to be considered for each form of pharmacotherapy.

7

OUTCOMES AND APPLICATION OF INTERVENTIONS

To evaluate the validity of a treatment intervention, it is necessary to consider its efficacy as well as other factors. This chapter identifies counseling and pharmacological interventions for the treatment of nicotine dependence that are supported by efficacy studies. In addition, counseling interventions are discussed that, although not supported by efficacy studies, are effective in clinical practice. Treatment parameters with demonstrated efficacy are also described relating to treatment intensity, type of clinician rendering treatment, format of treatment, and applicability of the interventions to all groups of smokers. Finally, the issue of patient motivation is discussed. It is hoped that by reading this chapter clinicians will learn about treatment interventions and parameters of treatment that work, as well as methods to address the crucial concern of patient motivation for cessation.

EVALUATING TREATMENT VALIDITY

As alluded to in the introduction to this book, there is no one single method to evaluate the validity of treatment interventions. Rather, there are two basic approaches to determining the validity of psychotherapy interventions. The two principal methods currently used in psychotherapy

153

outcome research are efficacy studies and effectiveness studies (Nathan et al., 2000; Seligman, 1995). An efficacy study is essentially an adaptation of the pharmaceutical testing model for the purpose of evaluating psychotherapy outcomes (Goldfried & Wolfe, 1996). These may be considered laboratory tests (Kazdin, 2001). As such they are conducted in the tradition of classic experimental design (Nathan et al., 2000; Seligman, 1995), as described in Exhibit 7.1.

The most serious criticism of efficacy studies relates to the inverse relationship between scientific rigor and application to real-world clinical practice. That is, as rigor is increased, generalizability to clinical practice is sacrificed. There are other problems with the use of efficacy studies in psychotherapy research (Seligman, 1995) relating to (a) the inability to have a true double-blind design (i.e., the therapist knows what treatment is being provided and the patient may as well); (b) limitations of manualized treatment, including the diminishment of interpersonal and therapeutic skills, judgment, and creativity; (c) the relatively brief treatment stints, meaning that certain types of treatment may never be validated by this method (e.g., psychoanalysis and psychodynamic psychotherapies); (d) methodological problems stemming from underlying assumptions that may themselves be invalid (Wampold, 1997); and (e) the focus on formal diagnostic categories and related symptoms to the exclusion of other relevant outcome measures such as general functioning, coping skills, and quality of life.

Effectiveness studies have also been used for the purpose of evaluating the validity of psychotherapy techniques. Effectiveness studies are more like field studies; the primary emphasis is on analyzing treatments as they are applied by the clinician in uncontrolled, real-world settings with actual patients (Seligman, 1995; Wampold, 1997). Although scientific rigor is compromised in this type of study, what is gained is information that is more readily accepted and applied by clinicians who render the treatment and patients who seek the treatment (Seligman, 1995). Because of the more

EXHIBIT 7.1
Key Characteristics of Psychotherapy Efficacy Studies

1. Treatment and control groups are comparable except one group receives the treatment under study (independent variable).
2. Participants are randomly assigned to treatment and control groups.
3. Differences within groups are minimized by the use of treatment manuals and strict inclusionary and exclusionary criteria for participants (e.g., participants may meet the clinical criteria for one disorder only).
4. Target measures (dependent variables) are precisely defined and reliably assessed.
5. Participants are treated for a fixed number of sessions only, and follow-up measures are taken after a fixed time posttreatment.

naturalistic style of effectiveness studies, they have limitations due to an absence of those factors that are most important in laboratory studies (random assignment to homogeneous groups, strict control of treatments rendered, etc.). As with other classic debates in psychology (e.g., mind/body, nature/nurture), there may never be complete resolution of the matter. Each side of the argument represents a legitimate viewpoint. Clinicians will not use artificial techniques developed in a laboratory that are not relevant to how they actually practice; on the other hand, they should not use techniques that cannot be supported by scientific study. To resolve the controversy about which method is superior, it has been suggested that studies be conducted that improve on existing methods: either "tighten up" effectiveness studies or alter efficacy studies to be more applicable and relevant to the practitioner; although logical, such methodologies do not currently exist (Nathan et al., 2000). It has also been suggested that the focus of study be changed to analyze processes related to patient change and therapist activities that influence these changes, rather than the more macroscopic study of different theoretical models of therapy (Beutler, 2000; Goldfried & Wolfe, 1996). Such an approach would have the advantage of cutting across established theoretical modes, and it would be of value to any clinician (Beutler, 2000). Others suggest that efficacy studies be the first step in a sequential validation process that would then be followed up with effectiveness studies in the field for those treatment procedures found to be efficacious in controlled settings (Kazdin, 2001; Kendall & Hudson, 2001). Given that a substantial body of evidence exists from efficacy studies, this seems a reasonable approach.

It may be stated, then, that the establishment of efficacy of a treatment intervention is only one step in the process of determining its true usefulness as a treatment method. Hughes (1993a) noted that other factors are important to consider in determining the value of a treatment intervention, including (a) acceptability, (b) availability, (c) cost-effectiveness, (d) indications for treatment, and (e) stability of treatment. *Acceptability* refers to a patient's willingness to undergo a specific treatment. It is a particular concern with aversive treatments but by no means exclusive to these methods. Any type of treatment requires some effort, discomfort, and cost; just the fact that the great majority of smokers prefer no treatment to any formal treatment suggests that patient acceptance is an issue (Klesges et al., 1996). In addition to patient acceptance, there is the issue of therapist acceptance. Not all therapists are comfortable rendering all types of treatment interventions; one may prefer not to use aversive techniques, another medication, and so on, for example.

Availability of treatment refers to personal resources (e.g., financial, transportation) as well as more general ones such as geography (e.g., rural areas are notoriously underserved for mental health problems). If access to treatment is blocked by a lack of availability, it is useless to some, so its efficacy means very little in such cases.

Cost-effectiveness of treatment is another major consideration in addition to efficacy. A smoker may be willing to seek treatment and it may be available, but if treatment is not cost-effective it may still be difficult to convince a patient of its worth to him or her. Fortunately, the cost-effectiveness of smoking-cessation treatment is easily demonstrated. First, cigarettes are costly enough that savings from cessation are immediately demonstrable. Second, savings in prevention of health care costs and quality of life are also obvious, so any short-term costs for treatment are amply compensated for in terms of intermediate- to long-term savings. It has been calculated that American smokers spend nearly as much on health care costs as they do on smoking, so for every dollar spent on cigarettes, they will incur that much more in medical costs resulting from the smoking (Klesges et al., 1996). In comparison to other commonly used health care procedures, smoking-cessation interventions (even the most intensive and costly) stack up favorably to other procedures: Treatment for hypertension is approximately 3 times more costly, and treatment for elevated cholesterol up to 10 times more expensive.

Indications for treatment interventions refer to circumstances or patient characteristics that, when present, suggest that a given treatment can be used. For example, indications for nicotine replacement therapy (NRT) are nicotine dependence and a desire to stop smoking. Hughes (1993a) noted that there are two general schemes to determine indications for treatment: stepped care and client–treatment matching. The stepped-care approach assumes that less costly, less intensive, simpler, and less risky procedures should be tried before more costly, intensive, complex, and more dangerous ones. The client–treatment matching approach attempts to match certain client characteristics to specific treatment interventions most likely to work. The use of the Fagerstrom Tolerance Questionnaire (FTQ; Fagerstrom, 1978) to identify level of nicotine dependence is a good example of a matching strategy; patients who are more dependent receive higher levels of nicotine when undergoing NRT.

Stability of treatment is a concept that relates to how long the effects of treatment can be expected to last. Naturally, all things being equal, one would prefer a treatment to have long-lasting effects. If treatment effects fade quickly, even the most efficacious treatment intervention will not be very attractive: Why bother with the effort and expense if the treatment effects are short-lived? For example, if NRT were found to be efficacious in promoting abstinence from smoking, but a 95% relapse rate could be expected within 3 days of completion of treatment, it would be much less attractive than if relapses were not expected for at least 1 year.

Recommendations from efficacy studies are not typically derived from individual investigations but are based on conclusions drawn from meta-analytic studies. Meta-analysis is a statistical method to measure the strength of a treatment method across a related set of studies. For a meta-analytic study to be performed, some selection process is necessary to determine minimum standards necessary to group studies together for analysis. Inclusionary criteria used for meta-analysis of smoking-cessation investigations (Lando, 1993; USDHHS, 2000b) are discussed in Exhibit 7.2.

The results of meta-analytic investigations are conventionally reported in the form of estimated odds ratios. The odds ratio represents the odds of an outcome of one variable (e.g., abstinence from a specified treatment intervention) given the status of another variable, usually the reference or control group (e.g., abstinence from no intervention) (USDHHS, 2000b). An example taken from the Clinical Practice Guideline (USDHHS, 2000b) will help clarify estimated odds ratios. A meta-analysis of various types of counseling and behavioral therapies yielded estimated odds ratios listed for the treatment groups, with corresponding 95% confidence intervals (CIs) in parentheses. The confidence interval associated with the estimated odds ratio provides a means to determine statistical significance of an intervention. If the lower limit of the confidence interval is greater than 1.0, then there is significance at the 0.05 level. The following confidence interval levels are excerpted from the Clinical Practice Guideline (USDHHS, 2000b):

1. No counseling or behavioral therapy: 1.0;
2. Relaxation/breathing: 1.0 (0.7–1.3);
3. General problem-solving: 1.5 (1.3–1.8);
4. Rapid smoking: 2.0 (1.1–3.5);

On the basis of the above figures, it can be stated that the odds of achieving abstinence by rapid smoking are two times the odds of achieving abstinence with no counseling or behavioral therapy. Furthermore, in the results presented above, relaxation and breathing yielded no better odds of achieving abstinence than no intervention, and odds of achieving abstinence through general problem-solving were one and one-half times more likely than with no intervention. Thus, the estimated odds ratio statistics provide a measure of treatment efficacy. In this example, relaxation is not efficacious, and general problem-solving and rapid smoking are; both general problem-solving and rapid smoking interventions are significantly better for achieving abstinence from smoking than no intervention. It may be further stated that rapid smoking demonstrated greater efficacy than general problem-solving in this statistical investigation.

COUNSELING INTERVENTIONS

The data presented in Table 7.1, based on extensive meta-analytic investigations of the smoking-cessation literature, are taken from two sources: the Clinical Practice Guideline (USDHHS, 2000b) and the Cochrane Library. The Cochrane Library publishes evidence-based medical databases

EXHIBIT 7.2
Criteria Considered for Inclusion of Smoking-Cessation Studies
in Meta-Analytic Investigations

1. *Publication status.* Analyses are usually confined to studies found in peer-reviewed professional publications.
2. *Assignment of subjects to groups.* Subjects, and sometimes therapists, are randomly assigned to groups.
3. *Existence of a control group.* Because we know that subjects can show improvement due to nonspecific factors, such as the provision of attention and support, suggestion, provision of structure and timing for a quit attempt, and so forth, to demonstrate its efficacy a treatment intervention must demonstrate that it contains a specific, active ingredient superior to the nonspecific factors that apply to the control group (Hajek, 1996).
4. *Definition of abstinence.* Two measures of abstinence are used in smoking cessation investigations: point prevalence and continuous abstinence. The more stringent measure is continuous abstinence: that is, subjects being abstinent continuously from the quit date to the follow-up date. With continuous abstinence there is disagreement over what lapses or slips are allowed (if any) before classifying a person as relapsed. Continuous abstinence may underestimate the actual number of abstinent subjects because it is possible that over the course of 6 to 12 months subjects may relapse then resume abstinence. With point prevalence, a unit of time is used as a reference point (usually 7 days, but it can be 24 hours, a month, etc.). With a 7-day point prevalence, for example, the person is classified abstinent if they have not smoked within the last 7 days of the follow-up measurement. The majority of efficacy studies use the point-prevalence definition of abstinence.
5. *Length of follow-up.* Because of the nature of nicotine dependence, and of the desire to obtain clinically meaningful information, a minimum follow-up of 6 months to 1 year is usually required. It is known that the further one measures from the quit date, the greater the number of relapses that will occur, and that most relapses occur shortly after treatment ceases, so 6 to 12 months is a sensible period of time to capture people who have survived the early pitfalls of abstinence from nicotine and reflect the influence of treatment. Measuring further out in time than 1 year would not be a fair evaluation of treatment effects, as many other influences may come to bear in the intervening time frame. Practical considerations sometimes influence the time frame used for study; for example, the Clinical Practice Guideline (USDHHS, 2000b) used a 5-month criterion (i.e., 5 months after the quit date) so that more studies could be included in its meta-analytic investigations. Lando (1993) pointed out that programs sometimes boast of very high abstinence rates, up to 60%; however, closer inspection shows that such numbers are obtained at the end of active treatment and will drop dramatically to 10% to 20% abstinence by 1-year follow-up.
6. *Validation of self-report of abstinence.* Abstinence at follow-up is usually measured by self-report. This may be considered adequate in clinical settings (USDHHS, 2000b). Although self-report does correlate with biochemical verification, outcomes research routinely demands the use of verification.
7. *Handling of dropouts and subjects lost to follow-up.* Results may vary significantly depending on how these subjects are handled statistically. The most conservative approach is to classify those who are treatment dropouts, or who completed treatment but are lost to follow-up contact, as relapsers (this is referred to as the "intent to treat" model). Very different, and misleading, results can be presented depending on the classification of these subjects. Lando (1993) gave an example of how a program may present inflated results

continues

EXHIBIT 7.2 *(Continued)*

depending on the classification of subjects who are dropouts or lost to follow-up. Say that 100 subjects are included in a smoking-cessation study: 50 complete the program, 30 of those completing the program respond to follow-up, and 20 of the 30 responders are abstinent at follow-up. Depending on how the numbers are presented, the reported abstinence rate could vary widely, from 20% to 67%. The more conservative rate of 20% is consistent with the recommended manner of reporting results, because those who did not complete treatment or provide follow-up data are assumed to have relapsed.

and conducts systematic reviews of these databases. Information on specific interventions discussed in chapter 6 for treatment of nicotine dependence is given in the table. For some interventions discussed in chapter 6, no meta-analytic data were available, reflecting the fact that an insufficient number of studies meeting the inclusionary criteria were available to conduct an analysis; this usually indicated low interest (as was the case for electric

TABLE 7.1
Efficacy Results of Counseling Interventions for Smoking Cessation

Intervention	Clinical Practice Guideline (USDHHS)	Cochrane Library
Aversive behavioral techniques		
Rapid smoking	2.0 (1.1–3.5)*	1.98 (1.36–2.90)*
Other aversive methods (rapid puffing, satiation, focused smoking, smoke holding, and covert sensitization)	1.7 (1.0–2.8)*	1.15 (0.73–1.82)
Silver acetate	–	1.05 (0.63–1.73)
Nonaversive behavioral techniques		
Contingency contracting	1.0 (0.7–1.3)	–
Nicotine fading	1.1 (0.8–1.5)	–
Coping skills (problem-solving, skills training, relapse prevention)	1.5 (1.3–1.8)*	–
Social support		
Individual counseling	1.7 (1.4–2.0)*	1.62 (1.35–1.94)*
Group counseling	1.3 (1.1–1.6)*	2.19 (1.42–3.37)*
Extra-treatment social support	1.5 (1.1–2.1)*	–
Referrals		
Brief physician advice	1.3 (1.0–1.6)*	1.69 (1.45–1.98)*
Acupuncture	1.1 (0.7–1.6)	1.50 (0.99–2.27)
Self-help	1.1 (0.9–1.3)	1.24 (1.07–1.45)*

Note. All data are estimated odds ratios (95% CI), compared to no-treatment control groups with odds ratios of 1.0. Dashes indicate that no data were available. CI = confidence interval. USDHHS = U.S. Department of Health and Human Services. Data in columns 1 and 2, respectively, are from *Treating Tobacco Use and Dependence: Clinical Practice Guideline*, U.S. Department of Health and Human Services, 2000, Rockville, MD, and *The Cochrane Library*, 2002 (Issues 1 and 4) and 2003 (Issues 1 and 2), Chichester, England: Wiley.
*$p < .05$.

shock, for example) or the fact that there was interest but too few acceptably designed studies (as in the case of hypnosis, for example). Thus, no specific data are provided for the interventions of electric shock, stimulus control, cue exposure, cognitive procedures (pledging, norm-referencing, and values clarification), commercial programs, Nicotine Anonymous, and hypnosis. For some interventions, only one of the two sources provided data, in which case only a single entry is provided. This was the case for silver acetate, contingency contracting, nicotine fading, coping skills, and extra-treatment social support. It will be noted that the odds ratio figures resulting from the different investigations are not identical (although they are very similar in most cases). The meta-analytic investigations used slightly different inclusionary criteria and were conducted at different dates, so they were not working with exactly the same data. All estimated odds ratio numbers in Table 7.1 are presented with reference to a no-treatment control group with an odds ratio value of 1.0, and with 95% confidence intervals indicated in parentheses.

As can be seen from the efficacy findings in Table 7.1, where quantitative data are available from both sources, there is general agreement; there are only two instances of one source finding a statistically significant odds ratio and the other not finding one. In both cases ("other aversive methods" and "self-help"), the finding of statistical significance was by a very small margin, so the discrepancy between the two sources was not of a large magnitude. A list of efficacious interventions (those with statistically significant odds ratios from both sources or from a single source, if that was all that was available) can be generated from the findings presented above: (a) rapid smoking; (b) coping skills; (c) social support (including both intra- and extra-treatment support; intra-treatment support includes individual and group counseling); and (d) brief physician advice. The list of interventions can be very helpful in guiding treatment decisions. However, the efficacy results do not tell the entire story. The limitations of efficacy studies for making treatment decisions may be illustrated by considering two interventions, stimulus control and rapid smoking. No data were reported on stimulus control, probably because it would not ever be considered as a stand-alone treatment, thereby drawing little or no attention from researchers. Yet, I consider stimulus control interventions an integral part of smoking-cessation treatment, and of recovery from other types of substance abuse, for that matter. On the other hand, rapid smoking produced strong efficacy results, yet there is very low acceptance of it by smokers attempting to quit, and by clinicians. Contingency contracting is another intervention that was not found to be efficacious, but as with stimulus control, I would use it without hesitation; providing extra incentives in treatment can only be positive. I recommend contingency contracting, either by providing the incentive directly (e.g., by payback of money paid up front at the start of treatment) or indirectly (having abstinent smokers treat themselves with a desired reward). I feel similarly about the cognitive procedures of pledging, values clarification, and norm-setting; these interventions take only minutes to apply but can significantly improve motivation and personal commitment to cessation.

Although it may be tempting to rank-order the interventions by magnitude of odds ratio results, it would not be proper. Although the odds ratio estimates give some measure of the relative efficacy of the different interventions, I do not recommend just rank-ordering the results and choosing the ostensibly more efficacious interventions, because of the manner in which the meta-analytic studies are conducted (noting statistical limitations and the fact that results derive from insufficient numbers of head-to-head comparisons) and in deference to the many factors beyond efficacy that must be considered when making treatment decisions. Rather, it is suggested that the clinician consider all the interventions with demonstrated efficacy as a pool of alternatives from which to choose for a given patient (USDHHS, 2000b).

Efficacy studies are necessarily conducted with individual interventions to evaluate the potential benefits and safety of specific treatment methods, but in actual practice most smoking-cessation programs combine interventions into multicomponent packages. Treatment programs can differ with respect to the particular elements that are used, but common methods used in multicomponent counseling programs include (Klesges et al., 1996; Lando, 1993) (a) setting of a quit date, (b) interruption of conditioned responses supporting cigarette use, (c) identification of high-risk situations and strategies for coping with these situations, (d) relapse prevention, (e) follow-up contact, and (f) social support. Multicomponent programs have been found to yield significantly higher abstinence rates than individual counseling interventions. A good multicomponent program can result in 6-month abstinence rates of approximately 50% and 1-year abstinence rates of about 40% (Lando, 1993). By comparison, estimated 5- to 6-month abstinence rates for specific interventions identified as efficacious are approximately (a) 20% for rapid smoking, (b) 16% for both problem-solving and extra-treatment social support, (c) 14% for intra-treatment social support, and (d) 10% for brief physician advice (USDHHS, 2000b). It is to be noted that aversive treatments are efficacious but unpopular. However, it is also important to note that multicomponent programs with too many elements are too complex and confusing and are ultimately rejected (Lando, 1993). Therefore, it is not advisable to simply pile on interventions with the intention of increasing abstinence rates with each new element.

TREATMENT PARAMETERS

In addition to the choice of interventions, meta-analytic investigations have been used to help make the following important treatment decisions:

1. *Treatment intensity*. Increasing the intensity of contact between patient and clinician was found to increase abstinence rates in a dose-dependent manner. That is, as contact was increased, so were abstinence rates (USDHHS, 2000b). Increasing intensity was accomplished by increasing session length or number of sessions. For example, the estimated odds ratio (relative to no-contact control) for less than 3 minutes of contact was 1.3 (1.01–1.06), but it was 2.3 (2.0–2.7) for session length greater than 10 minutes. Regarding the number of sessions and abstinence rates, the estimated odds ratio was 1.4 (1.1–1.7) for two or three sessions and 2.3 (2.1–3.0) for more than eight sessions. Looked at in terms of total contact time between clinician and patient, 1 to 3 minutes yielded an estimated odds ratio of 1.4 (1.1–1.8), and 91 to 300 minutes of contact resulted in an estimated odds ratio of 3.2 (2.3–4.6). Not only is the amount of contact a factor to consider, but so is when the contact is provided. Provision of contact around the quit date is critically important. Early behavior has been found to predict later abstinence, so it is absolutely necessary to provide clear instruction about the need for abstinence and to provide support in the early phase of treatment. Relapse within 2 weeks of the quit date is associated with greatly increased chances of smoking at 6-month follow-up (Kenford et al., 1994; Westman, Behm, Simel, & Rose, 1997).

2. *Type of clinician*. Treatment for smoking cessation can be effectively delivered by multiple clinician types (e.g., physician, dentist, nurse, psychologist, social worker), and treatment delivered by multiple types of clinicians to the same patient may be more effective than treatment by one type of clinician; this finding supports the value of therapist–physician collaboration (USDHHS, 2000b). The estimated odds ratio for one clinician type (relative to no-clinician control) was 1.8 (1.5–2.2); in contrast, two clinician types on one case resulted in an estimated odds ratio of 2.5 (1.9–3.4).

3. *Format of treatment*. Relative to no-format control groups, smoking-cessation interventions using two or more formats (i.e., individual and group counseling, self-help, telephone counseling) were more effective than interventions using only one format (USDHHS, 2000b). The estimated odds ratio for one format was 1.5 (1.2–1.8); for three or four formats it was 2.5 (2.1–3.0):

4. *Application to groups of smokers*. It has also been determined that counseling interventions (and pharmacological interventions, discussed below) are efficacious across diverse racial

and ethnic minorities and can thus be applied to all smokers (USDHHS, 2000b).

To summarize the meta-analytic results discussed directly above, an efficacious smoking-cessation counseling program endeavoring to produce the best odds of achieving abstinence should consist of at least eight sessions, with each session of at least 10 minutes duration. In addition, there should be at least two different types of clinicians involved, and treatment information should be delivered in multiple formats. There are many different ways that treatment can be organized and still satisfy these recommendations. The ideal structure of treatment is yet to be determined. We know that there is a dose–response relationship between treatment and efficacy, so more treatment is usually better. However, some patients, even those willing to undergo intensive treatment, cannot or will not make an indefinite commitment to treatment. Clinicians must determine session length and format (individual or group sessions). Smoking-cessation treatment may be conceived of as consisting of three phases: preparation, quit date, and maintenance. In providing a limited number of sessions (e.g., the minimum recommendation of eight), the clinician has to decide how to schedule the meetings (Abrams et al., 2003): Should treatment be front-loaded to develop skills in preparation for the quit date, or should more sessions be committed to management of early withdrawal and maintenance of abstinence after the quit date? No definite answer to this question has been found.

As a matter of personal preference, I usually conduct 45-minute, individual therapy sessions for smoking cessation. For someone requiring intensive treatment, I typically negotiate the length of treatment with the patient, advising at least eight sessions beyond two initial assessment sessions. I recommend apportioning the sessions depending partially on the history of the individual. For someone who appears to require more skill building and preparation (e.g., has tried only self-help or other minimal-assistance treatment and has never practiced stimulus control or developed a relapse prevention program), I would recommend that more sessions (four or five) be dedicated to preparation before the quit date. For individuals who appear to possess the requisite skills, more time is recommended for support after the quit date. Preference of the individuals seeking services is also taken into account. If they feel they need more time for preparation, or for support beyond the quit date, I am inclined to weigh this heavily in the scheduling of the treatment. In all aspects of the treatment, an attempt is made to help the patient remain actively involved in the process. The number of sessions, the quit date, and the scheduling of sessions are all discussed and negotiated. Incidentally, the setting of the quit date is important as a basic point of structure to begin to develop the rest of the treatment plan. Setting a definite quit date establishes the proper mindset for the process of quitting: It is not something to be done impulsively but rather a goal to be worked toward in very deliberate fashion.

Identifying a date to quit smoking also provides a certain concrete reality to the process, which is necessary to provide an alternative to the often vague general intention to stop smoking at some future point in time (which never comes). It is sometimes recommended to select quit dates that correspond with special days (e.g., birthdays, holidays, Saturdays).

PHARMACOLOGICAL INTERVENTIONS

Results of meta-analytic investigations of pharmacological treatments for smoking cessation are provided in Table 7.2. No results are provided for anxiolytic medications because there are too few studies to properly evaluate their efficacy (Hughes et al., 2003b).

As with the meta-analytic results for counseling interventions, it is tempting but improper to take the estimated odds ratio numbers for pharmacological interventions and rank-order them, due to the manner in which the investigations are conducted; all of the efficacious medications should be considered, among other factors, when developing an individual treatment plan. Although pharmacological treatment can be enhanced by combining it with counseling interventions, medications are efficacious without counseling and are helpful across a broad range of smokers, not just the most severely dependent (USDHHS, 2000b). Reported 5- to 6- month abstinence rates for pharmacological interventions are approximately (a) 31% for nicotine nasal

TABLE 7.2
Efficacy Results of Pharmacological Interventions for Smoking Cessation

Intervention	Clinical Practice Guideline (USDHHS)	Cochrane Library
Nicotine replacement therapy (NRT)		
Gum	1.5 (1.3–1.8)	1.66 (1.53–1.81)
Transdermal patch	1.9 (1.7–2.2)	1.74 (1.57–1.93)
Inhaler	2.5 (1.7–3.6)	2.08 (1.43–3.04)
Nasal spray	2.7 (1.8–4.1)	2.27 (1.61–3.20)
Lozenge	–	2.08 (1.63–2.65)
Combination of two NRTs	1.9 (1.3–2.6)[a]	–
Nonnicotine pharmacological treatments		
Bupropion SR	2.1 (1.5–3.0)	2.54 (1.90–3.41)
Nortriptyline	3.2 (1.8–5.7)	2.77 (1.73–4.44)
Clonidine	2.1 (1.4–3.2)	–

Note. Unless otherwise indicated, all data are estimated odds ratios (95% CI), compared to no treatment control groups with odds ratios of 1.0. Dashes indicate that no data were available. CI = confidence interval. USDHHS = U.S. Department of Health and Human Services. Data in columns 1 and 2, respectively, are from *Treating Tobacco Use and Dependence: Clinical Practice Guideline*, U.S. Department of Health and Human Services, 2000, Rockville, MD, and *The Cochrane Library*, 2003 (Issue 1), Chichester, England: Wiley. All results are significant at $p < .05$.
[a]Compared with control group using one form of NRT.

spray, (b) 24% for nicotine gum, (c) 23% for the nicotine inhaler, (d) 18% for the nicotine patch, (e) 31% for bupropion SR, (f) 30% for nortriptyline, and (g) 26% for clonidine. Concern about extending nicotine dependence is noted with NRT. For example, as many as 20% to 30% of those successful with nicotine gum have used it for 12 months or longer; this use of NRT, however, is still considered preferable to continued smoking.

Factors that may be helpful in deciding among the different pharmacological interventions include (USDHHS, 2000b)

1. *Safety record and side-effect profiles.* The U.S. Food and Drug Administration has identified as first-line medications for smoking cessation all forms of NRT and bupropion SR; designated as second-line medications are clonidine, nortriptyline, and combination NRT. Second-line medications carry greater concerns about safety than first-line medications and should be considered only after first-line interventions have been considered or used.

2. *Concern about weight gain.* Bupropion SR and NRT (especially gum) delay weight gain until the medication is discontinued.

3. *Degree of nicotine dependence.* The greater the nicotine dependence, the better the chance of successful treatment with 4-mg gum as compared with 2-mg gum. It is interesting to note that with combination NRT, there is higher dosing of nicotine than with only one form of NRT; however, the effect seems to derive not just from increased nicotine levels but from the use of two distinct delivery systems.

4. *History of depression.* Those smokers attempting to quit who have a history of depression may be especially responsive to treatment with the antidepressant, smoking-cessation medications bupropion SR and nortriptyline.

5. *Gender.* Although NRT is efficacious with women, it seems less so than for men.

There is empirical support for the fact that combining both pharmacological and counseling interventions enhances treatment outcomes above what is achieved by either approach alone (Hajek, 1996; Klesges et al., 1996; Stitzer & Walsh, 1997). Obviously, medication and counseling work by different mechanisms: Medications alter neurochemical systems and counseling works on thoughts, feelings, and behavior. There are several proposed reasons for why combining pharmacological and counseling treatment methods results in enhanced outcomes (Hughes, 1995; Klesges et al., 1996):

1. Counseling and medication address different components of smoking behavior.

2. Medication helps establish abstinence; counseling provides skills for coping and maintenance of abstinence.
3. Counseling and medication may be assisting two different sub-populations of smokers.
4. Each type of treatment may serve to improve adherence to the other (e.g., counseling reinforces the importance of medication compliance and behavior change; medication can reduce discomfort of withdrawal and allow for a focus on coping and behavior change).

The optimal length of pharmacological treatment has yet to be established. Efficacy studies are designed to validate methods of smoking-cessation treatment and evaluate their safety, not to determine the best possible use of treatment for maintenance of results. Therefore, other studies need to be conducted to determine the ideal duration of treatment for long-term abstinence (Sims & Fiore, 2002). To evaluate this treatment parameter, several factors come to bear: (a) the time course of withdrawal symptoms, (b) abuse liability of the medication, (c) possible added benefit of longer treatment, and (d) the safety of prolonged use of the medication. The time course and pattern of withdrawal symptoms may vary across individuals; usually symptoms gradually diminish with time, but for some abstinent smokers symptoms remain constant, last longer than the average, or worsen over time. For individuals with atypical withdrawal patterns, treatment may need to be lengthened. Abuse liability for all forms of pharmacotherapy typically used for smoking cessation is found to be low. There is some evidence, currently insufficient to be conclusive, that suggests added benefit for extended pharmacotherapy. For example, bupropion SR showed significantly improved abstinence rates over placebo when active treatment was given for 1 year (Hurt et al., 2002). Finally, too few data are available to draw firm conclusions about the safety of prolonged pharmacological treatment.

HARM REDUCTION AS A TREATMENT GOAL

Harm reduction refers to the practice of promoting reduced use of a substance to minimize the related risks. It is thought that decreased use, as opposed to complete abstinence, may be easier to achieve and may attract smokers to treatment who might otherwise not seek any assistance. In the broader domain of substance abuse treatment, harm reduction has been a controversial topic. The strongly addictive nature of nicotine rightfully inclines clinicians to promote abstinence as a treatment goal. In addition, because morbidity and mortality from smoking accrue in a dose–response manner, it makes sense that to stop smoking is the best policy. However, there remain smokers who are either unwilling or unable to stop completely.

A convincing rationale for harm reduction can be made (Etter, Laszlo, Zellweger, Perrot, & Perneger, 2002): Quitting is easier for lighter smokers, so cutting down may provide an advantage for a later quit attempt. Also, health risks are reduced with a reduction in smoking. Finally, self-efficacy and motivation for a quit attempt are sometimes elevated with success in reduction of smoking. The primary concerns about harm reduction versus total abstinence as a treatment goal are that smokers will not be able to maintain the reduction (due to the irresistible force of nicotine addiction) and that continued smoking will eliminate motivation for future cessation attempts (Etter et al., 2002; Hughes, Cummings, & Hyland, 1999). More data are needed to answer these questions, but studies do find that smokers can reduce the number of cigarettes smoked, realize improvements in respiratory functioning (Jimenez-Ruiz et al., 2002), and maintain the reduction for as long as 2 years (Hughes et al., 1999) without influencing cessation attempts in any way. For whom harm reduction goals would be appropriate remains an open question; for the time being, total abstinence is the goal promoted by most programs.

WEIGHT CONTROL

Concern about weight gain has been identified as a significant obstacle to the maintenance of abstinence from smoking (Mizes et al., 1998; USDHHS, 2000b). Many people believe that smoking is a way to control weight and that cessation will result in weight gain. To a degree, they are correct; the typical postcessation weight gain is 7 to 10 lbs. It appears that women in general may be more concerned about postcessation weight gain than men. Identification of this concern as a possible barrier to cessation efforts is advised. Certain medication options and behavioral strategies (e.g., an exercise plan) as well as education about the weight gain (i.e., causes, how much can be expected, low risk posed by weight gain) are recommended.

MOTIVATING SMOKERS TO QUIT

There can be no doubt that although nicotine dependence is a pernicious addiction that gets a strong hold on its victims, there are effective treatments available. Unfortunately, however, at any point in time many smokers are not thinking about stopping in the foreseeable future, and the large majority of those who are prefer self-help or minimal assistance if any at all (Fiore et al., 1990; Lando, 1993). Approximately 90% of cessation attempts are unassisted and are associated with poor success rates; smokers usually make many cessation attempts (approximately six) before they are successful at maintaining long-term abstinence. Only a small portion of the total population of quitters uses cessation programs; those seeking formal treatment services tend to be more heavily nicotine dependent, poor, less educated; to have psychiatric problems; and to suffer from smoking-related medical problems (Brandon, 2001; Fiore et al., 1990). Half the battle would be won if smokers identified nicotine dependence as a problem and sought treatment. The point at which clinicians discuss treatment options with a smoker is a relatively advanced stage in the quitting process. More often, we are dealing with smokers earlier in the cessation process who are marginally motivated to stop smoking, at best. The question, then, is what is to be done with the smoker who is not yet ready to discuss treatment options? Traditionally, in the treatment of substance abuse, an all-or-nothing conception of readiness for treatment has been applied. Simply put, smokers who were open to discussion about treatment alternatives and compliant with treatment recommendations were ready; if they resisted, they were not ready. Those considered not ready were aggressively challenged in an attempt to break their denial, and if this failed, they could be discharged from treatment, if they hadn't already dropped out. The idea then was to hope that when the negative consequences of continued substance abuse ensued, abusers would "hit bottom," reassess their abuse, and reconsider treatment. Clinicians in this conceptualization were in the position of passively waiting for life's circumstances and the natural consequences of addiction to alter the motivation of the substance abuser. The passive approach is undesirable from the perspectives of both patient and therapist: Patients leave treatment as failures and must endure negative consequences they might otherwise have been spared if they could have remained in treatment. For therapists, the passive approach fosters helplessness and a corresponding feeling of failure.

The Stages of Change (Transtheoretical) Model provides a conceptual framework to understanding the changing of unhealthy behavior as a dynamic process, open to influence. Of greater importance than merely describing points along the continuum of behavior change, interventions are suggested that can influence movement along the continuum. (The reader is referred to chapter 5 for a description of the five stages of change defined by Prochaska and DiClemente [1983].) The stages of change essentially describe intentions to change behavior. Summarizing the stages as applied to smoking cessation, *precontemplators* are smokers who do not intend to quit in the next 6 months; *contemplators* intend to quit in the next 6 months, but not in the next month; *preparers* intend to quit in the next month and have made at least one quit attempt in the last year; those in the *action stage* have currently not smoked for less than 6 months; those in the *maintenance stage* have not smoked for more than 6 months.

Having defined the stages, it becomes possible to assess prevalence of smokers by stage. Studies vary in their findings of the distribution of smokers by stage, depending on factors such as country and setting (e.g., clinical vs. nonclinical population). Some representative findings comparing smokers who are not yet abstinent are as follows (Etter, Perneger, & Ronchi, 1997): In the United States, mean percentages across four studies found 43% of smokers were precontemplators, 39% contemplators, and 18% preparers. Corresponding percentages in Switzerland (mean percentages across two studies) were 73% precontemplators, 21% contemplators, and 6% preparers. Results from other studies in European countries are closer to those of Switzerland than of the United States, possibly reflecting the greater anti-smoking sentiment in the United States. Although the assessment results are more favorable in the United States—a higher percentage of current smokers are further along in the change process relative to their European counterparts—there are still a significant portion in the precontemplation stage, and a large majority occupying the first two stages. The relevance of identifying stage of change of a smoker is fourfold:

1. It reminds us of the unfortunate fact that most treatment programs are set up to treat smokers at the preparation or action stages, although most are not yet there.
2. It gives an indication of an individual's receptivity to influence to change.
3. The stage that a person occupies turns out to have implications for likelihood of stopping smoking.
4. It becomes possible to track movement between stages and factors responsible for this movement.

Particularly relevant to treatment is receptivity to influence to change. There is evidence that stage-matched interventions may be more effective than generic interventions. For example, precontemplators perceive significantly fewer advantages to quitting, more pros to continued smoking, have lower self-efficacy expectations about stopping, and experience less social support for stopping than do smokers at later stages (Dijkstra, Bakker, & DeVries, 1997; DeVries, Mudde, Dijkstra, & Willemsen, 1998). Therefore, precontemplators will benefit more from interventions designed to increase their knowledge of the benefits of quitting, raise awareness of the consequences of continuing to smoke, teach them how to garner social support, and enhance their self-efficacy than from discussion about methods of treatment.

With respect to the relation of stage to likelihood of quitting, it has been found that a higher stage of change at baseline is associated with greater chances of participating in a treatment program, making a serious quit attempt, and successful quitting (Dijkstra et al., 1997; Dijkstra, Roijackers, & DeVries, 1998; Hennrikus, Jeffery, & Lando, 1995). For example, Dijkstra et al. (1997) found that 6 months after a stop-smoking intervention, 20% of precontemplators had made a quit attempt; this compares to 38% of smokers in the contemplation stage and 67% in the preparation stage at the time of intervention. The implications of these findings are significant in terms of intervention goals: Instead of attempting to move every smoker immediately into action, interventions might instead be used to more realistically stimulate movement to the next stage. There is evidence that matching interventions to stage can facilitate stage movement and, ultimately, quitting behavior (Perz, DiClemente, & Carbonari, 1996). Carpenter, Watson, Raffety, and Chabal (2003) reported an encouraging statistic: Smokers who can progress one stage toward readiness to quit smoking in a 6-month period can double their chances of making a quit attempt by Month 6.

The setting in which services are provided is an important factor regarding readiness for change behavior. In addition, the setting partly defines the role of the treatment provider. For example, a clinician working in a smoking-cessation clinic or program, or who offers such services as a specialized part of a more general practice, should expect to see a higher percentage of smokers further along the stages of change than someone in a different setting. Naturally, those identifying themselves as smokers who want to quit and explicitly seeking services for this are by definition at the preparation stage. The clinician's role is quite clear in this instance. Those who provide services in medical settings and programs, such as those in oncology, cardiac care, and diabetes care, for example, might also expect to deal with smokers who are more highly motivated to quit than average because of the immediate health- or life-threatening consequences of continued smoking. Again, the role of the clinician is clear.

Things get a little trickier in more traditional mental health settings when smokers do not identify themselves as smokers interested in treatment, or even in discussing the matter at all. More precontemplators will be encountered in this setting than in the settings described above. The role of the therapist in this setting is also less clear. Psychologists as a group are generally more loath than are medical professionals to introduce problems into the treatment that are not at least acknowledged first by the patient. However, it is not the case that therapists will never discuss problems not first introduced by the patient. Even with psychoanalytic treatments, in which therapists tend to be especially reluctant to bring material to the treatment, it is thought proper to initiate discussion of treatment-destructive behavior even if the patient never directly discusses it on his or her own. *Treatment-destructive behavior* refers to behavior that threatens to harm the patient or the treatment, including self-destructive behavior like uncontrolled substance abuse and suicidal behavior. Although it may seem a stretch to challenge patients' smoking on the grounds it will someday disable or kill them, their smoking can be relevant to other issues discussed that currently concern them. For example, patients presenting with anxiety or depressive symptoms, two of the most common presenting symptoms, might be surprised and interested to know of the anxiety- and depression-enhancing effects of smoking (see chap. 1 for more discussion of this topic); this provides an avenue for making cigarette smoking relevant to treatment even though it may not have been previously thought of this way by the patient. The same holds true for substance abuse, a problem of very high prevalence; patients may benefit from learning of the role of cigarettes in maintaining addiction to other substances. For this reason, as part of a comprehensive diagnostic assessment, it is advisable to inquire about substance abuse, and tobacco use in particular. If patients are currently smoking, it is important to assess their current desire to stop. If they are interested in treatment, options should be discussed; if they are not currently interested in treatment, stage of change should be assessed (see chap. 5 for assessment of stage of change) and interventions guided appropriately.

Because the proportion of precontemplators is so large, especially in Europe, and because they present the biggest treatment challenge, investigators have attempted to further analyze and subclassify them. For example, Dijkstra et al. (1998) identified an additional group of precontemplators, referred to as *immotives*, who are the least motivated to change smoking behavior: They are smokers not planning to quit for at least 5 years, if ever. Reading the literature on stages of change gives the impression that a level of precision is being sought that distinguishes one group of smokers from another so that exact interventions can be made; this level of precision is unrealized at present, and possibly unrealistic altogether. At any rate, the Stages of Change Model does provide a system to assess intention and level of motivation to stop smoking and corresponding suggestions for how to intervene according to a smoker's current stage of change. Smokers actively seeking treatment for cessation are at the preparation stage and can be guided to conventional cessation treatment. Smokers at earlier stages should be approached with the intermediate goal of moving them toward a higher stage, not immediately into abstinence as a goal. Some suggestions are provided in Exhibit 7.3.

SUMMARY

Meta-analytic investigations of efficacy studies have been used to assess the validity of both counseling and pharmacological interventions. However, caution should be exercised in using the results of meta-analytic research. Efficacy studies provide potentially useful information to the clinician attempting to determine the best treatment practice for the nicotine-dependent patient, but other factors need to be considered, including acceptability, availability, cost-effectiveness, indications for treatment, and stability of treatment. Furthermore, clinician experience and skill in establishing a productive working relationship with the patient are vitally important; the greatest techniques in the world are of limited or no use in the wrong hands. Finally, some interventions that are not currently validated by means of efficacy studies may still be properly used by the skilled

- *Precontemplation.* Precontemplators are not spontaneously thinking about their smoking. The goal with these smokers is to stimulate them to do so. Inquiries such as the following may help initiate desired cognitive activity: "Have you ever thought of stopping?"; "Can you imagine any benefits to quitting smoking?"; "Can you think of any consequences of continued smoking?"
- *Contemplation.* These smokers are thinking about stopping, but the time frame is too distal. The goal is to focus on the time frame to make it more proximal. Some questions that may be used are, "When were you planning to quit?"; "Can you think of any advantages of stopping in the next month?"; "Is there any reason you should not quit in the next month?"
- *Preparation.* Preparers are ready to quit in the near term. They can benefit from the establishment of a concrete quit date, discussion of treatment options, and discussion of previous quit attempts (focusing on previous difficulties and anticipated obstacles).
- *Action.* Smokers in this stage are assisted by applying the techniques discussed earlier in this chapter, or by referring for such services if they are not rendered by the therapist.
- *Maintenance.* Smokers in this stage are helped by relapse-prevention interventions (discussed in chap. 8).

clinician. Because many smokers are marginally motivated to stop smoking, the greatest clinical skill is called for in maintaining their interest in treatment and moving them forward on the continuum of readiness for behavior change.

Counseling interventions identified as efficacious include rapid smoking, coping skills, social support, and brief physician advice. Although not supported by efficacy studies, stimulus control, contingency contracting, and certain cognitive procedures are highly recommended. Multicomponent treatment programs are recommended above single-component programs. Several treatment parameters have been shown to improve treatment efficacy. For example, more intense treatment is more efficacious than less intense treatment. A minimum of at least eight sessions, each lasting at least 10 min, is suggested. Treatment by at least two clinician types is recommended (supporting the clinician–physician collaboration). Use of multiple treatment formats is superior to only one format, so clinicians should deliver treatment by different methods.

Pharmacological interventions identified as efficacious include all five forms of NRT and non-nicotine pharmacological medications, including bupropion SR, nortriptyline, and clonidine. All forms of NRT and bupropion SR are identified by the U.S. Food and Drug Administration as first-line medications for treatment of nicotine dependence; clonidine, nortriptyline, and combination NRT are designated as second-line medications. Second-line medications carry greater safety concerns than first-line medications, and so should only be used after first-line medications have been used or considered.

Harm reduction as a treatment goal remains a controversial topic. Although a solid rationale exists for considering harm reduction instead of complete abstinence, total abstinence remains as the goal most often promoted in treatment programs.

8

CRAVING AND
RELAPSE PREVENTION

In this chapter cravings for cigarettes (also referred to as *urges*) are defined and their causes are discussed. Cravings are necessary to study owing to the fact that they play a significant role in maintaining smoking, and in relapse to smoking among the abstinent. Methods of assessing cravings are presented, as are counseling and pharmacological interventions to cope with them.

The achievement of abstinence from cigarettes means very little if it is not maintained for a substantial period of time. Relapse prevention training, also described in this chapter, is designed to equip abstinent individuals to combat influences that incline them to resume smoking. In understanding cravings and how to cope with them and being able to apply relapse prevention principles, clinicians can help their patients maintain abstinence from smoking.

CRAVING

Craving, once thought to be just one of the symptoms of nicotine withdrawal, now occupies its own niche in the literature on nicotine addiction. The terms *craving* and *urge* (to smoke) are synonymous for all practical purposes (and are used as such in this book), although fine distinctions in definition are sometimes found in the literature. *Craving* is defined as a subjectively experienced motivational state (i.e., desire) to use nicotine (Miyata & Yanagita, 2001; Sayette, Martin, Hull, Wertz, & Perrott, 2003; Tiffany & Drobes, 1991); with its neurobiological underpinnings and correlates, craving has been likened to other biologically motivated states like hunger for food (Shiffman et al., 1997). Craving is not unique to nicotine dependence and is common to all substances of abuse.

Why is craving of such interest in the study and treatment of nicotine dependence? Craving is found to be a central factor in the maintenance of ongoing cigarette smoking and is highly related to relapse to smoking behavior for abstinent individuals (Doherty, Kinnunen, Militello, & Garvey, 1995; Durcan et al., 2002; Shiffman et al., 2002). Abstinent smokers with strong cravings are more likely to relapse by 1 month postcessation than those abstinent smokers with lower levels of reported craving (Durcan et al., 2002). Doherty et al. (1995) assessed craving from quit date to Day 30 postcessation (conducting assessments on Days 1, 7, 14, and 30). They found that reported cravings were strongest on Day 1, consistently decreasing to Day 30. They also found a significant relationship between strength of craving at time of assessment and smoking status by the next assessment; that is, those abstinent smokers reporting higher levels of craving were more likely to relapse by the next assessment date. Similarly, Killen and Fortmann (1997) reported the results of three separate prospective studies that found a significant relationship between level of postcessation craving (measured immediately after cessation) and ability to maintain abstinence. Intensity of reported craving was strongly predictive of relapse within the first week of cessation. To address the question of whether an increase in craving necessarily precedes lapses, or if lapses occur more or less automatically and without conscious thought, Catley, O'Connell, and Shiffman (2000) required abstinent smokers to record their cravings at random times throughout the day for 14 days during a quit attempt (or fewer days if they returned to regular smoking). They found that the large majority (94%) of lapses were preceded by conscious, strong cravings. Very few lapses to smoking were attributed to "absent-minded," automatic processes. This finding is actually good news because it means that most of the time there is an opportunity to intervene and interrupt the process of moving from craving to smoking behavior. If there is a conscious struggle between craving and a desire to remain abstinent, the smoker has some chance to cope; if the process were conscious less often, it would be much more difficult to alter. Smokers can be educated to recognize the experience of cravings as a reliable signal to use coping strategies. It has been contended that morning urges, specifically, are a particularly strong predictor of relapse, suggesting that the control of these urges is a special target for intervention efforts (Shiffman et al., 1997, 2000).

If craving is not a withdrawal symptom, then what is it? Craving was listed as a withdrawal symptom of nicotine dependence in earlier versions of the *Diagnostic and Statistical Manual of Mental Disorders* (e.g., *DSM–III–R*; American Psychiatric Association, 1987). However, it is not listed as a symptom of nicotine withdrawal in the *DSM–IV* (American Psychiatric Association, 1994; Teneggi et al., 2002) and is not considered a withdrawal symptom by most experts in the field. Evidence that craving is not a classic withdrawal symptom comes mainly from the reports of both active and abstinent smokers. Reports from active smokers have revealed that cravings are high during ad libitum smoking (Shiffman et al., 1997); they may spike in intensity during initial abstinence but are close to peak during regular smoking. If cravings were withdrawal based, they would be nonexistent, or close to it, while smoking. In addition, cravings over the course of sustained abstinence do not follow the typical pattern of nicotine withdrawal symptoms. Withdrawal symptoms usually appear within several hours of abstinence, peak in 1 to 4 days, and progressively diminish over approximately 4 weeks' time (Durcan et al., 2002). Cravings present differently. They also peak in early abstinence in terms of frequency and intensity and diminish over time. However, they last much longer than the approximate 1-month period of time typical of classic withdrawal symptoms, appearing for up to 6 months or longer (Durcan et al., 2002). Not only do cravings endure much longer than withdrawal symptoms, they also show episodic spikes that appear independent of duration of abstinence and are related to certain cues. Cues identified as evoking acute increases in cravings are referred to as *smoking-related cues* and include smoking, smoking paraphernalia, affective disturbance, eating, and drinking alcohol (Shiffman et al., 1997, 2003).

Cravings, then, appear to be of two different types: There is steady, moderate craving that diminishes over time, not unlike a classic withdrawal symptom; there is also craving that is episodic and acute in nature and can be experienced at any time, for a much longer period of time than withdrawal-based symptoms, and in response to smoking-related cues (sometimes referred to as *cue-provoked cravings*) (Shiffman et al., 2003). It has been suggested that cravings derive from two different processes: One is withdrawal based and characterized by negative affect resulting from reduced intake of nicotine after dependence has been established (relief of this negative state through consumption of nicotine is negatively reinforcing); the other is based on positive affect and appetitive processes (i.e., positive reinforcement) relating to the direct reinforcing action of nicotine on the mesolimbic dopamine system (reward center) of the brain (el-Guebaly & Hodgins, 1998; Zinser, Baker, Sherman, & Cannon, 1992). It is the latter process that is present during active smoking, so current smoking appears to cue or prime further smoking, resulting in high levels of craving even when the smoker is not nicotine-deprived. Thus, cues may become associated with smoking through both negative and positive reinforcement processes. The cues become powerful evocative agents capable of stimulating urges long after the typical withdrawal period has passed. Support for both types of craving can be found in the literature. For example, in support of withdrawal-based craving, a strong relationship has been found between nicotine blood levels and degree of craving for a cigarette (Jarvik et al., 2000). Higher nicotine blood levels result in lower levels of reported nicotine craving.

Other studies show the influence of conditioning factors on craving. For example, it has been demonstrated that neutral cues, when paired with smoking in a laboratory environment, can become conditioned stimuli that evoke conditioned responses such as increased craving and positive affect. A study using denicotinized cigarettes further demonstrates the role of learning in the experience of cravings (Dallery, Houtsmuller, Pickworth, & Stitzer, 2003). Smoking denicotinized cigarettes (not identified as such to the smokers) suppressed craving scores the same as smoking regular, nicotine-containing cigarettes, underscoring the power of stimuli associated with smoking to influence craving. Lazev, Herzog, and Brandon (1999) pointed out that the opportunities for the conditioning of stimuli to smoking are ample: The average dependent smoker consumes 20 or more cigarettes per day, taking approximately 11 puffs per cigarette, totaling in excess of 80,000 puffs per year. Few behaviors receive such reinforcement and provide such abundant opportunity for conditioning to cues. So, because of the learned association of nicotine administration by smoking with cues (internal and external), these stimuli may evoke cravings to smoke.

Cravings are not experienced exactly the same way by everyone, because they are multidimensional. Craving can be experienced across different domains, so the experience may be quite variable from person to person, especially at lower levels of nicotine dependence (Shadel, Niaura, Brown, Hutchison, & Abrams, 2001). Cravings manifest across the following domains: (a) physiological (e.g., lightheadedness, tiredness); (b) affective (e.g., irritability, nervousness); (c) cognitive (e.g., difficulty concentrating); and (d) behavioral (e.g., associating smoking with certain acts such as eating or driving an automobile). With increasing intensity of urges, responses tend to covary, so more domains are involved (Sayette et al., 2003); with so many different areas affected, especially as craving intensity increases, it is easy to see why they result in a felt sense of urgency to smoke.

Summarizing briefly, craving is important to study because (a) it is a prominent, aversive experience; (b) smokers anticipate it to be a significant impediment to abstinence; and (c) it predicts relapse to smoking for abstinent smokers. Like all important phenomena, it is critical that cravings be assessed properly. Cravings have typically been measured by one, sometimes two, face-valid items, with subjects requested to simply rate the degree of craving they are experiencing on a Likert-type scale or visual analogue scale (Anton & Drobes, 1998; Tiffany & Drobes, 1991). These typical methods of assessment are fast and easy to use, and for these reasons enjoy wide use. However, they have weaknesses: With one-item scales, internal consistency cannot be evaluated; moreover, brief scales assume a unidimensional nature for cravings, although it has been clearly established that urge manifestations are many and diverse. A scale has been developed that recognizes the multidimensional nature of cravings and is psychometrically sound: the Questionnaire of Smoking Urges (QSU; Tiffany & Drobes, 1991). The scale consists of 32 items, assessing responses across four categories (eight items per category), requiring subjects to respond to statements on a 7-point Likert-type scale (with 1 = *strongly disagree*; 7 = *strongly agree* with the statement). The four categories assessed, with sample items, are (Tiffany & Drobes, 1991, p. 1469)

1. Desire to smoke—"All I want right now is a cigarette."
2. Anticipation of positive outcomes from smoking—"Smoking would make me feel very good right now."
3. Anticipation of relief from nicotine withdrawal or from associated negative affect—"I would be less irritable now if I could smoke."
4. Intention to smoke—"I will smoke as soon as I get the chance."

The QSU has demonstrated sensitivity to both types of craving, withdrawal-based and those provoked by cues (Morgan, Davies, & Willner, 1999).

Time constraints may limit the application of the QSU in clinical and research contexts. In response to concern about the time of administration, an abbreviated version of the QSU was developed, the QSU–Brief (Cox, Tiffany, & Christen, 2001). The QSU–Brief consists of 10 items from the original scale and takes only approximately 2 minutes to apply. The QSU–Brief strongly correlates with the QSU, is psychometrically sound, and has the advantage of brevity compared with the longer scale.

The all-important question about urges remains to be discussed: How can they be managed to safeguard abstinence? Cognitive–behavioral coping strategies (see chap. 6 for discussion of coping strategies), stimulus control, and pharmacological interventions can all be used to combat urges to smoke. The experience of strong cravings is a high-risk situation for a smoker attempting to maintain abstinence; a failure to attempt coping when feeling the urge to smoke is related to relapse (Shiffman et al., 1997). In fact, the more rapidly coping is attempted and the more coping strategies that are used, the better able a person is to maintain abstinence (Drobes, Meier, & Tiffany, 1994). Craving intensity also appears to be modified by a commitment to not smoke (Dols, van den Hout, Kindt, & Willems, 2002); it is true that urges may be stimulated by smoking-related cues, but a strong, conscious commitment not to smoke can attenuate their degree of intensity. In other words, an abstinent (ex-)smoker need not necessarily be a helpless victim of craving; active cognitive efforts in the form of a firm commitment to abstinence can significantly temper the urge to smoke. In addition, clinical experience has taught me that urges are time-limited. An urge for a cigarette, once stimulated, does not last indefinitely, but rather approximately 20 minutes. This information can be helpful to abstinent smokers because they will know they only need to cope for 20 minutes or so, and not forever. Because classical conditioning of cues is a significant component of craving, extinction (cue-exposure) techniques would logically be indicated; however, their efficacy has not been established.

The following coping strategies are important in the management of craving: Patients should be educated about types of cravings, which provides them with a framework to understand what they are experiencing, and should use cognitive–behavioral coping strategies when urging. It is probably less important which particular strategies are used, so following one's personal preference is advised. The rapid employment of whatever strategies are used is important, so anticipation of high-risk situations is helpful, as is rehearsing using a range of strategies so that coping becomes automatic. Stimulus control principles (i.e., avoidance of high-risk situations) should be used to minimize contact with cues to diminish the strength of the cues. Finally, patients should be educated about the time-limited nature of cravings and realize that although they have limited control over what happens to them, maintaining a conscious commitment not to smoke, no matter how they feel, helps to quell the craving.

With regard to pharmacological interventions for the management of urges, the efficacy of nicotine replacement therapy (NRT) and bupropion SR (discussed in chaps. 6 and 7) has been demonstrated. NRT in the forms of nicotine gum and transdermal patch has been shown to reduce intensity of background, withdrawal-based craving (Jarvik et al., 2000; Shiffman et al., 2003; Teneggi et al., 2002). The 24-hour transdermal patch is particularly effective in managing morning craving (Shiffman et al., 2000). The use of NRT for reduction of acute, cue-stimulated craving has shown promise, so some researchers regard nicotine gum as a possible "rescue medication" in high-risk situations (Shiffman et al., 2003).

Bupropion SR has also demonstrated efficacy for curtailing intensity of cravings (Durcan et al., 2002). Because bupropion SR reduces craving and supports abstinence, it is recommended not only for supporting early abstinence but as a longer-term relapse prevention medication (Hurt et al., 2002).

RELAPSE PREVENTION

Use of common terminology is necessary in discussing abstinence and relapse to ensure clarity and minimize misunderstanding. The following definition of terms related to the discussion of relapse was recommended by the 1986 National Working Conference on Smoking Relapse (discussed in Curry & McBride, 1994): (a) quit episode—at least 24 hours of continuous abstinence; (b) lapse or slip—not more than 6 consecutive days of smoking at least one puff following at least 24 hours of abstinence; (c) relapse—at least 7 consecutive days of smoking at least one puff following a quit episode; (d) relapse crisis—any situation in which it is tempting to smoke.

The statistics discussed in chapter 7 on cessation rates achieved through formal treatment programs might leave one with a sense of optimism that nicotine dependence can be effectively treated. Statistics on maintenance, or rather the failure to maintain abstinence (i.e., relapse), threaten to negate this optimism. Relapse continues to be the bane of nicotine dependence treatment, as for substance abuse treatment in general. Estimates of relapse to smoking range to upwards of 80% within 1 year post-cessation (Brigham, Henningfield, & Stitzer, 1991; Carmody, 1992; Curry & McBride, 1994). The rate of relapse over the course of time is not constant; relapse rates decelerate with time (Curry & McBride, 1994; Ockene et al., 2000). A high proportion of relapses occur within the first 3 months post-cessation, and the rate stabilizes by about 6 months, at which point relapses continue, but at a slower pace. For example, relapses occur at a rate of 34% for the first 2 days postcessation, and at a rate of 1% per day by the 6-month point. Unfortunately, although the rate declines with time, there is not a safe point beyond which relapse stops altogether. Any use of cigarettes (i.e., any lapse) appears to lead almost inevitably to a relapse; the relapse rate following a lapse has been reported to be as high as 88% (Brandon, Tiffany, Obremski, & Baker, 1990). The silver lining, if there is any, is that lapses usually do not lead to immediate and complete relapse. Findings suggest that typically, after a lapse occurs, it may be about 2 to 6 weeks before a second cigarette is smoked, and smoking is intermittent at first. This means that, from a treatment standpoint, there is time to intervene to manage the lapse so as to prevent or minimize a relapse.

One of the most important lessons learned from the relapse numbers is that quitting smoking is a process that includes several attempts at abstinence before it can be successfully maintained, and this process may take as long as 7 years for a given individual (Curry & McBride, 1994). It would constitute a major misunderstanding of nicotine addiction to view a lapse, or even full-blown relapse, as a failure of treatment, or a personal failure for the smoker, because nicotine dependence is a chronic, relapsing condition. One of the biggest challenges is to keep from losing hope and breaking off the treatment relationship; hopelessness after a lapse or relapse is a threat to patient and therapist alike.

Methods of Investigating Relapse

It should come as no surprise that the investigation of relapse to cigarette smoking is a focus of tremendous research and clinical interest. Relapse has been studied through three general methods: prospective identification of variables to predict relapse, retrospective recall, and near real-time or real-time reporting. The goal of these investigations is to identify factors that cause relapse and can be targets of intervention efforts. Variables measured at baseline that predict later relapse include degree of nicotine dependence, education level, commitment to abstinence, psychiatric status (presence of anxiety and depressive disorders in particular), and existence of family and social support (Curry & McBride, 1994; Killen, Fortmann, Kraemer, Varady, & Newman, 1992; Nides et al., 1995; Piasecki, Jorenby, Smith, Fiore, & Baker, 2003). As severity of nicotine dependence increases (measured, for instance, by number of cigarettes smoked per day or by assessment of withdrawal symptoms), so does the likelihood of relapse. Lower educational achievement is associated with increased chances of relapse, as are the existence of depression and anxiety conditions, low commitment to abstinence, and low levels of family and social support for cessation. Findings such as these from prospective investigations may be thought of as describing predisposing factors for relapse to smoking. These factors tend to be static (i.e., they exist or they do not and are not likely to change when treatment is initiated), so for treatment purposes they serve as markers for treatment-matching; once marked, smokers possessing any of these variables should be guided to appropriate treatment interventions (e.g., more intensive treatment in general, NRT for the highly nicotine-dependent smoker, psychiatric treatment for anxiety or depression).

The retrospective method of study of relapse is best exemplified by the research of Marlatt and associates (e.g., Marlatt & Gordon, 1985). With this method relapsers are requested to provide narrative accounts of events (internal, subjective events and external, objective ones), which are coded according to predetermined relapse categories. Through the retrospective method it has been discovered that the majority of relapses (approximately three fourths) occur in response to the following high-risk situations (Marlatt & Gordon, 1985): (a) negative emotional states (35%), (b) social pressure to smoke (20%), and (c) interpersonal conflict (16%). Compared to data provided by the prospective method discussed above, this method produces information about more dynamic, proximal determinants of relapse, referred to as high-risk situations; once these situations have been identified, the coping skills the individual uses in these situations become the focus of interest.

Investigations of near real-time and real-time methods of studying relapse prevention have been conducted by Shiffman and colleagues (e.g., Shiffman, Gnys, Richards, Paty, Hickcox, & Kassel, 1996). Shiffman has used telephone hotlines for near real-time assessment, and more recently, electronic diaries (hand-held computers) that smokers carry with them for real-time assessment (referred to as *ecological momentary assessment* [EMA]). With telephone hotlines, smokers were required to call the hotline during temptation crises or shortly afterward to report data. With the EMA method, smokers carried the electronic diaries with them at all times during the investigation and were asked to record responses based on events (during or immediately following temptation crises or lapses), or when beeped to provide baseline data. The near real-time and real-time methods have the advantage (over retrospective recall methods) of minimizing memory distortion and of getting more fine-grained details of events. As with the results of retrospective recall, the focus of these methods is the identification of the proximal situational determinants contributing to relapse. Among the many important findings attained by these methods are those relating to the relationship between cravings and relapse (discussed earlier in this chapter) and the relevance to relapse of high-risk circumstances such as negative affect and positive affect (for example, celebrations), eating, consuming alcohol, and social situations where smoking is taking place.

The different assessment methods possess strengths and weaknesses relative to one another and can produce different results. However, some common findings can be determined across all three methods (McKay, 1999):

1. The experience of negative emotional states (e.g., anxiety, depression, frustration, anger) is strongly associated with a lapse.
2. Cravings are high before a lapse.
3. Conflict is associated with a lapse.
4. An absence of coping efforts during a temptation crisis is associated with a lapse.
5. Cognitive factors that precede a lapse include low self-efficacy and low commitment to abstinence.

Relapse Prevention Model

Models of relapse prevention can be seen in the literature; the two most frequently encountered are by Marlatt (Marlatt & Gordon, 1985) and Shiffman (Shiffman, Read, Maltese, Rapkin, & Jarvik, 1985). Both are considered cognitive–behavioral models; Marlatt's model is the prominent, more widely discussed, and more influential of the two. The Marlatt relapse prevention model has been referred to as the prototype on which most other relapse prevention programs are based (Rawson, Obert, McCann, & Marinelli-Casey, 1993) and so will be presented in more detail. The Marlatt model was first developed in the treatment of alcoholics but applies to all substances of abuse, including nicotine (Marlatt, 1996). In contrast to the view in traditional substance abuse treatment, relapse is not seen as an endpoint or treatment failure, but as a point on the continuum of recovery; a lapse or relapse indicates the need for more learning. The process of relapse is thought to begin before the actual resumption of use of a substance and to continue beyond the use of the substance. In other words, the behavior of smoking is one observable component of the relapse process that involves the interaction of several factors. According to the model, there are two broad categories of factors that contribute to relapse: immediate determinants and covert antecedents (Larimer, Palmer, & Marlatt, 1999).

Immediate determinants are high-risk situations, outcome expectancies, and the abstinence violation effect, or AVE (Marlatt & Gordon, 1985). High-risk situations are those that present the greatest temptation to use cigarettes; the most common high-risk situations were presented above (negative emotional states, social pressure, and interpersonal conflict). Exposure to high-risk situations is one aspect of a potential lapse; another is the person's response. If a cognitive or behavioral coping response is used in the situation, a lapse can be averted; if not, a lapse may ensue. Successful coping usually results in a bolstering of self-efficacy. A challenge in high-risk situations is resisting the influence of attendant positive expectations—a focus on the short-term positives associated with immediate use of the substance (e.g., relief from stress or other discomfort), while ignoring the intermediate- to long-term negative consequences.

If a lapse occurs, it may or may not become a relapse, depending on the emotional response to the lapse and causal attributions. Feelings of guilt and other negative emotions contribute to further use of the substance for relief. Regarding attributions, the AVE may manifest, also contributing to further substance use. The AVE indicates that the individual has essentially given up on the commitment to control use of the substance because abstinence has been violated. With the AVE the person is saying, in effect, "Now that I have smoked, I might as well go all the way." Causal attributions associated with the manifestation of the AVE are internal (originating in the self), stable (lapse is due to an unchanging trait), and global (other situations will result in a lapse) (Marlatt & Gordon, 1985); a statement such as the following would reflect the presence of the AVE: "*I* am a *loser* with no self-control who will *always* smoke when I get the chance."

Covert antecedents of relapse are less obvious and immediate and relate to more general factors such as lifestyle (e.g., high stress levels) and cognitive factors such as excessive or inappropriate use of defenses (like rationalization or denial) or a habit of seeking immediate gratification (i.e., satisfying cravings). The covert antecedents are thought to contribute to relapse by increasing exposure to high-risk situations and eroding desire to resist temptation.

Relapse prevention interventions are designed to address both immediate determinants and covert antecedents. Regarding immediate determinants, the following interventions are recommended (Larimer et al., 1999):

1. Provide an overview of the model as an aid to comprehension and enlist the patient as an active participant in the process.
2. Identify high-risk situations for that person. It may help to suggest common situations of risk, but it is best to identify those

situations most tempting for each individual. It is sometimes helpful to review past relapse scenarios and relapse fantasies. Having the individual keep a record of smoking behavior can also be helpful in this process. For at least a week, smokers can be asked to record each cigarette smoked, the time of day, where they were, who was present, and how they felt. In this way antecedents to smoking may be identified.

3. Help the patient develop coping strategies to avoid lapsing in high-risk situations. Coping strategies may be cognitive, behavioral, or both, and the patient should play a significant role in choosing responses to be used. Bolstering of self-efficacy may be necessary because someone may recognize tempting situations and have a plan of action but feel unable to execute the plan under duress. Self-efficacy can be enhanced by focusing on previous incidents reflecting successful coping, and by reducing the challenge to a more manageable one (i.e., one day at a time). In addition, to bolster the individual against the influence of positive expectations that threaten to diminish commitment to abstinence, it can be helpful to address some common myths about nicotine and to construct a decision matrix. One example of addressing a myth is pointing out (as discussed in chap. 1) that research has convincingly demonstrated that, despite appearances to the contrary, nicotine is ultimately anxiety- and depression-causing. To construct a decision matrix, individuals are asked to list the pros and cons of remaining abstinent or resuming smoking behavior; they should do this for both the immediate future and for the long term. The matrix can be referred to at times of temptation to help objectify the situation and move the individual away from making a decision based only on the narrow, immediate circumstances.

4. Prepare the individual to control a lapse, should one occur, and avoid a full-blown relapse. Several techniques can be useful here. To combat the AVE, cognitive restructuring can be used by explaining the problem as one resulting from ineffective coping or as a consequence of a highly tempting situation, both of which can be dealt with (rather than the lapse being the result of the person being a helpless, hopeless failure with no willpower who can never stop smoking). Also, the patient should be made aware that maintaining contact with the therapist is important to reinforce the notion that treatment is not over with the resumption of smoking and so that an individual can begin to search for the causes of the lapse (which further supports the idea that the situation can be changed).

Interventions for covert antecedents involve encouragement to structure one's life to be less stressful and more satisfying. This may involve skills training to assist the individual to more effectively manage his or her life, such as relaxation training, stress management, assertiveness training, and development of "positive addictions" (e.g., exercise, meditation, or yoga). A form used to teach relapse prevention to patients, "Managing Temptation and Relapse," is presented in Exhibit 8.1. A case example illustrating use of the form is provided in Exhibit 8.2.

Some smokers may have difficulty recognizing coping responses they use or need assistance to develop new coping skills. I find that the Coping With Temptations Inventory (CWTI; Shiffman, 1988) is helpful in this respect. I do not request that patients fill out the form, but share it with them to facilitate active thinking and discussion that, it is hoped, will lead to the choosing of preferred coping methods to use when needed. The CWTI is shown in Exhibit 8.3.

Meta-analytic studies (e.g., Carroll, 1996) support the use of cognitive–behavioral relapse prevention models such as that described by Marlatt and Gordon (1985). Relapse prevention training, either as an abstinence initiation intervention or maintenance treatment, produces favorable treatment outcomes compared to outcomes for no-treatment control groups; it is comparable to other active treatments with respect to the achievement of abstinence. Although relapse prevention may not be superior to other active treatment methods in preventing relapse, it is superior with respect to other outcome measures:

1. It appears to reduce the severity of relapse when it occurs.
2. It shows delayed emergent effects. In other words, the benefits are of longer duration than those of other treatments, and its superiority is more apparent over time (e.g., more than 1 year postcessation).
3. Relapse prevention may be particularly helpful with vulnerable groups that have greater nicotine dependence and those most deficient in coping. Although all of the elements of the Marlatt model are not supported by research, it is still clinically valid and useful for treatment (Kadden, 1996).

The cognitive–behavioral relapse prevention models of Marlatt, Shiffman, and their respective associates are not the only relapse prevention methods. Relapse prevention interventions that have also been used include booster sessions and extended contact, and use of intervention supplements (Curry & McBride, 1994). Booster sessions involve the offering of treatment sessions at some point after formal treatment has concluded. The rationale behind booster sessions is to prevent the decay of treatment effects that occurs over time by offering more of the treatment originally received. Results achieved by booster methods have been unimpressive, with problems of

EXHIBIT 8.1
Managing Temptation and Relapse Form

MANAGING TEMPTATION AND RELAPSE

Quitting smoking is quite an accomplishment. The goal of treatment, however, is much bigger than that. It is quitting and staying quit. There are three key parts to staying quit that can be learned and practiced to maintain your cessation goal:

1. Identification of situations that are most likely to tempt you to resume smoking.
2. Engaging in behaviors other than smoking at these tempting times that allow you not to smoke and to endure the situations without an intolerable struggle.
3. If you happen to slip up and smoke, preventing the fact that you smoked from becoming the launching point for resumption of regular smoking.

There are some situations that seem to be more tempting than others when it comes to smoking. For example, experiencing negative feelings, celebrating, drinking alcohol, being around other smokers, and having an argument with someone are common circumstances that evoke strong cravings to smoke.

Exercise 1. Please list the situations that you consider most likely to create the greatest temptation for you to smoke. If you have attempted to quit before, it is usually a good idea to consider those situations that led to a resumption of smoking after past cessation attempts.

_____
_____
_____
_____

Fortunately, you need not be helpless in dealing with tempting situations. You may not have control over whether or not you experience cravings, but you have total control over how you respond to craving and temptation. It may help to know that once a craving is felt, it does not last forever (usually not more than 20 min). You don't have to hold on indefinitely. Coping methods that are used to combat temptation are usually classified as mental and behavioral. Mental coping strategies that may be used to resist the urge to smoke include actively thinking of the benefits of quitting and negative consequences of smoking; deliberately pushing aside thoughts of smoking; not considering smoking an option no matter how you feel; using positive, relaxing mental images; and mentally anticipating tempting situations and your successful response. Behavioral coping strategies that may be used include eating or chewing (for example, gum, candy), distracting activities (for example, reading, crossword puzzles, watching TV), leaving tempting situations, relaxation exercises, physical exercise, rewarding yourself for maintaining abstinence, seeking social support, and referring to your decision matrix.

Exercise 2. Please list at least one strategy to assist you to effectively manage each tempting situation identified above.

_____
_____
_____
_____

continues

EXHIBIT 8.1 *(Continued)*

While the goal of treatment is permanent freedom from smoking, it is an unfortunate fact that there are sometimes slips or lapses when a cigarette is smoked. The most important thing to remember is that smoking one cigarette does not mean you must resume regular smoking. To prevent a fallback into regular smoking, you should do the following:

1. Contact your counselor and by all means do not drop out of treatment. If you have already completed the treatment program, or stopped for other reasons, call your counselor to discuss treatment options.
2. Understand that the slip was the result of a highly tempting situation or poor coping, both of which can be dealt with. The slip is not an indication of an unalterable condition you have, or unalterable circumstances.

Note. From *Stop Smoking System*, by C. E. Dodgen, 2004, Florham Park, NJ. Unpublished manuscript. Reprinted by permission.

attendance and difficulty determining the proper timing of sessions (Curry & McBride, 1994).

Extended contact refers to interventions that are conducted through contact that is scheduled and ongoing but less frequent than that of the initial formal treatment episode. The contact often comes in different forms, including written feedback, telephone counseling, support groups, and ongoing biological monitoring for nicotine use. Extended contact methods show some promise in the ability to maintain abstinence and may serve as useful adjuncts to treatment.

Intervention supplements are interventions proactively directed to those consequences of cessation known to be obstacles to the maintenance of abstinence: withdrawal, weight gain, stress, depression, and weak or no social and family support. Withdrawal discomfort is eased pharmacologically: Nicotine and non-nicotine medications have been used to alleviate withdrawal distress, with success not only at initiation but also in the maintenance phase of treatment (see the section above on craving). Concern about weight gain may be an obstacle to treatment, especially for women (U.S. Department of Health and Human Services, 2000b). Provision of traditional weight management interventions does not appear efficacious in supporting maintenance of abstinence in general and so should probably be reserved for individuals who express significant concerns about weight gain. Elevated levels of stress, anxiety, and depression are associated with relapse and should be addressed in treatment through skill training, standard psychotherapy, or pharmacotherapy. Finally, an absence of family and social support is very dangerous to the individual attempting to remain abstinent; arranging support either in the individual's natural environment or in treatment is vitally important.

EXHIBIT 8.2
Case Example: Caitlin M.

BRIEF BACKGROUND AND SMOKING HISTORY

Caitlin M. is a 57-year-old married woman. At her physician's request she was seeking treatment for nicotine dependence. On a recent, routine physical, her physician expressed concern about her smoking because she was positive for several health risk factors. Her family history included a mother who was a smoker and died from lung cancer and a father who was a nonsmoker and died of a heart attack. Mrs. M. is obese and a longtime smoker. She has smoked since she was 13 years old and currently consumes about a pack of cigarettes (20) per day. She was previously employed as an administrative assistant at an insurance company and accepted a retirement package at age 55. Since her retirement she has experienced a sense of purposelessness and feels more bored than ever. Her husband still works full time, and she feels she does little but wait for him to come home during the week. Smoking has actually increased over the 2 years since she retired. Mrs. M. had attempted to quit smoking two times previously. Prior to getting married, she quit on her own for about 2 months. Then, after her mother's death, she quit for approximately 4 years. This cessation episode was aided by the involvement of her physician and use of nicotine gum.

SMOKING-CESSATION INTERVENTIONS

When she attempted to complete the first exercise of the "Managing Temptation and Relapse" form, it was apparent that she had difficulty with the assignment from the beginning. She had smoked for so long and it was such an automatic behavior that she could not initially think of any specific circumstances that represented elevated risk or temptation. This was where keeping a smoking record was especially helpful. On her smoking record she noted several times when feelings of boredom and loneliness were associated with smoking, as was relief from withdrawal symptoms that included hunger and craving. After some discussion with her about this, she agreed that for her the cigarette acted like a soothing, reliable companion. Review of Mrs. M.'s quit history led to a similar conclusion: After the previous 4-year hiatus she started smoking within several months after her sister, her only sibling and best friend, moved out of state. Mrs. M. also reported concern about compensatory eating and weight gain if she should stop smoking. Discussion about addiction to nicotine and relief from symptoms of withdrawal provided a context within which to understand motivations for smoking.

For Exercise 2 of the form, Mrs. M. was asked to list one or more strategies to cope with the tempting situations. Because she had found chewing nicotine gum helpful in the past, she expressed interest in using that again. Because the greatest temptation appeared to stem from an internal feeling state, rather than an observable event, it became necessary for Mrs. M. to maintain a record of feelings even after the quit date so as to be able to identify risky times for herself. In recording her feelings every 1 to 2 hours, she consciously took notice of how she felt. When she felt an urge to smoke or any other withdrawal symptoms, she agreed to use the nicotine gum. When she felt lonely or bored, feelings apt to lead to an urge to smoke, she chose the strategy of seeking social support. She agreed to call her husband, sister, or me when necessary.

In addition to specific interventions to cope with acute temptation, it was also necessary to work on a more global level. That is, coping strategies described above were agreed on to more effectively manage high-risk situations. In addition, global

continues

EXHIBIT 8.2 *(Continued)*

interventions were developed in an attempt to reduce, avoid, or eliminate high-risk situations. To help with her boredom and sense of purposelessness, we discussed ways for her to spend her time more meaningfully. In addition, to relieve her sense of loneliness, increased social interaction was recommended. Mrs. M. was able to meet both needs by obtaining a part-time job at a local supermarket. She enjoyed cooking and several nights per week worked at the supermarket, giving cooking demonstrations. To deal with concerns about her weight, we discussed the fact that nicotine gum helps to prevent weight gain from cessation as long as the gum is used. For weight management beyond the time period she would use the gum, she agreed to seek services at a nationally known weight management program.

Two weeks after her quit date, Mrs. M. reported having a couple of cigarettes. Her honesty was applauded, as was her commitment to treatment, as evidenced by her continuing treatment after the slip. She expressed embarrassment, a sense of failure, and hopelessness, stating that maybe certain people are not capable of stopping. It was explained to her that slips do occur even in ultimately successful cessation, and that the important thing was to understand what went wrong and to take corrective action. In this particular situation the lapse occurred on a weekend when she felt bored and strongly craved a cigarette. She did not think of anything else at the time other than how good it would be to have the cigarette. We discussed the importance of reaching out for help when she feels such intense urges, and of her consciously remembering her motivation for attempting to stop smoking to begin with: not wanting to die of lung cancer, like her mother did.

COMMENTS

Mrs. M.'s situation was a classic case of someone who has been smoking for a very long period of time. The smoking behavior becomes so generalized and woven into his or her life that the smoker cannot easily see any reason for smoking—or for stopping, for that matter. Smoking just seems to become a natural part of life like bathing and eating. With such cases the smoking record and quit history can be helpful in identifying patterns that can provide clues about how to intervene with specific coping strategies. Both specific and global interventions are needed to help achieve and maintain abstinence. If a lapse occurs, it is crucial to frame it in a constructive way: Slips occur, and they can be understood and dealt with in treatment. There is no shame in having a slip and remaining in treatment to correct the situation. This case demonstrates that relapse prevention goes beyond smoking behavior per se, requiring much skill in evaluating sometimes complex and subtle clinical situations, and maintaining the individual's involvement in treatment, especially after a slip.

SUMMARY

Achievement of abstinence is a significant accomplishment and involves both management of cravings and relapse prevention. Craving is a factor in maintaining active smoking and is strongly related to relapse for abstinent smokers. Cravings appear to derive from two different sources, one related to withdrawal from nicotine, the other to the learned association of smoking with cues. The withdrawal-based craving presents like a classic

EXHIBIT 8.3
The Coping With Temptations Inventory (CWTI)

BEHAVIORAL COPING RESPONSES

Alternatives
  Alternative Consumption
    Food and drink
      Allow yourself to eat more to
        avoid smoking
      Chew gum
      Drink a lot of water
      Eat more fruit
    Nicotine
      Chew nicotine gum
      Use snuff
  Alternative activities
    Exercise
      Exercise
      Lift weights
      Take walks
    Distraction
      Keep busy
      Distract yourself
      Crochet
      Doodle when on phone to avoid
        smoking
    Relaxation
      Do deep-breathing exercises
      Engage in more relaxing activities
      Listen to tape on relaxation
      Take hot showers to relax
Self-Care—activities to promote well-
being
  Stress reduction
    Isolate yourself for a weekend of
      peace and quiet
    Keep out of stressful situations
    Remove yourself from stressful
      situations
    Scream to relieve frustration
  Other self-care activities
    Eat better
    Go shopping to feel better
    Set aside time for yourself
    Spend more of your free time doing
      things for yourself
Stimulus Control
  Cigarettes and paraphernalia
    Buy cigarettes by pack rather than
      by carton
    Do not keep cigarettes in house
    Leave cigarettes in a part of the
      house that is away from you

Get rid of ashtrays
  Other substances
    Avoid alcohol
    Avoid coffee
    Drink juice instead of coffee so as
      not to smoke
  People
    Avoid friends who smoke
    Do not visit any smokers
  Situations
    Avoid situations where you used to
      smoke
    Change places of relaxation at
      home (favorite chair, etc.)
    Leave tempting situations
    Sit in nonsmoking section of
      restaurants
Help from Others
  Social support
    Ask kids to throw away your
      cigarettes if you are smoking
    Call a "buddy" from the clinic
    Get support from someone else
      who quit
  Wagers, dares
    Arrange a wager with a friend as a
      motivator
    Arrange a dare with a friend as a
      motivator
  Treatment
    Attend a clinic
    Enroll in a clinic
    Sign up for four-session course with
      a hypnotist
Direct Control of Smoking
  Cut down—includes rules restricting
    smoking, reduction of tar and
    nicotine
    Buy low-tar cigarettes
    Cut down from 20 to 10 cigarettes
      a day
    Eliminate your least important
      cigarettes
    Do not smoke in car or socially
  Satiation
    Smoke cigar to make you sick
    Smoke until sick prior to quitting

continues

EXHIBIT 8.3 *(Continued)*

Other Techniques
Self-reward
Put $1 in jar for each day quit
Reward yourself for 3-hour
abstinence periods
Focus on techniques—behaviors
meant primarily to cue cognitions

Get out and read list of reasons for
quitting
Look at jar of cigarette butts when
tempted
Make a list of reasons, hang it on a
mirror
Other responses

COGNITIVE COPING RESPONSES

Consequences
Health consequences
Your own health
Positive consequences
Future—large-scale, abstract,
future consequences
Think about wanting a longer
life
Think about being here for a
grandchild
Think that by quitting you will
improve your health
Immediate—small-scale,
concrete, immediate
consequences
Think how much better you
will feel if you quit
Think how nice it will be to be
able to breathe deeply
Notice that you feel better
physically
Think about no longer
waking up coughing
Negative consequences
Future—large-scale, abstract,
future consequences
Think about getting cancer,
dying, and leaving kids
alone
Think of someone who died
of lung disease
Think, "I don't want
emphysema"
Think about the possibility of
lung cancer
Immediate—small-scale,
concrete, immediate
consequences
Think, "I don't feel well when
smoking"
Think about not being able to
breathe deeply

Think, "I get colds because
of smoking"
Think, "My lungs hurt from
smoking"
Others' health—smoking's effects
on others
Think, "It would be nice for kids to
have fresh air"
Think, "My son's health problems
are due to my smoking"
Social consequences—including
modeling and social reactions
Positive
Try to set example for daughter
who is pregnant
Think, "Quitting would make my
spouse happy"
Think that your family will be
proud
Negative
Think about getting grief from
friends about not being able to
quit
Think, "A relapse would
disappoint my doctor"
Think, "My daughter will know if I
smoke and be disgusted"
Financial consequences
Think, "I can use the money for
something else"
Remember that smoking is an
expensive habit
Think about the money you are
saving
Other consequences—sensory,
sanitary, etc.
Positive
Think, "Food tastes better"
Think, "The whole house smells
cleaner"
Think, "I want my complexion to
look better"

continues

EXHIBIT 8.3 (Continued)

Notice that you're not as nervous now

Negative

Notice you don't like the smell of smoke in the house

Think, "The smell is offensive"

Think about yellow teeth from smoking

Think, "My mouth tastes like a garbage can"

Devaluation of Smoking—downplaying value of smoking

General devaluation ("not worth it")

Tell yourself it's not worth it to have a cigarette

Think, "Smoking is disgusting"

Think, "I'm sick of cigarettes"

Disappointment of expectations of smoking

Remind yourself that cigarettes are not a solution to problems

Think, "Smoking didn't make me feel better"

Think, "Smoking won't improve anything"

Sensory devaluation

Think, "Smoking tasted bad"

Remember that cigarettes didn't really taste good

Self-Talk

Self-motivation

Denying want or need— restatements of motivation

Keep telling yourself that you don't really want to smoke

Think, "I don't need them"

Think, "I must quit"

Reviewing reasons for quitting

Remind youself that you wanted to quit to breathe better

Remind yourself of why you quit

Willpower—solely expression of mental effort

Give yourself orders not to smoke

Resolve to quit

Tell yourself "no" when tempted, using willpower

Self-redefinition

Tell yourself, "I'm a nonsmoker"

Think of yourself as a nonsmoker

Visualize yourself as a nonsmoker

Positive thoughts

Self-confidence, efficacy

Think, "I can do it"

Think, "I can be in smoking situations—no problem"

Think, "If others can do it, so can I"

Accomplishment

Feel good because you've done this

Think about your enjoyment of quitting

Pat yourself on the back for abstinence

Hopeful prospects—expectation of improvement

Think, "It will get better"

Tell yourself that after 4–6 weeks the urges won't be so severe

Think, "It will get easier"

General positive attitudes

Encourage yourself

Keep a positive attitude

Take a positive attitude toward the quit attempt

Orienting Thoughts

Planning—higher-order cognitive activities

Methods, plans—including plans for other responses

Plan on substituting exercise when you feel tempted

Think, "I'll use nicotine gum"

Think about getting rid of cues for smoking

Think, "I can get antianxiety pills from my doctor"

Setting a quit date

Decide to quit on the National Smoke-Out Day

Set a new quit date

Think, "I can quit if I set a date 2 weeks hence"

Self-monitoring, awareness, analysis

Feel aware every time you light a cigarette

Be aware of tension and anxiety

Think about particular situations responsible for temptation

Understand situations under which you smoke

continues

EXHIBIT 8.3 *(Continued)*

Temporal orientation
Hour or day at a time
Think about not smoking an hour at a time
Think, "One day at a time"
Think that you only have to make it through the day
Stages
Think, "If this quit doesn't work, the next one will"
Think, "I will encounter strong temptations for some time"
Think that it has been easier these last 2 weeks
Think, "I'm not safe from relapse yet"

Alternative Cognitions
Distraction
Actively push thoughts about smoking out of your head
Keep the urge out of your mind
Keep your mind busy
Think about other things when there is an urge to smoke
Relaxation
Fantasize about a cabin
Try to stay calm
Try to relax

Other Cognitions
Remorse
Self-punitive—has an insulting, punitive aspect
Accuse yourself of being weak-minded, lacking willpower
Say to yourself, "You fool, you've started again!"
Think, "I'm an idiot"

Guilt-remorse—may include reasonable reconsideration
Feel guilty about relapsing
Think, "I wasted the last 2 weeks of work by relapsing"
Think, "I haven't really tried hard enough"

Consequences of lapses
Lead to relapse
Say to yourself, "Don't start, you'll go right back"
Think, "If I have one cigarette, I will relapse"
Think, "It must be all or nothing"
Undo progress
Think, "I do not want to go through withdrawal again"
Think, "I've been off 4 weeks—it would be a shame to start again"
Think, "I got to this point, it's not worth blowing it"
Promote feeling of failure
Concentrate on how guilty you will feel if you smoke
Think, "I don't want to relapse because it would be a defeat"
Think how sorry you will be if you relapse

Minimizing of lapses
Remember prior relapse—it wasn't as major as you thought
Think, "One cigarette does not mean complete relapse"
Think, "Holding it down to 20 per day is keeping it in hand"
Think, "Just one is not the end of the world"

Note. From "Behavioral Assessment" (pp. 163–168), by S. Shiffman, 1988, in D. M. Donovan and G. A. Marlatt (Eds.), *Assessment of Addictive Behaviors*, New York: Guilford Press. Copyright 1988 by the Guilford Press. Reprinted with permission.

withdrawal symptom; these cravings spike initially after reduction or cessation of nicotine intake, then diminish over time. The cravings stemming from the learned association of smoking with cues is more episodic in nature and last for much longer than typical withdrawal symptoms. Cravings can be assessed with psychometric instruments or by clinical interview.

Cravings are known to predict relapse; those abstinent smokers with strong cravings are more likely to relapse. The experience of cravings may be thought of as a high-risk situation for relapse to smoking, so cravings are integrally related to relapse prevention. Although relatively impressive abstinence rates may be achieved in smoking-cessation treatment, the fact remains that maintenance of abstinence is notoriously difficult, and the further out one goes in time from treatment, the less likely an individual is to remain abstinent.

Research has identified situations that tend to place an abstinent smoker at risk for relapse, and this knowledge may serve as a starting point for training in relapse prevention. Personal high-risk situations for a given individual should be identified. High-risk situations are those that evoke strong cravings to smoke. Coping strategies should be planned and rehearsed for rapid application in high-risk situations. Abstinent smokers benefit from knowing that (a) lapses and relapses are a reality for almost all smokers and treatment should not end because a lapse or relapse occurs; (b) cravings are feelings that do not have to be acted on; (c) cravings are time-limited; and (d) taking active steps to cope while experiencing cravings is very important.

An effective relapse prevention program requires the adoption of a comprehensive approach to relapse whereby relapse behavior is treated as reflecting processes (biological, psychological, and/or environmental) active both before and after any resumption of nicotine use. In addition to being trained to cope with cravings (whose presence signals the existence of a high-risk situation), individuals should also be taught to cope with lapses (or relapses) if they occur. Furthermore, if indicated, the individual should receive pharmacological and psychotherapeutic assistance to cope with withdrawal symptoms and psychiatric symptoms of stress, anxiety, or depression. Finally, it would be advisable to provide for extended contact beyond the formal treatment period, and also to arrange for social and/or family support for the abstinent individual.

9

SPECIAL POPULATIONS

The treatment of any condition requires exploration for the possible existence of subpopulations that may deserve special consideration for treatment. Barriers to the provision of appropriate, special services for certain groups of smokers may be created or supported by misunderstanding or lack of consideration of such variables as psychiatric status, race and ethnicity, and gender. The purpose of this chapter is to remind clinicians of the need to consider all relevant variables to develop and effectively apply a truly individualized treatment plan.

PSYCHIATRIC STATUS

In the United States there is growing public sentiment against smoking. Antismoking messages come from many sources now: health care professionals, friends, family, media, schools, and laws restricting public smoking (Royce, Corbett, Sorensen, & Ockene, 1997). As the pressure to not smoke increases, there is more incentive for smokers to stop. Naturally, those who can stop probably will; those who remain smokers in the face of rising pressure to stop will, in all likelihood, be individuals less able to stop, such as the more severely nicotine dependent or individuals who are more limited in coping resources, like smokers with psychiatric problems (Irvin & Brandon, 2000). Despite the fact that the prevalence of smoking in the adult general population of the United States has declined over the past two decades, no such drop has been found in the number of smokers with psychiatric conditions (including substance abuse) (Kalman, 1998; Ziedonis & Williams, 2003). Rates of smoking for individuals with substance abuse problems and other psychiatric conditions remain alarmingly high. The ensuing discussion addresses the reasons this subpopulation experiences such high smoking rates and may have particular difficulty stopping, as well as possible special treatment needs.

Substance Abuse and Nicotine Dependence

A very large proportion of substance abusers are current smokers, estimated as high as 84% (Kalman, 1998); this compares with approximately 27% of the general population of U.S. adults who were smokers in 1998. Broken down by primary substance of abuse for which they were seeking substance abuse treatment services, current smokers accounted for 74% of alcoholics, 77% of cocaine addicts, and 85% of heroin addicts (discussed in Sees & Clark, 1993). As can be seen by these statistics, current substance abusers are about two to three times more likely to be smokers than are non–substance-abusing individuals. In addition to their higher rates of smoking, substance abusers tend to be heavier smokers; they are not only more likely to smoke, but when they smoke, they smoke more cigarettes. A serious consequence of the elevated rates and amount of smoking among substance abusers is the resulting increase in mortality and morbidity rates in this population (Gill & Bennett, 2000; Hughes, 1993c; Sees & Clark, 1993). Substance abusers are more likely to die from the consequences of nicotine dependence than they are from addiction to their primary drug of choice. Annual death rates in the United States attributed to cigarettes are in excess of 430,000; the annual U.S. death tolls from other drugs are (Sees & Clark, 1993) (a) alcohol: 125,000 to 150,000; (b) cocaine: 2,000 to 4,000; (c) heroin: 4,000; and (d) marijuana: 75.

Substance abusers are at higher risk for smoking-related diseases than non–substance-abusing smokers. For example, the particular combination of alcohol and nicotine dependence produces very high cancer rates. In addition, smoking is positively correlated with substance abuse such that heavier smoking is associated with a greater likelihood of abusing other substances.

With the very high rates of smoking for substance abusers, and correspondingly high morbidity and mortality rates, one would think that treatment of this population would be a priority. Sadly, this has not been the case. Until recently, substance abusers have been an underserved group with respect to the treatment of nicotine dependence. This is the case despite the fact that there are tremendous incentives for substance abusers to seek abstinence from nicotine, including improved health and longevity, and increased probability of achieving abstinence from other substances of abuse.

The relative neglect of substance abusers appears to derive principally from two sources: bias on the part of treatment professionals and the inherent difficulty of treating comorbid conditions of nicotine dependence and other addictions. A survey of attitudes of addiction professionals toward offering treatment for nicotine dependence to individuals receiving treatment for substance abuse found a majority (about 58%) who thought treatment for nicotine dependence would improve chances of recovery from other substances of abuse (Gill & Bennett, 2000). However, a substantial minority (about 18%) thought simultaneous treatment would negatively affect recovery from substance abuse, or would have no effect (about 20%) on substance abuse treatment, neither enhancing nor impeding it. That ignorance or prejudice contributed to the treatment professionals' bias was illustrated by the fact that reported attitudes toward nicotine dependence treatment were significantly related to the amount of nicotine treatment education received and to personal smoking history. That is, the more nicotine treatment education received, the more likely was the treatment worker to consider nicotine dependence treatment important; and current smokers thought nicotine dependence treatment in their patients less important. Others have reported that even substance abuse counselors who report an interest in promoting smoking cessation frequently demonstrate behaviors that are inconsistent with their stated intentions (Burling, Ramsey, Seidner, & Kondo, 1997).

A variety of commonly encountered, unfounded beliefs that serve as grounds for not providing treatment for nicotine dependence together with substance abuse treatment are presented in Exhibit 9.1.

There is reason to believe, however, that the tide may be turning in terms of awareness of the need to address both comorbid conditions in treatment. Hughes (1993c) suggested that providers are recognizing that a growing number of people recovering from substance abuse are dying from smoking-related illnesses, substance abusers are reporting more interest in nicotine-dependence treatment, and many facilities and substance abuse treatment programs are smoke-free, all of which provide impetus to treat nicotine dependence. With increasing attention, improved treatment should follow; there are significant questions yet to be definitively answered as to how best to treat this subpopulation of smokers. To review what appears certain about treatment, see Exhibit 9.2.

What appears less certain is exactly when nicotine dependence treatment should be offered relative to substance abuse treatment. Early abstinence from nicotine increases stress and symptoms of anxiety and depression, which can increase the challenge of recovery from nicotine and other substances; on the other hand, abstinence from nicotine, once achieved, appears to be a potential asset to recovery at a later point in treatment. Because readiness to quit is an important variable in the treatment of nicotine dependence, smoking-cessation treatment should be offered to substance abusers in substance abuse treatment with a full discussion of the

EXHIBIT 9.1
Some Misconceptions About Substance-Abusing Smokers
That Are Obstacles to Treatment

1. *Substance abusers do not want treatment for nicotine dependence.* In actuality, when queried a majority of substance abusers in treatment do report interest in smoking cessation (Kalman, 1998; Sees & Clark, 1993).
2. *Substance abusers cannot benefit from treatment of nicotine dependence.* As one would expect, considering the existence of comorbid conditions, nicotine-dependence treatment is more difficult, but smoking-related outcomes can be improved with current and past substance abusers who smoke (el-Guebaly et al., 2002; Hughes, 1993), although probably not with the degree of success found with non–substance abusers (Hurt et al., 1994; Kalman, 1998). It has also been observed that the offering of simultaneous substance abuse and nicotine-dependence treatment leads to increased motivation to stop smoking and attempts to stop; even if initial cessation outcomes are relatively modest, longer-term prospects may be improved (Hurt et al., 1994).
3. *Treatment for nicotine dependence will jeopardize recovery from other substance abuse.* It has been very convincingly demonstrated that providing treatment for nicotine dependence, for substance abusers already abstinent from other substances or in treatment to achieve abstinence, does not negatively impact the traditional substance abuse treatment when the treatment for nicotine dependence is voluntary (Gariti et al., 2002; Hughes, 1993c; Kalman, 1998; McCarthy, Collins, & Hser, 2002; Sees & Clark, 1993). In fact, those individuals able to maintain abstinence from nicotine were more likely to also maintain abstinence from their primary substance of abuse at follow-up points; when abstinent smokers relapsed, they usually relapsed to smoking, not to other substances. It is noted that the experience of symptoms of stress, anxiety, and depression may increase early in abstinence due to withdrawal from nicotine, and this can challenge treatment. Taken all together, the evidence indicates that treatment for nicotine dependence does not negatively influence substance abuse recovery, but rather positively influences abstinence efforts with other substances.
4. *Nicotine dependence is different from dependence on other substances, so it cannot easily be integrated with traditional substance abuse treatment.* In chapter 4 of this book, the scientific basis was presented for classifying nicotine as a classic substance of abuse like alcohol, cocaine, and heroin. Therefore, education about nicotine dependence and its treatment can be discussed in a manner consistent with that used for other substances of abuse.
5. *Use of pharmacological agents, a significant component of nicotine dependence treatment, is not consistent with traditional substance abuse treatment.* This may be true in some cases in which the use of any psychotropic substance is considered dangerous to recovery. However, how consistent is the message to not use any psychoactive substances during recovery but to allow substance abusers to smoke cigarettes and drink beverages with caffeine freely? Furthermore, the same rationale has sometimes been applied to the absurd degree of challenging the use of psychiatric medications for those in substance abuse treatment. The argument seems equally thin for smokers in substance abuse treatment: If they can be assisted to stop smoking by pharmacological intervention they should be, especially when the alternative is to allow unrestricted consumption of nicotine via cigarettes.
6. *It is too difficult to give up all addictions at once, and because it is not necessary to become abstinent from nicotine to be abstinent from other substances, treatment for nicotine dependence should be deferred.* This concern can be addressed with several points, one already mentioned: Nicotine dependence

continues

EXHIBIT 9.1 *(Continued)*

treatment does not appear to jeopardize or weaken substance abuse treatment. In addition, substance abusers are asked to give up all other substances of abuse; including nicotine in this endeavor is completely consistent with treatment. Substance abusers would not be asked to ignore a heroin addiction while treating a cocaine addiction, and they should not be asked to neglect nicotine dependence treatment for other treatments.

pros and cons of simultaneous treatment. If individuals are not currently ready, treatment should proceed, as with any other patient, with the goal of motivating them for a future quit attempt. If they are ready for a quit attempt, treatment should commence.

Other Psychiatric Conditions and Smoking

Like substance abusers, patients with other psychiatric conditions are heavily overrepresented in the smoking population; this is the case in the United States as well as other countries. For example, Poirier et al. (2002) reviewed statistics in the United States and compared them with results they obtained in France. According to their findings, psychiatric outpatients in the United States have a prevalence of smoking of 52%, compared with 33%

EXHIBIT 9.2
Established Facts About Treatment of Smokers
Who Are Substance Abusers

1. Nicotine-dependence treatment is sorely needed due to the very high prevalence of smoking among substance abusers and the severe health consequences they suffer.
2. When offered on a voluntary basis, nicotine dependence treatment does not negatively influence substance abuse treatment.
3. Substance abusers already abstinent or in treatment for substance abuse can improve outcomes with both their primary substance of abuse and with nicotine from treatment for nicotine dependence.
4. Substance abusers tend to be heavy smokers and so should automatically be directed to more intense treatment options. No special methods of treatment are needed as long as treatment is of sufficient intensity. Because substance abusers tend to have less supportive environments with respect to smoking cessation (they have a higher percentage of smoking friends and family, with more positive attitudes about smoking and more negative attitudes about cessation, than do non–substance abusers), the provision of social support in treatment is of particular importance (Burling et al., 1997). A stronger case for the need for intense, comprehensive treatment is made by the fact that substance abusers also have a higher prevalence of psychiatric problems than nonabusers, and these problems need to be appropriately assessed and treated.

in the general population for the time period being evaluated. Reported rates of smoking in American adults, broken down by diagnosis, were (a) schizophrenia—88%, (b) bipolar disorder—70%, (c) major depression—49%, (d) anxiety disorder—47%, (e) personality disorder—46%, and (f) adjustment disorder—45%. The results from the United States were somewhat similar to those obtained with the French sample of inpatients and outpatients receiving psychiatric services; approximately 58% were smokers, compared to 33% in the general population. By diagnosis, results from the French sample were (a) schizophrenia—66%, (b) anxiety disorder—55%, (c) mood disorder—51%, and (d) personality disorder—50%.

Other reviews of studies from Europe, Australia, and Asia have found similar elevations in smoking rates among psychiatric patients (Ziedonis & Williams, 2003). Some trends across the studies can be described:

1. Overall, the majority of individuals receiving psychiatric treatment smoke.
2. The more severe the psychiatric diagnosis, the more likely the individual is to smoke (el-Guebaly et al., 2002; Ferrell et al., 2003).
3. Psychiatric patients tend to smoke more heavily than nonpsychiatric patients (Resnick, 1993).
4. As a result of heavier smoking, they, like substance-abusing smokers, experience higher morbidity and mortality rates than smokers not experiencing psychiatric problems.

In addition to increased morbidity and mortality, smoking poses special problems for patients receiving psychotropic medications. Smoking affects liver functioning, resulting in an alteration of the effects of psychotropic medications (Resnick, 1993). More specifically, it appears as though the metabolism of tar in cigarettes generates the release of enzymes that increase liver metabolism of many antipsychotic, antidepressant, and anxiolytic drugs (Ziedonis & Williams, 2003). As a result of this biochemical action, smokers require higher doses of medications than nonsmokers. This may become a treatment complication if the smoking rate changes after a medication dose has been established. When smokers are abstinent, for example, blood levels of psychiatric medications may increase, with a result of increased side effects.

Just like substance-abusing smokers, smokers with other psychiatric conditions are an undertreated population. Again, like substance-abusing smokers, the insufficient attention they receive by treatment professionals reflects bias on the part of the professionals as well as the inherent difficulty treating comorbid conditions. Rationales encountered to explain why nicotine dependence treatment has not been appropriately pursued (Resnick, 1993) are described in Exhibit 9.3.

EXHIBIT 9.3
Some Misconceptions About Treatment of Psychiatric Patients for Nicotine Dependence

1. *Psychiatric patients are too fragile and need smoking as a coping aid.* It is true that cessation of smoking will increase stress initially and exacerbate psychiatric symptoms of anxiety and depression, but there are other coping aids that can be used, in the form of both psychiatric medications and pharmacological products used for treatment of nicotine dependence that are available to soften the withdrawal experience and are not as dangerous as continued smoking.
2. *Psychiatric patients are unwilling or unable to benefit from nicotine dependence treatment.* Psychiatric patients do, in fact, express interest in smoking cessation (el-Guebaly et al., 2002) and usually for the same reasons as other smokers (i.e., health concerns) (Resnick, 1993). The same level of success may not be achieved with psychiatric patients compared to the general population of smokers, but they can still benefit from smoking-cessation treatment (el-Guebaly et al., 2002; Ziedonis & Williams, 2003).
3. *Smoking can be a positive activity, shared with staff as a way to overcome barriers to communication.* Comments like this probably reflect a desire of staff to justify their continued smoking with the patients. There are other less destructive, more constructive methods of establishing rapport than to smoke with someone. Perhaps it will come as no surprise that Stubbs, Haw, and Garner (2004) found that smoking status correlated with worker attitudes toward smoking in a psychiatric hospital. As expected, smoking staff members were more permissive of smoking by patients on hospital wards.
4. *With more severely impaired inpatients, cigarettes can actually be used as a reward to help improve behavior and functioning.* For that matter, alcohol and cocaine could also probably be used as rewards, but who would resort to such means? Cigarettes cannot be justified as a reinforcing agent when other reinforcers surely can be used; besides, most facilities are smoke-free, anyway.

Regarding the difficulty treating comorbid psychiatric conditions and smoking, real challenges exist. A chronic psychiatric condition or nicotine dependence alone is tough enough to treat, so both together can only be a taller order. There appears to be a bidirectional relationship between smoking and psychiatric conditions such that cigarette smokers are more likely to develop psychiatric conditions, and individuals with psychiatric conditions are more likely to smoke. This bidirectional relationship has been observed with adolescents and adults alike (Upadhyaya, Deas, Brady, & Kruesi, 2002), and it has been found that the presence of one worsens the course and prognosis of the other. Depression, for example, has been shown to be associated with heavier smoking, more difficulty quitting, and increased risk of aggravation of the depressive condition upon cessation (Patten et al., 2001). It appears that withdrawal symptoms reported by abstinent smokers are related to coexistent psychological symptoms: Individuals high on measures of anxiety, depression, or disordered eating are more likely to experience an exacerbation in those specific symptoms rather than other symptoms of nicotine withdrawal (Pomerleau, Marks, & Pomerleau, 2000).

The co-occurrence of nicotine dependence and psychiatric conditions may be the result of several factors (Ziedonis & Williams, 2003):

1. *Genetic inheritance.*
2. *Psychological factors.* Psychiatric patients often report that smoking cigarettes reduces psychiatric and cognitive symptoms. Subjective reports that anxiety can be quelled, depression relieved, and some improvement in cognitive functioning achieved in anxious individuals, depressives, and schizophrenics, respectively, suggest that smokers use cigarettes to self-medicate psychiatric symptoms (D'Mello & Flanagan, 1996; Johnson et al., 2000; Smith, Singh, Infante, Khandat, & Kloos, 2002). There are some who suggest that schizophrenics may smoke to regulate neurotransmitter receptor sensitivity, thus reducing positive and negative symptoms (Patkar et al., 2002; Procyshyn, Patel, & Thompson, 2004). Interestingly, cigarette smoking is found to be depressogenic and anxiogenic, so after the initial withdrawal period, decreases in depression and anxiety are usually found (Patten et al., 2001; West & Hajek, 1997). As discussed in chapter 1, smokers may only be relieving anxiety or depression created by nicotine (withdrawal) in the first place. Also to be considered, the presence of significant psychiatric symptoms suggests the existence of poor coping skills; smoking may be used as a coping mechanism in those with inadequate coping skills.
3. *Social factors.* Individuals experiencing psychiatric conditions tend to have fewer resources: They are often lacking in family and social support, education, and financial resources (Resnick, 1993). All of these factors may work against an individual already handicapped with poor coping skills, making the giving up of cigarettes an even greater task.

Because of the historical undertreatment of this population of smokers, best treatment practices are yet to be clearly defined. It is interesting to note that smoking bans on inpatient psychiatric units have not resulted in the anticipated exacerbation of symptoms, indicating that even the most impaired psychiatric patients can survive abstinence without major regression in their psychiatric status (Resnick, 1993). Despite the fact that there is still more to learn on the subject, some kernels of knowledge exist to guide treatment interventions (Resnick, 1993; Ziedonis & Williams, 2003), as shown in Exhibit 9.4.

EXHIBIT 9.4
Some Guidelines for the Treatment of Psychiatric Patients for Nicotine Dependence

1. Standard treatment interventions, including the full range of pharmacological interventions, can be used safely and effectively with these patients.
2. Because psychiatric patients are heavier smokers on average, more intense treatment options should be automatically considered (including higher-dose pharmacological interventions).
3. Both conditions must be treated. It would not be appropriate to treat nicotine dependence and ignore a mental health problem, or vice versa. The best timing has not been established (whether one treatment should precede the other or both be conducted simultaneously). As recommended with substance abusers, because readiness to quit is always an important factor in nicotine-dependence treatment, it should be discussed with the patient and determined on an individual basis. It is important to prepare patients for the withdrawal-based symptoms that may present as psychiatric symptoms, help them understand the time-limited nature of these symptoms, and offer assistance in coping with these symptoms through pharmacological interventions or counseling techniques.
4. Treatment is ideally provided by clinicians trained in mental health and nicotine-dependence treatments. The clinician will need to consider the effects of cessation on psychiatric symptoms, medication levels, and side effects and prepare the patient accordingly. For example, patients should be advised to inform the physician prescribing their psychiatric medications of their plans to stop smoking. In addition, the clinician should consider treatment interventions that will address both conditions. For example, expecting an increase in anxiety (due to a positive history) early in nicotine dependence treatment, assist the individual to cope with the anxiety by providing interventions such as relaxation training and stress management and enhanced social support, in addition to pharmacological interventions. The same should be done for an anticipated increase in depression in those individuals with a history of mood symptoms. There is some evidence to suggest that psychotherapeutic interventions focusing on mood management do improve smoking-cessation outcomes in individuals with a history of depression (Hall, Munoz, & Reus, 1994), although later research by the same group indicates that the intensity of contact associated with the mood management interventions may be more important than the specific content of the interventions (Hall et al., 1996), further underscoring the importance of high-intensity treatment for this subpopulation of smokers. Of course, pharmacological interventions also need to be considered for patients with a history of depression. Antidepressants bupropion SR and nortriptyline may be especially helpful to address depression and nicotine dependence.

RACE AND ETHNICITY

There are four major racial or ethnic minority groups in the United States, as identified by the U.S. Department of Health and Human Services (1998): (a) African American, (b) Hispanic, (c) American Indian and Alaska Native, and (d) Asian American and Pacific Islander. Race and ethnicity form an important variable to discuss for treatment of nicotine dependence for a couple of reasons. For one thing, the four groups combine to equal a large population of smokers. Altogether, they made up about 25% of the total U.S. population in 1998 (approximately 60 million people), and this proportion is expected to grow to about half of the total U.S. population by 2050. In addition to the demographic significance of racial and ethnic minorities, there is evidence that race and ethnicity may be related to smoking behaviors and response to treatment.

In the Clinical Practice Guideline (USDHHS, 2000b), it is stated that the interventions promoted in the publication may be effectively applied to all smokers, including members of racial and ethnic minority groups. There is some question as to whether enough empirical evidence has been generated to support this claim (Lawrence, Graber, Mills, Meissner, & Warnecke, 2003). Most of the research on smoking cessation has been done using predominately White, middle-class subjects (Benowitz, 2002), and when research is conducted with minority populations, it is usually with African Americans, to the relative neglect of the three other minority groups (Lawrence et al., 2003). That interventions have been developed and tested with primarily majority-population subjects does not invalidate the results or mean that the successful interventions will not also be efficacious with minority-status smokers; it means only that more direct empirical evidence of this fact may be necessary before reaching firm conclusions.

Prevalence of current adult smoking by racial and/or ethnic group is as follows (USDHHS, 1998):

1. American Indian and Alaska Native—36.0%
2. African American—26.5%
3. White—26.4%
4. Hispanic—18.0%
5. Asian American and Pacific Islander—14.2%

In addition to smoking rates, group differences are observed in terms of smoking behaviors. For example, comparing African American smokers to White smokers, Benowitz (2002) noted that African Americans smoke fewer cigarettes per day; they are more likely to smoke mentholated cigarettes; they have higher rates of lung cancer; they appear to be more heavily addicted; and although they express a similar desire stop and make as many quit attempts as White smokers, they are less successful in their cessation efforts.

The devastating consequences of smoking are indistinguishable between all racial and ethnic groups, with the noted exception that African Americans experience an elevated risk of lung cancer. All racial and ethnic groups experience addiction to nicotine. However, White smokers do evidence higher quit rates than members of all four minority groups (USDHHS, 1998). The differential success in quitting smoking is an important finding. Reasons for the observed differences that have been offered include (Benowitz, 2002; USDHHS, 1998) (a) genetic differences (e.g., African Americans and Whites do appear to metabolize nicotine differently, which may have implications for addiction liability); (b) differences in language and health literacy; (c) the fact that minority smokers are less affluent and live in areas with higher rates of smoking, psychological stress, and substance abuse (i.e., socioeconomic status is inversely related to smoking); (d) the racism with which minority smokers contend, which is a significant source of stress; (e) the distrust of research by government and educational authorities that is common in minority groups; (f) the aggressive cigarette advertising targeted at minority groups; and (g) the lower educational levels of minority smokers, and the inverse relationship between education and smoking.

There are two different levels on which changes need to be made to improve treatment outcomes with minority smokers: removing barriers to treatment and improving access to providers and programs; and providing interventions that are effective once the person presents for treatment. Barriers to treatment include cost, lack of transportation, need for child care, lack of language skills, distrust of researchers and clinicians, and lack of energy from the physical demands of blue-collar jobs. Overcoming barriers is more a matter for social policy makers than for treatment providers, but the effectiveness of interventions is an issue clinicians can more directly address. Racial and ethnic sensitivity is important in guiding the clinician to provide the most effective treatment interventions and messages to a member of a given group (USDHHS, 1998). One obvious method is to provide material and services in the language of the patient. In addition, Hispanic patients are known to be most responsive to ideas that involve protection of the family (e.g., underscoring the point that smoking places children at risk to smoke and harms their health with secondhand smoke). African Americans respond to the use of prayer at cessation meetings, American Indians are reportedly not responsive to direct confrontation, and Chinese Americans are responsive to the use of martial arts as a behavioral alternative to smoking.

Self-help materials have been prepared that target different racial and ethnic groups and appear to be well received (see USDHHS, 1998, for titles and descriptions of materials for Hispanic, African American, Vietnamese, Chinese, and American Indian smokers). The self-help materials include pictures of members of the specific minority group addressed with messages determined by research to be most important for that group, and written in the appropriate language.

Interventions proven effective with the majority population may or may not be as effective with members of different racial and ethnic groups. This is still an open question to be answered empirically. However, practically speaking, those methods that are effective with majority-status smokers remain the best place to start when treating members of racial and ethnic minorities. Although there is a need for more research, standard counseling and pharmacological interventions have been found effective with minority populations, and there is no consistent evidence that modified programs result in improved outcomes. Exercising racial and ethnic sensitivity in applying services is really a specific example of a general practice already strongly recommended in treatment: to make interventions personally relevant to the patient.

Much research is still necessary to generate specific recommendations for each racial or ethnic group. Clinicians are well advised to keep in mind that there is significant diversity within groups, so broad generalizations may not even apply for a given minority population. In general it may be stated that to maximize clinical effectiveness it behooves the clinician to provide treatment and supportive materials in the appropriate language at the appropriate reading level, and to increase acceptance of treatment through awareness of the culture and psychosocial correlates of smoking attendant on minority status, such as increased stress and decreased coping resources. Clinicians providing services to an ethnically diverse population or a population with a high percentage of individuals from a specific minority group need to be aware of whom they are serving and to educate themselves accordingly to best serve their patients. For example, if I have an office in an area with a large Hispanic population, it is critical that I learn about the culture and obtain support materials that will be most relevant and appealing to my patients.

GENDER

Gender has been investigated as a variable that may indicate the need to modify treatment. Just as most smoking-cessation studies have been done with majority-status smokers, most of these studies have also been conducted with men; thus it remains to be demonstrated that the results apply to women as well.

Overall in the United States, women are less likely to be smokers than are men (Royce et al., 1997). For example, in 1998 prevalence was estimated at about 26% for men and 22% for women (USDHHS, 2001). The gender gap is much smaller now than it used to be; historically, women started using cigarettes later than men but have all but caught up. In 1965, men smoked at a much greater rate than women (approximately 52% for men to 34% for women). Elevated prevalence of smoking for men relative to women is found across all racial and ethnic groups except American Indians (USDHHS, 1998). Women carry the same risk of adverse medical consequences as men, as well as additional ones owing to anatomical differences: cervical cancer, early menopause, osteoporosis, reduced fertility, increased rate of spontaneous abortions, premature births, and low-birth-weight infants (King, Borrelli, Black, Pinto, & Marcus, 1997). By 1987, lung cancer had supplanted breast cancer as the leading cause of cancer death in women, a trend that continues to the present time (USDHHS, 2001). For women, as for men, socioeconomic status and education level are inversely related to smoking.

Early results evaluating response to treatment were mixed (USDHHS, 2001), but more recent research suggests that women are not as successful as men at stopping smoking (discussed in Wetter, Kenford, et al., 1999). For example, two national surveys have shown that the percentage of former smokers is higher for men (about 50% and 48% in the two studies) than for women (approximately 46% and 42% in the same two studies) (USDHHS, 2001). The superior cessation results for men do not appear to be due to less desire or fewer attempts by women to stop or to reflect different motivations for wanting to stop, all of which are about the same for both groups; it is rather a reflection of an overall poorer performance in cessation attempts by women. Particularly with nicotine replacement therapy (NRT), women have been less successful than men at achieving and maintaining abstinence (Swan, Jack, & Ward, 1997; Wetter, Kenford, et al., 1999). With NRT, women tend to relapse more quickly and at higher rates than men, a difference found across various follow-up points (i.e., early and late postcessation).

Many possible explanations have been entertained in an attempt to account for the observed differences in treatment outcomes (Royce et al., 1997): Women show less confidence in their ability to quit; they are different from men with respect to smoking behavior and withdrawal response; women rely more on smoking as a coping aid; women experience a higher prevalence of anxiety and depressive disorders; they do not persist in quit attempts to the same degree as men; and they experience and cope with stress differently than men do. One idea receiving particular attention and support in the literature suggests that gender differences in quitting reflect the fact that NRT is more effective in suppressing withdrawal symptoms in men, and that the effects of nicotine are inherently more rewarding for men than women (i.e., the non-nicotine aspects of smoking play a greater role for women than for men; discussed in Wetter, Fiore, et al., 1999). In support of this hypothesis, Wetter, Fiore, et al. (1999) found that on an objective measure of a withdrawal symptom (sleep disturbance), men received greater benefit from NRT than women did (i.e., the NRT reversed sleep disturbance caused by withdrawal more effectively for men than for women).

In the absence of abundant evidence to suggest that treatment should be altered for women, standard treatment recommendations apply. The data showing that women tend to be less successful than men with NRT are not so strong as to support a recommendation that NRT not be attempted with women. The full complement of counseling interventions should always be considered in the treatment planning process for anyone, and these interventions are available to address the non-nicotine aspects of smoking that may be more important to women. Motivation to stop smoking and success at stopping are greatest during pregnancy. This is a particularly opportune time to intervene, and intervention has positive consequences for mother and developing fetus alike. An intensive counseling program is recommended due to the potential consequences of not stopping during pregnancy.

Owing to concerns about negative side effects to mother and fetus resulting from pharmacotherapy, it should only be used after intensive counseling has failed and under the close supervision of a physician.

SUMMARY

In this chapter the question is addressed as to whether or not the standard treatment interventions for nicotine dependence apply to special populations of smokers, including smokers with a positive psychiatric history, racial and ethnic minorities, and women. The question still awaits empirical research before a definitive answer can be provided for each subpopulation of smokers, but generally speaking, the standard treatment interventions do apply. Smoking levels are disproportionately high for individuals with psychiatric and substance abuse histories. Both populations are undertreated, partially owing to misconceptions by treatment providers. Traditional psychiatric patients and substance abusers desire nicotine dependence treatment and can benefit from it. Treatment of nicotine dependence does not appear to adversely affect treatment for either substance abuse or psychiatric conditions. The standard treatment interventions for nicotine dependence apply with the following special considerations: Patients with psychiatric and substance abuse histories require intensive treatment options; both the nicotine dependence and the psychiatric or substance abuse problems should be treated, although exact timing must be worked out sensitively with the patient, with full understanding of the possible exacerbation of psychiatric symptoms due to withdrawal effects, as well as complications of psychiatric medications.

The four major racial and ethnic minority groups in the United States make up a large and growing population. Meta-analytic research suggests that smoking-cessation interventions developed and applied to mostly majority-group smokers are efficacious across all groups. Common sense is supported by other research indicating that interventions and treatment materials that are culturally sensitive will improve patient acceptance of treatment.

Although women are, and have historically been, less likely to be smokers than men, the gap has been closing considerably. There is some research to suggest that men are more successful at smoking cessation than women. In particular, men may receive more benefit from NRT due to more effective suppression of withdrawal symptoms. Some have suggested that women are more concerned about weight gain and that they are more influenced by non-nicotine aspects of smoking than are men. All things considered, it is still recommended that all standard treatment interventions be considered in the treatment of women for nicotine dependence.

10

ADOLESCENT SMOKING

The goal of this chapter is to identify and understand the special treatment needs of adolescent smokers. Differences between and commonalities of adolescent and adult smokers are reviewed with a focus on factors that translate into the alteration of traditional treatment practices for adolescent smokers.

Adolescent smokers may be the single most important subpopulation of them all. As all adults were adolescents at one time, this is the well from which all smokers spring. In the United States, almost all initial use of cigarettes occurs before high school graduation, and approximately two thirds of American adolescents have tried smoking by age 18 (Rohde, Lewinsohn, Brown, Gau, & Kahler, 2003; USDHHS, 1994). Because the health consequences of smoking are largely a function of the duration and amount of smoking, it is obvious why adolescent smoking is of serious concern. The earlier smoking is initiated, the heavier the ensuing smoking behavior, and the more difficulty there is in quitting. Adolescence is the time when the addiction to nicotine is usually established, but the major health consequences are not experienced until much later; this combination of far-off consequences and currently developing dependence makes it particularly difficult to motivate adolescents to stop using once they have tried smoking.

Prevention of smoking is an extremely important pursuit. Preventing use altogether, or even delaying onset of smoking, can result in a significant reduction in negative health outcomes. Unfortunately, despite our efforts at prevention, many adolescents are still currently smoking, and there are new initiates every day. For example, it is estimated that in the United States between 2,000 and 6,000 adolescents per day try cigarettes for the first time (Colby, Tiffany, Shiffman, & Niaura, 2000a; Vickers, Thomas, Patten, & Mrazek, 2002). After years of decline, in the 1990s adolescent smoking rose substantially in the United States and worldwide (Shadel, Shiffman, Niaura, Nichter, & Abrams, 2000). Depending on the survey and year conducted, between one fourth and one third of U.S. students are current smokers by high school graduation, and the prevalence is as high as 7 out of 10 for school dropouts (Moolchan, Ernst, & Henningfield, 2000; Prokhorov et al., 2001). Until prevention can be more effective, there is still a large need for treatment of adolescent smokers. Important as prevention of smoking is, it is a topic beyond the scope of this book. Readers interested in prevention of adolescent smoking are referred elsewhere (e.g., USDHHS, 1994).

Because smoking starts in adolescence and is common by the end of high school, and early onset is associated with heavier use and more difficulty quitting, adolescence is a good time to intervene (Rohde et al., 2003). It may take up to 2 years from time of initiation to become a regular smoker, so there is ample opportunity to intervene. However, if their smoking is not interrupted, a large majority (approximately 75%) of adolescent daily smokers will continue to smoke well into adulthood (Colby et al., 2000a). Owing to obvious physical and developmental differences between adolescents and adults, the following questions are suggested for consideration with respect to adolescent smoking:

1. Are adolescents' smoking behaviors and patterns the same as adults?
2. Do adolescents develop addiction to nicotine and, if so, in the same way as adults?
3. Are there different motivating factors with respect to quitting?
4. Are the same interventions that are effective with adults effective with adolescents?

Regarding smoking behavior and patterns, adolescents are known to have much more variable smoking habits than adults (Colby et al., 2000a). Adolescents are in the process of developing dependence; adults have been dependent for some time. Adult smoking behaviors are, therefore, more routinized. External factors (i.e., smoking restrictions) exert a more significant influence on the smoking behavior of adolescents; they are not as free as adults to smoke. In addition to legal restrictions, and disapproval by authorities (e.g., parents, school personnel), social factors play a more important role early in the development of nicotine dependence than they do later. So adolescents may smoke many cigarettes all weekend when in the company of friends but not smoke all week, for example; or, they may smoke frequently during summer vacation when they are in the presence of other smoking peers and less visible to authorities. Restricted access to smoking is an important factor to consider in the assessment process because it may lead to an underestimation of nicotine dependence in adolescents (Colby et al., 2000b). For example, time to first cigarette and number of cigarettes smoked per day are two commonly used indicators of nicotine dependence (from the Fagerstrom Tolerance Questionnaire; Fagerstrom, 1978). Many adolescents are not free to smoke on awakening even if they want to; nor are they usually free to smoke other times during the day, so it is likely the case that if they had unlimited freedom to smoke they would consume more cigarettes per day and smoke sooner after awakening in the morning. I have had more than a few parents of adolescents earnestly challenge the suggestion that their child is nicotine dependent because he or she was not smoking daily, or consistently smoking a high number of cigarettes, as an adult would. What the parents of adolescents may fail to realize is that until adolescent smokers get to the advanced stage of daily smoking, they do not present as adult smokers; and, if the early smoking is not stopped, dependence can develop that will very likely progress to adultlike dependence.

A review of studies assessing nicotine dependence in adolescents (Colby et al., 2000a) found that adolescents report symptoms consistent with criteria in the *Diagnostic and Statistical Manual of Mental Disorders* (4th ed.; *DSM–IV*; American Psychiatric Association, 1994) and the Fagerstrom Tolerance Questionnaire. Signs of nicotine dependence are evident with adolescents well before daily smoking (DiFranza et al., 2002). Adolescents engaging in monthly smoking have been found to be positive for one or more symptoms of nicotine dependence (Backinger & Leischow, 2001); one fifth of adolescents report symptoms of nicotine dependence within 4 weeks of initiating at least monthly smoking.

So even though adolescents early in their smoking histories do not usually smoke daily, they definitely develop dependence on nicotine, which manifests in the same way as it does with adults. With adults, dependence is evidenced by several symptoms but is generally characterized by loss of control and compulsive use, that is, a desire to cut down or stop but an inability to do so. Interestingly, only a small percentage of adolescent (daily) smokers expect to be smoking by 5 years post–high school graduation, when in actuality three fourths will still be smoking (Colby et al., 2000a). The majority of adolescent smokers express a desire to stop and have made at least one unsuccessful cessation attempt (Klesges, Johnson, Somes, Zbikowski, & Robinson, 2003; USDHHS, 1994). In addition to difficulty quitting, adolescents experience withdrawal symptoms. Most adolescent smokers report at least one withdrawal symptom subsequent to a reduction in smoking or a quit attempt, and about 1 in 3 report three or more symptoms (Colby et al., 2000a). Withdrawal symptoms are often cited as impediments to smoking-cessation efforts. The withdrawal symptoms reported by adolescent smokers are more likely to be experienced by daily smokers than occasional smokers, as expected. Overall, then, adolescents are less likely to engage in daily smoking, they smoke with less regularity, and they smoke fewer cigarettes per day than adults. Nonetheless, adolescents do develop dependence on nicotine in the same ways as adults do, and the commonalities in the manifestation of nicotine dependence become more evident as smoking continues for the adolescent.

Adolescent smokers are also like adult smokers in terms of the high prevalence of comorbid problems. As seen with adults who smoke (see chap. 9), adolescent smokers are observed to experience higher rates of psychiatric problems, including traditional psychiatric disorders and substance use disorders (USDHHS, 1994); presence of conduct disorder and impulsivity are strong predictors of adolescent smoking.

Motivations for quitting smoking are similar for adolescents and adults, although there are some notable differences. For adults, the most commonly reported reason for quitting is concern for health. Concern about the negative impact of smoking on health is a primary motivating force for adolescents to quit as well (Moolchan et al., 2000; Riedel, Robinson, Klesges, & McLain-Allen, 2002b). Reasons for quitting reported by adolescents are presented in Exhibit 10.1.

Compared to adult smokers, adolescents tend to do more poorly in smoking cessation (Horn, Fernandes, Dino, Massey, & Kalsekar, 2003; Lawrence, 2001; Moolchan et al., 2000; Patten et al., 2001; Riedel et al., 2000a). A multitude of reasons has been proposed to account for the unsatisfactory results with adolescent smokers. Adolescents are greater risk takers than

---

EXHIBIT 10.1
Motives to Stop Smoking Reported by Adolescents

1. *Health.*
2. *Cost of smoking.* Not having independent means of income, many adolescents find paying for cigarettes a challenge. This is perhaps why taxing of cigarettes, which drives up cost, effectively reduces adolescent smoking.
3. *Peer pressure.* At a time in normal development when the opinions and behavior of peers are highly valued, having friends and associates who do not smoke and do not approve of smoking can be a strong motive to not smoke.
4. *Smoking behavior and attitudes of parents toward smoking.* Because adolescents are still dependent on parents, parental nonsmoking behavior and attitudes of disapproval toward smoking can be deterrent factors to adolescent smoking.
5. *Appearance.* For adolescents, being of dating age and with a heightened interest in appearance, effects of smoking on physical appearance and appearance-related disapproval from a boyfriend or girlfriend can be reasons to stop smoking.
6. *Athletic performance.* Adolescents are generally more physically active than adults; the negative impact of smoking on conditioning and athletic performance has been cited as a reason to stop smoking.

---

adults, which may reflect developmental differences (incomplete development of the frontal lobes and executive function), and they have experienced relatively minor negative consequences from smoking, so there is less to dissuade them from risking addiction and all that it entails. Also, in many cases treatment for adolescents is initiated by parents or school authorities. With any condition, the best situation is one in which the person in question is a willing participant in the treatment. Therefore, treatment of adolescents is often undertaken in less than ideal circumstances.

Adolescents are found to use poor cessation techniques. First of all, they prefer no-help or self-help methods of cessation. No-help methods include such things as having a pact with friends to quit or agreeing to a no-smoking contract with someone. Successful self-initiated smoking-cessation rates are estimated at between 0% and 11%, very low success rates on average. Adolescents are notoriously difficult to recruit and maintain in formal treatment programs. When formal techniques are used, adolescents tend not to use ones traditionally recommended, such as stimulus control or relapse prevention. When adolescents do complete treatment programs, they tend to do better in terms of achievement of abstinence than self-quitters.

One of the main options available to adults, nicotine replacement therapy (NRT), is a controversial intervention for adolescents. The safety, efficacy, and tolerability of NRT (as well as other forms of pharmacotherapy) are not as well established for adolescents as for adults (McNeill, Foulds, & Bates, 2001; Moolchan et al., 2000; Sargent, Mott, & Stevens, 1998). In fact, the manufacturers of NRT products recommend a cutoff age for use of 18 years old. Because of the more variable smoking patterns of adolescents, a legitimate question is raised about introducing nicotine on a daily basis with NRT. For example, an adolescent who smokes a pack of cigarettes per day over the weekend but does not smoke much if at all during the week would be receiving significantly more nicotine on NRT during the week than he or she receives from smoking. Although such an individual would require treatment, NRT would not be appropriate. Adolescent smokers who have more advanced dependencies with daily smoking, more like the typical adult, would be appropriate for NRT. The point has been made that, measured against the alternative of allowing continued smoking, NRT is a safe option. Why shouldn't adolescents be able to receive the most effective methods of treatment available? Some researchers have recommended that the cutoff age to use NRT be lowered to 12 years old (McNeill et al., 2001). Studies that have been conducted with adolescents using NRT (specifically, nicotine patch) have found the treatment to be safe and well tolerated but not very effective (Hurt et al., 2000; Smith et al., 1996). With adolescents it is especially important to have the family consult with a physician before undertaking any pharmacological interventions.

It is thought that part of the observed resistance to formal smoking-cessation treatment is due to having to inform parents and other adults of the smoking behavior. School-based smoking-cessation programs may circumvent the disclosure issue because parents are already informed when the child is caught smoking at school (Riedel et al., 2002a). Schools often do two things that support smoking-cessation efforts: They punish smoking behavior at school through disciplinary procedures, and they are smoke free. The provision of a smoke-free environment is very important, as it protects everyone from secondhand smoke, disallows modeling of smoking behavior, and adds to the perception of nonsmoking behavior as the norm. Smoking at school should be viewed as something more than a rules infraction. Studies find that the majority of students caught smoking at school are nicotine dependent. One longitudinal study found that nicotine dependence usually develops first, before smoking at school (Soteriades, DiFranza, Savageau, & Nicolaou, 2003). In other words, the behavior of smoking at school is driven by nicotine dependence and an inability to resist the temptation to smoke. Therefore, students caught smoking at school, in addition to being seen as rule violators, should also be viewed as nicotine dependent and referred to treatment. The situation with smoking at school is directly analogous to laws prohibiting the operation of a motor vehicle while under the influence of a psychoactive substance. To dissuade the behavior, stiff penalties are applied to violators. However, it is also recognized that a high percentage of the violators are symptomatic for a substance use disorder; in addition to being punished for the behavior of driving under the influence, they are referred for treatment. Treatment for substance abuse will not only help the individual to not drive under the influence in the future but also properly address the problem that underlies the punishable behavior.

TREATMENT CONSIDERATIONS

As seen with other subpopulations of smokers (see chap. 9), direct empirical support for the use of interventions found to be efficacious with the majority population (i.e., White, male adults) still need to be compiled for adolescent smokers. Until the time when the evidence suggests otherwise, the interventions recommended for adults remain the best place to start (see chap. 6 and 7 of this book for discussion of efficacious treatment interventions). One significant component of smoking-cessation treatment for adults, NRT, raises particular concerns with adolescents (see discussion of NRT earlier in this chapter).

Results from the "Truth" campaign discussed in chapter 2 indicate that adolescent motivation to stop smoking can be elevated through education. Raising awareness about the targeting of youths, the self-serving motivations of tobacco companies, and their disregard for the health of smokers results in increasing negative attitudes toward smoking and a reduction in smoking behavior (Farrelly et al., 2002; Zucker et al., 2000).

As with adults, adolescents who are more nicotine dependent have more difficulty stopping. Adolescents are not adults, however, and because they are at an earlier developmental phase in life, certain differences can be expected. For example, adolescents are still dependents and have relatively little control over some aspects of their environment; siblings or parents who smoke (or parents who do not disapprove of their smoking for other reasons) pose a significant obstacle to their being abstinent. Adolescents also tend to be particularly sensitive to social pressures and the behavior and attitudes of peers. Having peers who smoke is a major obstacle to abstinence. Adolescence is also a time of well-known stress and anxiety, so the provision of emotional support for a quit attempt is particularly critical for smokers in this stage of life. A barrier to treatment for adolescents not encountered by adults is that smoking is illegal and disapproved of for them. Adolescents can be in a bind about whether to seek help for fear of sanction because they are admitting to the use of cigarettes.

A key to successful treatment of adolescents, as with any other group member or individual, is to focus on areas already important to them to maximize their motivation to remain with treatment and to stop smoking (Riedel et al., 2002a). The assessment phase is crucial, as always, in helping to make treatment interventions relevant for a given individual. Because of the high prevalence of psychiatric comorbidity and the stress of adolescence, the possible presence of psychiatric symptoms needs to be evaluated; if symptoms exist they should be directly addressed as a part of the smoking-cessation treatment. The factors motivating each individual for a quit attempt should be identified so that the treatment may be personalized. We know that some concerns are common for most adolescents (health, cost, etc.), but it is important to find out what specific concerns exist for each individual. I always ask an individual expressing a desire to stop smoking to tell me how he or she came to the decision and also to provide a list of the pros and cons of smoking; through these means the most personally relevant motives for seeking smoking cessation can be identified. Once identified, they become useful to refer to for maintaining interest in treatment and abstinence. In traditional substance abuse treatment, reminding recovering addicts of the negative consequences of their addiction, referred to as "keeping it green," is a standard method of motivating them to maintain their commitment to abstinence.

Involving parents in treatment is very important with adolescents. Parents can assist in the treatment process by learning the value of their disapproval of smoking and how best to express this disapproval. They need to be explicitly supportive of smoking abstinence, and explicitly disapproving of smoking. Generally speaking, parents should not be put in the position of treatment professionals for their children. More appropriately, they need to bring the child to treatment, and they can be the "eyes" and "ears" of the treatment to report observations to the treating professional that suggest compliance or noncompliance. Parents who smoke often report discomfort with challenging their child's smoking because they feel hypocritical. I recommend to these parents that they present the situation in the same way they would the use of alcohol (about which they tend to be less ambivalent). Alcohol is legal to consume for individuals of the proper age. Likewise, tobacco products can be legally purchased by anyone at least 18 years of age. Until that time, adolescents are not free to make their own decisions about use of cigarettes any more than they should be to make decisions regarding alcohol.

There is a potential risk in actively including parents in treatment: Adolescents may feel inhibited about disclosing sensitive, private material to the clinician, wondering if the clinician is working to help them or their parents. Sound judgment and great care must be exercised by the clinician in balancing the adolescent's need for privacy and the parent's right to know. I find it necessary to be very explicit about my role from the first contact. I usually recommend privacy concerning what is talked about by me and the adolescent, with three exceptions: danger of harm to the adolescent (and I make it clear that I consider any use of psychoactive substances, including nicotine, dangerous); danger to someone else; and anything that the adolescent and I agree to share with his or her parents.

Social and emotional support for abstinence is helpful for adolescents and adults alike. However, because of the central role social activity assumes for the adolescent, it is especially important for the treatment provider to be sensitive to these matters. The direct provision of support in the form of individual or group counseling is highly advised. In addition, evaluation of the adolescent's social environment is necessary. If adolescents have many smoking friends, or key people in their lives are smokers (e.g., best friend, boyfriend, or girlfriend), this is a major problem for them. In traditional substance abuse treatment, abusers in recovery are advised to avoid people, places, and things that are associated with their former substance use. I recommend to parents that the adolescent do the same with smoking. This is often where their commitment to their child's abstinence from cigarettes can really be tested. More than once the recommendation has been perceived as unduly extreme, as if to say that forcing a separation from certain friends is not called for over something as insignificant as smoking. However, the parents will admit that if drug use involving marijuana, alcohol, or cocaine were taking place with the same associates and their child, they would feel comfortable intervening. Parents in this position may benefit from education about the long-term outcomes of cigarette smoking (including risk of abuse of other substances). In situations in which the parents do not accept the recommendation to separate their child from peers who smoke, I advise they allow only supervised contact. For example, while in school contact may be allowed because it is a smoke-free environment and there are responsible adults present; the same is true of most formal extracurricular activities. Regarding informal, leisure activities, contact with known smoking associates should take place only when chaperoned. This is a cumbersome and inconvenient setup, but one that is well worth it in the long run.

SUMMARY

Adolescents develop nicotine dependence that manifests in symptoms much the same way as with adults; adolescents may smoke as infrequently as monthly and still develop symptoms of nicotine dependence. Consistent with the development of nicotine dependence, adolescents experience withdrawal symptoms that serve as an impediment to cessation efforts. Adolescents share with adults concern about their health as a motive to quit smoking but cite other motives more characteristic of their stage of life, including cost, peer influences, attitude and behavior of parents regarding smoking, appearance, and athletic performance. Adolescents are difficult to recruit and engage in nicotine dependence treatment, partially because they are often compelled to treatment by others. On their own, adolescents usually use poor cessation techniques. In treatment there is provider reluctance to use pharmacological interventions, especially with younger adolescents. The current recommendation for pharmacological interventions is to use them only for adolescents 18 years of age and up. It has been proposed by some that NRT be considered with a cutoff age of 12 years old rather than the current 18 years, as the alternative is to allow nicotine intake via cigarettes. Standard treatment interventions apply to adolescents, although as with other subpopulations, some sensitivity to their special status needs to be exercised; for example, the social issues of the younger adolescent and significant stressors attendant to later adolescence need to be addressed to assure relevance of the treatment. Parental involvement in the treatment of adolescents is recommended.

APPENDIX:
BASIC OUTLINE OF
A TREATMENT PLAN

Out of respect for the complexity of treatment, and the competence and autonomy of clinicians, I am reluctant even to attempt to outline a detailed, cookbook-style treatment plan. At the same time, I am aware that having some structure (to adhere to or deviate from as seen fit by the clinician) may be useful. Therefore, I provide below a basic, schematic treatment plan to assist the clinician in applying the information presented throughout the present book. All of the assessment and treatment techniques and tools mentioned here are discussed earlier in the book.

ASSESSMENT
(CONDUCTED OVER TWO SESSIONS)

- Full psychosocial history via clinical interview using diagnostic criteria. Make referrals for substance abuse or psychiatric services if necessary.
- Nicotine assessment.

Screening. Screening for nicotine use can be achieved with a very brief clinical interview or biological testing (less commonly used, except for research).

Diagnosis. A diagnosis of nicotine dependence can be established by using the *Diagnostic and Statistical Manual of Mental Disorders* (4th ed.; *DSM–IV*; American Psychiatric Association, 1994) and gathering the information via interview or with a psychometric tool (Structured Clinical Interview for *DSM–III–R*, Composite International Diagnostic Interview, or the Diagnostic Interview Schedule). Degree of nicotine dependence can be assessed with the Fagerstrom Tolerance Questionnaire or other versions of the FTQ. Also, assessment of withdrawal is relevant to diagnosis and treatment planning. Criteria from the *DSM–IV* can be used for this purpose, as can psychometric measures (the Minnesota Nicotine Withdrawal Scale or the Wisconsin Smoking Withdrawal Scale).

Triage. Treatment intensity can be determined through information already obtained, including degree of nicotine dependence, psychiatric history, family and social environment, prior treatment, and quit history. Smokers who are more severely nicotine dependent, positive for a psychiatric or substance use disorder, or have an unsupportive environment should be directed to intensive treatment. Smokers with no quit history, or a quit history with some success (i.e., at least one quit attempt of a year's duration and a quit attempt in the last year lasting at least 1–2 weeks), may be appropriate for less intensive treatment in the absence of the other factors.

Treatment planning. For treatment planning purposes, it is advised to assess the stage of change and cognitive processes (such as outcome expectancy and values) in addition to information already gathered. Stage of change can be assessed clinically or with psychometric tools such as the University of Rhode Island Change Assessment scale (McConnaughy, Prochaska, & Velicer, 1983). Outcome expectancy can be measured via interview or with the Smoking Consequences Questionnaire (Brandon & Baker, 1991). It is also recommended to have the patient begin to keep a record of smoking behavior.

The assessment process should determine the individual's motivation for treatment, the presence of comborbid symptoms or disorders, degree of nicotine dependence, nicotine dependence treatment history, and degree of support in the social and family environment. If the individual is nicotine dependent but not yet ready to discuss treatment, then interventions are applied in an attempt to instigate further movement toward readiness for behavior change. If the clinician is practicing in a setting where he or she is providing service to the smoker for reasons other than smoking cessation, this is easier to do. For example, I provide services in an independent practice setting. I rarely have people referred solely for smoking cessation; they are referred for other reasons, and nicotine dependence may also be identified as a problem to be addressed in treatment. Even if the patient is not interested in nicotine-dependence treatment, there is still ongoing contact for the main referral problem, so there are future opportunities to address the nicotine dependence. If the clinician works in a setting specializing in smoking cessation, then an attempt should be made to schedule at least one follow-up appointment to reassess the patient and reapply motivation-enhancing interventions. For individuals interested in smoking-cessation treatment who do not require intensive treatment, low-intensity treatment options are discussed (please refer to chap. 6 for discussion of low-intensity alternatives). For individuals requiring and willing to undergo intensive treatment, the following treatment schedule is recommended. Exercises specified by session may be done in session if time allows. If sessions are relatively brief owing to time limitations, the exercises may be completed as homework and reviewed in session. The eight sessions are not necessarily conducted on consecutive weeks for the entire treatment period. The treatment schedule is worked out with the patient. I usually prefer that sessions be held on the quit date and for the 2 weeks following the quit date due to the importance of the first 2 weeks postcessation. Any additional sessions beyond this point may be spread out to provide longer coverage in treatment.

TREATMENT
(EIGHT SESSIONS ARE RECOMMENDED)

Session 1

- Identify the negative consequences of smoking. Use of the "What Smoking Does to Me" form is recommended.
- Discuss what the smoker likes about smoking. The "Smoking Consequences Questionnaire" may be used or the "What I Like About Smoking" form.
- Discuss the benefits of smoking cessation.
- Discuss the social support contract. The "Support Agreement" form may be used.
- Review values clarification and norm-setting. The "Personal Values" form may be used for the purpose of values clarification.
- Establish the quit date and quit method. If non–nicotine replacement pharmacotherapy is to be used, it should be started; if nicotine replacement therapy is used, it should start on the quit date. Also, if nicotine fading is decided on as a quit method, it should start now. The "cold turkey" stopping method is started on the quit date.
- Have the smoker sign the pledge.

Session 2

- Complete stimulus control education and exercises. The "Reducing Temptation" form may be used.
- Develop the reward contract. Rewards for abstinence are recommended at key points: quit date, each of first 2 weeks post-cessation, and any other points agreed on.
- Assist in preparing the letter to the patient's physician (or in finding a physician, if necessary).
- Review the smoking record

Session 3

- Educate the patient about pharmacology, withdrawal, and addiction to nicotine. The "Nicotine Addiction" form may be used.

Session 4

- Complete the relapse prevention/coping strategies exercises. The "Managing Temptation and Relapse" form is used for this purpose. The "Coping With Temptations Inventory" may also be used.

Session 5

- Quit date.
- Review withdrawal education material.
- Start nicotine replacement therapy (if applicable).
- Review reward contract.

Session 6

- Review relapse prevention/coping strategies exercises.
- Review reward contract
- Provide support.

Session 7

- Review relapse prevention/coping strategies exercises.
- Review reward contract.
- Provide support.

Session 8

- Review relapse prevention/coping strategies exercises.
- Review reward contract.
- Provide support.

REFERENCES

Abbot, N. C., Stead, L. F., White, A. R., Barnes, J., & Ernst, E. (2001). Hypnotherapy for smoking cessation (Cochrane Review). In *The Cochrane Library* (Issue 1). Chichester, England: Wiley.

Abrams, D. B., Niaura, R., Brown, R. A., Emmons, K. M., Goldstein, M. G., & Monti, P. M. (2003). *The tobacco dependence treatment handbook: A guide to best practices*. New York: Guilford Press.

Abramson, D. J. (2001). Treatment efficacy and clinical utility: A guidelines model applied to psychotherapy research. *Clinical Psychology: Science and Practice*, 8(2), 176–179.

Acker, C. J. (1993). Stigma or legitimation? A historical examination of the social potentials of addiction disease models. *Journal of Psychoactive Drugs*, 25(3), 193–205.

Alcoholics Anonymous. (1952). *Twelve steps and twelve traditions*. New York: Alcoholics Anonymous World Services.

Al-Delaimy, W. K., Cho, E., Chen, W. Y., Colditz, G., & Willet, W. C. (2004). A prospective study of smoking and risk of breast cancer in young adult women. *Cancer, Epidemiology, Biomarkers & Prevention*, 13, 398–404.

Al-Delaimy, W. K., Crane, J., & Woodward, A. (2000). Questionnaire and hair measurement of exposure to tobacco smoke. *Journal of Exposure Analysis and Environmental Epidemiology*, 10, 378–384.

Allen, J. P., & Mattson, M. E. (1993). Psychometric instruments to assist in alcoholism treatment planning. *Journal of Substance Abuse Treatment*, 10, 289–296.

Allison, K. R., Adlaf, E. M., & Mates, D. (1997). Life strain, coping, and substance abuse among high school students. *Addiction Research*, 5, 251–273.

Altman, G. A., Levine, D. W., Howard, G., & Hamilton, H. (1997). Tobacco farming and public health: Attitudes of the general public and farmers. *Journal of Social Issues*, 53(1), 113–128.

American Cancer Society. (1982). *The fifty most often asked questions about smoking and health and the answers*. Atlanta, GA: American Cancer Society.

American Cancer Society. (2000). *Cancer facts and figures*. Atlanta, GA: Author.

American Lung Association. (1984). *Freedom from smoking in 20 days*. Washington, DC: Author.

American Lung Association. (1986). *A lifetime of freedom from smoking: A maintenance program for ex-smokers*. New York: Author.

American Medical Association. (1994). *American Medical Association guidelines for the diagnosis and treatment of nicotine dependence: How to help patients stop smoking*. Washington, DC: Author.

American Psychiatric Association. (1987). *Diagnostic and statistical manual of mental disorders* (3rd ed., rev.). Washington, DC: Author.

American Psychiatric Association. (1994). *Diagnostic and statistical manual of mental disorders* (4th ed.). Washington, DC: Author.

American Psychiatric Association. (1996). Practice guideline for treatment of patients with nicotine dependence. *American Journal of Psychiatry, 153*(10), S1–S31.

Anton, R. F., & Drobes, D. J. (1998). Clinical measurement of craving in addiction. *Psychiatric Annals, 28,* 553–560.

Arnett, J. J. (1999). Adolescent storm and stress, reconsidered. *American Psychologist, 54,* 317–326.

Ashmead, G. G. (2003). Review: Smoking and pregnancy. *Journal of Maternal-Fetal & Neonatal Medicine, 14,* 297–304.

Ayanian, J. Z., & Cleary, P. D. (1999). Perceived risks of heart disease and cancer among cigarette smokers. *Journal of the American Medical Association, 281,* 1019–1021.

Backinger, C. L., & Leischow, S. J. (2001). Advancing the science of adolescent tobacco use cessation. *American Journal of Health Behavior, 25,* 183–190.

Balfour, J. K., & Ridley, D. L. (2000). The effects of nicotine on neural pathways implicated in depression: A factor in nicotine addiction? *Pharmacology Biochemistry and Behavior, 66*(1), 79–85.

Bandura, A. (1997). *Self-efficacy: The exercise of control.* New York: Freeman.

Becona, E., & Garcia, M. P. (1993). Nicotine fading and smokeholding methods to smoking cessation. *Psychological Reports, 73,* 779–786.

Becona, E., & Garcia, M. P. (1995). Relation between the Tolerance Questionnaire (nicotine dependence) and assessment of carbon monoxide in smokers who participated in treatment for smoking. *Psychological Reports, 77,* 1299–1304.

Bell, A., & Rollnick, S. (1996). Motivational interviewing in practice: A structured approach. In F. Rotgers, D. S. Keller, & J. Morgenstern (Eds.), *Treating substance abuse: Theory and technique* (pp. 266–285). New York: Guilford Press.

Bell, C. M., & Khantzian, E. J. (1991). Contemporary psychodynamic perspectives and the disease concept of addiction: Complementary or competing models? *Psychiatric Annals, 21,* 273–281.

Benowitz, N. L. (1996). Pharmacology of nicotine: Addiction and therapeutics. *Annual Review of Pharmacology & Toxicology, 36,* 597–613.

Benowitz, N. L. (1997). Treating tobacco addiction: Nicotine or no nicotine? *The New England Journal of Medicine, 337,* 1230–1231.

Benowitz, N. L. (1998). Pharmacology of nicotine. In R. E. Tarter & R. T. Ammerman (Eds.), *Handbook of substance abuse: Neurobehavioral pharmacology* (pp. 283–297). New York: Plenum Press.

Benowitz, N. L. (1999). Nicotine addiction. *Primary Care, 26,* 611–631.

Benowitz, N. L. (2002). Smoking cessation trials targeted to racial and economic minority groups. *Journal of the American Medical Association, 288,* 497–499.

Berkow, R., & Fletcher, A. J. (Eds.). (1987). *The Merck manual of diagnosis and therapy* (15th edition). Rahway, NJ: Merck & Co.

Best, J. A., Owen, L. E., & Trentadue, L. (1978). Comparison of satiation and rapid smoking in self-managed smoking cessation. *Addictive Behaviors, 3,* 71–78.

Beutler, L. E. (2000). David and Goliath: When empirical and clinical standards of practice meet. *American Psychologist, 55,* 997–1007.

Biener, L., & Abrams, D. B. (1989). *The Contemplation Ladder: Validation of a measure of readiness to quit smoking.* Unpublished manuscript, Brown University, Providence, RI.

Bier, I. D., Wilson, J., Studt, P., & Shakleton, M. (2002). Auricular acupuncture, education, and smoking cessation: A randomized, sham-controlled trial. *American Journal of Public Health, 92,* 1642–1647.

Blum, K. (1984). *Handbook of abusable drugs.* New York: Gardner Press.

Brandon, T. H. (2001). Behavioral tobacco cessation treatments: Yesterday's news or tomorrow's headlines. *Journal of Clinical Oncology, 19*(Suppl.), 64s–68s.

Brandon, T. H., & Baker, T. B. (1991). The Smoking Consequences Questionnaire: The subjective expected utility of smoking in college students. *Psychological Assessment: A Journal of Consulting and Clinical Psychology, 3,* 484–491.

Brandon, T. H., Tiffany, S. T., Obremski, K. M., & Baker, T. B. (1990). Postcessation cigarette use: The process of relapse. *Addictive Behaviors, 15,* 105–114.

Brewington, V., Smith, M., & Lipton, D. (1994). Acupuncture as a detoxification treatment: An analysis of controlled research. *Journal of Substance Abuse Treatment, 11,* 289–307.

Brigham, J., Henningfield, J. E., & Stitzer, M. L. (1991). Smoking relapse: A review. *The International Journal of the Addictions, 9A–10A,* 1239–1255.

British Thoracic Society. (1998). Smoking cessation guidelines and their cost-effectiveness. *Thorax, 53,* S1–S19.

Brown, R. A., Larkin, J. C., & Davis, R. L. (2000). Current concepts in the management of smoking cessation. *The American Journal of Managed Care, 6,* 394–401.

Bukstein, O. (1995). *Adolescent substance abuse: Assessment, prevention and treatment.* New York: Wiley.

Burling, T. A., Ramsey, T. G., Seidner, A. L., & Kondo, C. S. (1997). Issues related to smoking cessation among substance abusers. *Journal of Substance Abuse, 9,* 27–40.

Carmody, T. P. (1989). Affect regulation, nicotine addiction, and smoking cessation. *Journal of Psychoactive Drugs, 21,* 331–342.

Carmody, T. P. (1992). Preventing relapse in the treatment of nicotine addiction: Current issues and future directions. *Journal of Psychoactive Drugs, 24,* 131–158.

Carpenter, K. M., Watson, J. M., Raffety, B., & Chabal, C. (2003). Teaching brief interventions for smoking cessation via interactive computer-based tutorial. *Journal of Health Psychology, 8*(1), 149–160.

Carroll, K. M. (1996). Relapse prevention as a psychosocial treatment: A review of controlled clinical trials. *Experimental and Clinical Psychopharmacology, 4*(1), 46–54.

Catley, D., O'Connell, K. A., & Shiffman, S. (2000). Absentminded lapses during smoking cessation. *Psychology of Addictive Behaviors, 14*(1), 73–76.

Centers for Disease Control and Prevention. (2000). Trends in cigarette smoking among high school students—United States, 1991–1999. *Journal of the American Medical Association, 284,* 1507–1508.

Chassin, L., Presson, C. C., Rose, J. S., & Sherman, S. J. (1996). The natural history of cigarette smoking from adolescence to adulthood: Demographic predictors of continuity and change. *Health Psychology, 15,* 478–484.

Choi, W. S., Patten, C. A., Gillin, J. C., Kaplan, R. M., & Pierce, J. P. (1997). Cigarette smoking predicts development of depressive symptoms among U.S. adolescents. *Annals of Behavioral Medicine, 19*(1), 42–50.

Cocores, J. (1993). Nicotine dependence: Diagnosis and treatment. *Psychiatric Clinics of North America, 16*(1), 49–60.

Colby, S. M., Monti, P. M., Barnett, N. P., Rohsenow, D. J., Weissman, K., Spirito, A., et al. (1998). Brief motivational interviewing in a hospital setting for adolescent smoking: A preliminary study. *Journal of Consulting and Clinical Psychology, 66,* 574–578.

Colby, S. M., Tiffany, S. T., Shiffman, S., & Niaura, R. S. (2000a). Are adolescent smokers dependent on nicotine? A review of the evidence. *Drug and Alcohol Dependence, 59*(Suppl. 1), S83–S95.

Colby, S. M., Tiffany, S. T., Shiffman, S., & Niaura, R. S. (2000b). Measuring nicotine dependence among youth: A review of available approaches and instruments. *Drug and Alcohol Dependence, 59*(Suppl. 1), S23–S39.

Collins, R. L., Emont, S. L., & Zywiak, W. H. (1990). Social influence processes in smoking cessation: Postquitting predictors of long-term outcome. *Journal of Substance Abuse, 2,* 389–403.

Copeland, A. L., Brandon, T. H., & Quinn, E. P. (1995). The Smoking Consequences Questionnaire—Adult: Measurement of smoking outcome expectancies of experienced smokers. *Psychological Assessment, 7,* 484–494.

Corelli, R. L., & Hudman, K. S. (2002). Medicine cabinet. Medications for smoking cessation. *Western Journal of Medicine, 176*(2), 131–135.

Council on Scientific Affairs. (1987). Scientific issues in drug testing. *Journal of the American Medical Association, 257,* 3110–3114.

Covino, N. A., & Bottari, M. (2001). Hypnosis, behavioral theory, and smoking cessation. *Journal of Dental Education, 65,* 340–347.

Cox, L. S., Tiffany, S. T., & Christen, A. G. (2001). Evaluation of the brief Questionnaire of Smoking Urges (QSU–brief) in laboratory and clinical settings. *Nicotine and Tobacco Research, 3,* 7–16.

Cramer, P. (1991). *The development of defense mechanisms: Theory, research and assessment.* New York: Springer.

Cramer, P. (2000). Defense mechanisms in psychology today. *American Psychologist, 55,* 637–646.

Curry, S. J. (1993). Self-help interventions for smoking cessation. *Journal of Consulting and Clinical Psychology, 61,* 790–803.

Curry, S. J., & McBride, C. M. (1994). Relapse prevention for smoking cessation: Review and evaluation of concepts and interventions. *Annual Review of Public Health, 15,* 345–366.

Daeppen, J. B., Smith, T. L., Danko, G. P., Gordon, L., Landi, N. A., Nurnberger, J. I., et al. (2000). Clinical correlates of cigarette smoking and nicotine dependence in alcohol-dependent men and women. *Alcohol and Alcoholism*, *35*(2), 171–175.

Dallery, J., Houtsmuller, E. J., Pickworth, W. B., & Stitzer, M. L. (2003). Effects of cigarette nicotine content and smoking pace on subsequent craving and smoking. *Psychopharmacology*, *165*, 172–180.

Dani, J. A., & DeBiasi, M. (2001). Cellular mechanisms of nicotine addiction. *Pharmacology, Biochemistry, and Behavior*, *70*, 439–446.

Davidson, R. (1996). Motivational issues in the treatment of addictive behavior. In G. Edwards & C. Dare (Eds.), *Psychotherapy, psychological treatments and the addictions* (pp. 173–188). New York: Cambridge University Press.

Davis, A. L., Faust, R., & Ordentlich, B. A. (1984). Self-help smoking cessation and maintenance programs: A comparative study with 12-month follow-up by the American Lung Association. *American Journal of Public Health*, *74*, 1212–1217.

Dawley, H. H., Fleischer, B. J., & Dawley, L. T. (1985). Attitudes toward smoking and smoking rate: Implications for smoking discouragement. *The International Journal of the Addictions*, *20*, 483–488.

deRidder, D., & Schreurs, K., (2001). Developing interventions for chronically ill patients: Is coping a helpful concept? *Clinical Psychology Review*, *21*, 205–240.

Dermer, M. L., & Jacobsen, E. (1986). Some potential negative social consequences of cigarette smoking: Marketing research in reverse. *Journal of Applied Social Psychology*, *16*, 702–725.

DeVries, H., Mudde, A. N., Dijkstra, A., & Willemsen, M. C. (1998). Differential beliefs, perceived social influences, and self-efficacy expectations among smokers in various motivational phases. *Preventive Medicine*, *27*, 681–689.

DiFranza, J. R., Savageau, J. A., Rigotti, N. A., Fletcher, K., Ockene, J. K., McNeill, A. D., et al. (2002). Development of symptoms of tobacco dependence in youths: 30 month follow-up data from the DANDY study. *Tobacco Control*, *11*, 228–235.

Dijkstra, A., Bakker, M., & DeVries, H. (1997). Subtypes within a sample of precontemplating smokers: A preliminary extension of the stages of change. *Addictive Behaviors*, *22*, 327–337.

Dijkstra, A., Roijackers, J., & DeVries, H. (1998). Smokers in four stages of readiness to change. *Addictive Behaviors*, *23*, 339–350.

D'Mello, D. A., & Flanagan, C. (1996). Seasons and depression: The influence of cigarette smoking. *Addictive Behaviors*, *21*, 671–674.

Dodgen, C. E., & Shea, W. M. (2000). *Substance use disorders: Assessment and treatment*. San Diego, CA: Academic Press.

Dodgen, C. E. (2004). *Stop smoking system*. Unpublished manuscript.

Doherty, K., Kinnunen, T., Militello, F. S., & Garvey, A. J. (1995). Urges to smoke during the first month of abstinence: Relationship to relapse and predictors. *Psychopharmacology*, *119*, 171–178.

Dols, M., van den Hout, M., Kindt, M., & Willems, B. (2002). The urge to smoke depends on the expectation of smoking. *Addiction, 97,* 87–93.

Drobes, D. J., Meier, E. A., & Tiffany, S. T. (1994). Assessment of the effects of urges and negative affect on smokers' coping skills. *Behavior Research and Therapy, 32*(1), 165–174.

Dugan, S., Lloyd, B., & Lucas, K. (1999). Stress and coping as determinants of adolescent smoking behavior. *Journal of Applied Social Psychology, 29,* 870–888.

Durcan, M. J., Deener, G., White, J., Johnston, J. A., Gonzales, D., Niaura, R., et al. (2002). The effect of bupropion sustained-release on cigarette craving after smoking cessation. *Clinical Therapeutics, 24,* 540–551.

Dykstra, L. (1992). Drug action. In J. Grabowski & G. R. VandenBos (Eds.), *Psychopharmacology: Basic mechanisms and applied interventions* (pp. 59–96). Washington, DC: American Psychological Association.

el-Guebaly, N., Cathcart, J., Currie, S., Brown, D., & Gloster, S. (2002). Smoking cessation approaches for persons with mental illness or addictive disorders. *Psychiatric Services, 53,* 1166–1170.

el-Guebaly, N., & Hodgins, D. (1998). Substance-related cravings and relapses: Clinical implications. *Canadian Journal of Psychiatry, 43,* 29–36.

Erickson, L. M., Tiffany, S. T., Martin, E. M., & Baker, T. B. (1983). Aversive smoking therapies: A conditioning analysis of therapeutic effectiveness. *Behavior Research and Therapy, 21,* 595–611.

Etter, J., Duc, T. V., & Perneger, T. V. (1999). Validity of the Fagerstrom Test for Nicotine Dependence and of the Heaviness of Smoking Index among relatively light smokers. *Addiction, 94,* 269–281.

Etter, J., Humair, J., Bergman, M. M., & Perneger, T. V. (2000). Development and validation of the Attitudes Towards Smoking Scale (ATS–18). *Addiction, 95,* 613–625.

Etter, J. F., Laszlo, E., Zellweger, J. P., Perrot, C., & Perneger, T. V. (2002). Nicotine replacement to reduce cigarette consumption in smokers who are unwilling to quit: A randomized trial. *Journal of Clinical Psychopharmacology, 22,* 487–495.

Etter, J. F., Perneger, T. V., & Ronchi, A. (1997). Distribution of smokers by stage: International comparison and association with smoking prevalence. *Preventive Medicine, 26,* 580–585.

Fagerstrom, K. O. (1978). Measuring degree of physical dependence to tobacco smoking with reference to individualization of treatment. *Addictive Behaviors, 3,* 235–241.

Fagerstrom, K. O. (1991). Towards better diagnoses and more individual treatment of tobacco dependence. *British Journal of Addiction, 86,* 543–547.

Fagerstrom, K. O. (1994). Combined use of nicotine replacement products. *Health Values, 18*(3), 15–20.

Fagerstrom, K. O. (2002). The epidemiology of smoking: Health consequences and benefits of cessation. *Drugs, 62* (Suppl. 2), 1–9.

Farrelly, M. C., Healton, C. G., Davis, K. C., Messeri, P., Hersey, J. C., & Haviland, M. L. (2002). Getting to the truth: Evaluating national tobacco countermarketing campaigns. *American Journal of Public Health, 92*, 901–907.

Ferrell, M., Howes, S., Taylor, C., Lewis, G., Jenkins, R., Bebbington, P., et al. (2003). Substance misuse and psychiatric comorbidity: An overview of the POCS National Psychiatric Morbidity Survey. *International Review of Psychiatry, 15*, 43–49.

Fiore, M. C., Novotny, T. E., Pierce, J. P., Giovino, G. A., Hatziandreu, E. J., Newcomb, P. A., et al. (1990). Methods used to quit smoking in the United States. *Journal of the American Medical Association, 263*, 2760–2765.

Flay, B. R. (1993). Youth tobacco use: Risks, patterns, and control. In J. Slade & C. T. Orleans (Eds.), *Nicotine addiction: Principles and management*. New York: Oxford University Press.

Foxx, R. M., & Brown, R. A. (1979). Nicotine fading and self-management for cigarette abstinence or controlled smoking. *Journal of Applied Behavior Analysis, 12*(1), 111–125.

Frank, S. H., & Jaen, C. R. (1993). Office evaluation and treatment of the dependent smoker. *Substance Abuse, 20*(1), 251–268.

Frenk, H., & Dar, R. (2000). *A critique of nicotine addiction*. New York: Kluwer Academic Publishers.

Gamberino, W. C., & Gold, M. S. (1999). Neurobiology of tobacco smoking and other addictive disorders. *The Psychiatric Clinics of North America, 22*, 301–312.

Gariti, P., Alterman, A., Mulvaney, G., Mechanic, K., Dhopesh, V., Tu, E., et al. (2002). Nicotine intervention during detoxification and treatment for other substance use. *The American Journal of Drug and Alcohol Abuse, 28*, 671–679.

Gibson, B. (1997). An introduction to the controversy over tobacco. *Journal of Social Issues, 53*(1), 3–11.

Gift, A. G., Stommel, M., Jablonski, A., & Given, W. (2003). A cluster of symptoms over time in patients with lung cancer. *Nursing Research, 52*, 393–400.

Gill, B. S., & Bennett, D. L. (2000). Addiction professionals' attitudes regarding treatment of nicotine dependence. *Journal of Substance Abuse Treatment, 19*, 317–318.

Gill, D., & Hatcher, S. (2001). Antidepressants for depression in medical illness (Cochrane Review). In *The Cochrane Library* (Issue 3). Chichester, England: Wiley.

Glassman, A. H., Helzer, J. E., Covey, L. S., Cottler, L. B., Stetner, F., Tipp, J. E., & Johnson, J. (1990). Smoking, smoking cessation, and major depression. *Journal of the American Medical Association, 264*, 1546–1549.

Glover, E. D., & Glover, P. N. (2001). Pharmacological treatments for the nicotine dependent smoker. *American Journal of Health Behavior, 25*, 179–182.

Goldfried, M. R., & Wolfe, B. E. (1996). Psychotherapy practice and research: Repairing a strained alliance. *American Psychologist, 51*, 1007–1016.

Gori, G. B. (1996). Failings of the disease model of addiction. *Human Psychopharmacology, 11*, S33–S38.

Gostin, L. O., Arno, P. S., & Brandt, A. M. (1997). FDA regulation of tobacco advertising and youth smoking: Historical, social, and constitutional perspectives. *Journal of the American Medical Association, 277*, 410–418.

Haddock, C. K., Lando, H., Klesges, R. C., Talcott, G. W., & Renaud, E. A. (1999). A study of the psychometric and predictive properties of the Fagerstrom Test for Nicotine Dependence in a population of young smokers. *Nicotine & Tobacco Research, 1*, 59–66.

Hajek, P. (1994). Treatment for smokers. *Addiction, 89*(1), 1543–1549.

Hajek, P. (1996). Current issues in behavioral and pharmacological approaches to smoking cessation. *Addictive Behaviors, 21*, 699–707.

Hajek, P., & Stead, L. F. (2002). Aversive smoking for smoking cessation (Cochrane Review). In *The Cochrane Library* (Issue 4). Chichester, England: Wiley.

Hall, S. M., Munoz, R. F., & Reus, V. I. (1994). Cognitive-behavioral intervention increases abstinence rates for depressive-history smokers. *Journal of Consulting and Clinical Psychology, 62*(1), 141–146.

Hall, S. M., Munoz, R. F., Reus, V. I., & Sees, K. L. (1993). Nicotine, negative affect, and depression. *Journal of Consulting and Clinical Psychology, 61*, 761–767.

Hall, S. M., Munoz, R. F., Reus, V. I., Sees, K. L., Duncan, C., Humfleet, G. L., & Hartz, D. T. (1996). Mood management and nicotine gum in smoking treatment: A therapeutic contact and placebo-controlled study. *Journal of Consulting and Clinical Psychology, 64*, 1003–1009.

Hansen, W. B. (1992). School-based substance abuse prevention: A review of the state of the art in curriculum, 1980–1990. *Health Education Research: Theory & Practice, 7*, 403–430.

Heatherton, T. F., Kozlowski, L. T., Frecker, R. C., & Fagerstrom, K. O. (1991). The Fagerstrom Test for Nicotine Dependence: A revision of the Fagerstrom Tolerance Questionnaire. *British Journal of Addiction, 86*, 1119–1127.

Hebert, R. (2004). What's new in nicotine and tobacco research? *Nicotine & Tobacco Research, 6*(Suppl. 2), S95–S100.

Heishman, S. J., Taylor, R. C., & Henningfield, J. E. (1994). Nicotine and smoking: A review of effects on human performance. *Experimental and Clinical Psychopharmacology, 2*, 345–395.

Henningfield, J. E., Cohen, C., & Pickworth, W. B. (1993). Psychopharmacology of nicotine. In C. T. Orleans & J. Slade (Eds.), *Nicotine addiction: Principles and management* (pp. 24–45). New York: Oxford University Press.

Henningfield, J. E., Cohen, C., & Slade, J. D. (1991). Is nicotine more addictive than cocaine? *British Journal of Addiction, 86*, 565–569.

Henningfield, J. E., & Heishman, S. J. (1995). The addictive role of nicotine in tobacco use. *Psychopharmacology, 117*, 11–13.

Henningfield, J. E., & Keenan, R. M. (1993). Nicotine delivery kinetics and abuse liability. *Journal of Consulting and Clinical Psychology, 61*, 743–750.

Henningfield, J. E., & Woodson, P. P. (1989). Dose-related actions of nicotine on behavior and physiology: Review and implications for replacement therapy for nicotine dependence. *Journal of Substance Abuse, 1*, 301–317.

Hennrikus, D. J., Jeffery, R. W., & Lando, H. (1995). The smoking cessation process: Longitudinal observations in a working population. *Preventive Medicine, 24*, 235–244.

Herrera, N., Franco, R., Herrea, L., Partidas, A., Rolando, R., & Fagerstrom, K. O. (1995). Nicotine gum, 2 and 4 mg, for nicotine dependence: A double-blind placebo-controlled trial within a behavior modification support program. *Chest, 108*, 447–451.

Hoffman, E. H., Blackburn, C., & Cullari, S. (2001). Brief residential treatment for nicotine addiction: A five-year follow-up study. *Psychological Reports, 89*, 99–105.

Holmes, T. H., & Rae, R. H. (1967). The social readjustment rating scale. *Journal of Psychosomatic Research, 11*, 213–218.

Horn, K., Fernandes, A., Dino, G., Massey, C. J., & Kalsekar, I. (2003). Adolescent nicotine dependence and smoking cessation outcomes. *Addictive Behaviors, 28*, 769–776.

Howell, D. (2000). *The unofficial guide to quitting smoking.* New York: IDG Books Worldwide.

Hughes, J. R. (1992). Tobacco withdrawal in self-quitters. *Journal of Consulting and Clinical Psychology, 60*, 689–697.

Hughes, J. R. (1993a). Pharmacotherapy for smoking cessation: Unvalidated assumptions, anomalies, and suggestions for future research. *Journal of Consulting and Clinical Psychology, 61*, 751–760.

Hughes, J. R. (1993b). Smoking is a drug dependence: A reply to Robinson and Pritchard. *Psychopharmacology, 113*, 282–283.

Hughes, J. R. (1993c). Treatment of smoking cessation in smokers with past alcohol/ drug problems. *Journal of Substance Abuse Treatment, 10*, 181–187.

Hughes, J. R. (1995). Combining behavioral therapy and pharmacotherapy for smoking cessation: An update. In L. Onlan & J. Blaine (Eds.), *Integrating behavioral therapies with medication in the treatment of drug dependence.* (NIDA Research Monograph). Washington, DC: U.S. Government Printing Office.

Hughes, J. R., Cummings, K. M., & Hyland, A. (1999). Ability of smokers to reduce their smoking and its association with future smoking cessation. *Addiction, 94*(1), 109–114.

Hughes, J. R., & Hatsukami, D. K. (1986). Signs and symptoms of tobacco withdrawal. *Archives of General Psychiatry, 43*, 289–294.

Hughes, J. R., Stead, L. F., & Lancaster, T. (2003a). Antidepressants for smoking cessation (Cochrane Review). In *The Cochrane Library* (Issue 1). Chichester, England: Wiley.

Hughes, J. R., Stead, L. F., & Lancaster, T. (2003b). Anxiolytics for smoking cessation (Cochrane Review). In *The Cochrane Library* (Issue 1). Chichester, England: Wiley.

Hurt, R. D., Croghan, G. A., Beede, S. D., Wolter, T. D., Croghan, I. T., & Patten, C. A. (2000). Nicotine patch therapy in 101 adolescent smokers: Efficacy, withdrawal symptom relief, and carbon monoxide and plasma cotinine levels. *Archives of Pediatrics & Adolescent Medicine, 154,* 31–37.

Hurt, R. D., Eberman, K. M., Croghan, I. T., Offord, K. P., Davis, L. J., Jr., Morse, R. M., et al. (1994). Nicotine dependence treatment during inpatient treatment for other addictions: A prospective intervention trial. *Alcoholism: Clinical and Experimental Research, 18,* 867–872.

Hurt, R. D., Wetter, T. D., Rigotti, N., Hays, J. T., Niaura, R., Durcan, M. J., et al. (2002). Bupropion for pharmacologic relapse prevention to smoking: Predictors of outcome. *Addictive Behaviors, 27,* 493–507.

Hymowitz, N., & Eckholdt, H. (1996). Effects of a 2.5 mg silver acetate lozenge on initial and long-term smoking cessation. *Preventive Medicine, 25,* 537–546.

Irvin, J. E., & Brandon, T. H. (2000). The increasing recalcitrance of smokers in clinical trials. *Nicotine & Tobacco Research, 2,* 79–84.

Jarvik, M. E. (1995). The scientific case that nicotine is addictive. *Psychopharmacology, 117,* 18–20.

Jarvik, M. E., Caskey, N. H., Rose, J. E., Herscovik, J. E., & Sadeghpour, M. (1989). Anxiolytic effects of smoking associated with four stressors. *Addictive Behaviors, 14,* 379–386.

Jarvik, M. E., & Henningfield, J. E. (1988). Pharmacological treatment of tobacco dependence. *Pharmacology, Biochemistry, & Behavior, 30,* 279–294.

Jarvik, M. E., Madsen, D. C., Olmstead, R. E., Iwamoto-Schaap, P. N., Elins, J. L., & Benowitz, N. L. (2000). Nicotine blood levels and subjective craving for cigarettes. *Pharmacology, Biochemistry and Behavior, 66,* 553–558.

Jellinek, E. M. (1960). *The disease concept of alcoholism.* New Haven, CT: Hill House Press.

Jimenez-Ruiz, C., Solano, S., Viteri, S. A., Ferrero, M. B., Torrecilla, M., & Mezquita, M. H. (2002). Harm reduction: A treatment approach for resistant smokers with tobacco-related symptoms. *Respiration, 69,* 452–455.

Johanson, C. (1992). Biochemical mechanisms and biological principles of drug action. In J. Grabowski & G. R. VandenBos (Eds.), *Psychopharmacology: Basic mechanisms and applied interventions* (pp. 11–58). Washington, DC: American Psychological Association.

Johnson, J. G., Cohen, P., Pine, D. S., Klein, D. F., Kasen, S., & Brook, J. S. (2000). Association between cigarette smoking and anxiety disorders during adolescence and early adulthood. *Journal of the American Medical Association, 284,* 2348–2351.

Johnson, S. L. (1997). *Therapist's guide to clinical intervention: The 1–2–3s of treatment planning.* San Diego, CA: Academic Press.

Jorenby, D. (2002). Clinical efficacy of bupropion in the management of smoking cessation. *Drugs, 62*(Suppl. 2), 25–35.

Kadden, R. M. (1996). Is Marlatt's relapse taxonomy reliable and valid? *Addiction, 91*(Suppl.), S139–S145.

Kadden, R. M., & Mauriello, I. J. (1991). Enhancing participation in substance abuse treatment using an incentive system. *Journal of Substance Abuse*, 8, 113–124.

Kalman, D. (1998). Smoking cessation treatment for substance misusers in early recovery: A review of the literature and recommendations for practice. *Substance Use & Misuse*, 33, 2021–2047.

Kandel, D. (1975). Stages in adolescent involvement in drug use. *Science*, 190, 912–914.

Kawakami, N., Takatsuka, N., Inaba, S., & Shimizu, H. (1999). Development of a screening questionnaire for tobacco/nicotine dependence according to *ICD–10, DSM–III–R*, and *DSM–IV. Addictive Behaviors*, 24(2), 155–166.

Kazdin, A. E. (2001). Progression of therapy research and clinical application of treatment require better understanding of the change process. *Clinical Psychology: Science and Practice*, 8(2), 143–151.

Kellar, K. J., Davila-Garcia, M. L., & Xiao, Y. (1999). Pharmacology of neuronal nicotine acetylcholine receptors: Effects of acute and chronic nicotine. *Nicotine and Tobacco Research*, 1(Suppl. 2), S117–S120.

Kendall, P. C., & Hudson, J. L. (2001). Participating in a roundtable discussion on the science of psychotherapy research. *Clinical Psychology: Science and Practice*, 8(2), 184–185.

Kenford, S. L., Fiore, M. C., Jorenby, D. E., Smith, S. S., Wetter, D., & Baker, T. M. (1994). Predicting smoking cessation: Who will quit with and without the nicotine patch. *Journal of the American Medical Association*, 271, 589–594.

Kessler, D. A., Barnett, P. S., Witt, A., Zeller, M. R., Mande, J. R., & Schultz, W. B. (1997). The legal and scientific basis for FDA's assertion of jurisdiction over cigarettes and smokeless tobacco. *Journal of the American Medical Association*, 277, 405–409.

Killen, J. D., & Fortmann, S. P. (1997). Craving is associated with smoking relapse: Findings from three prospective studies. *Experimental and Clinical Psychopharmacology*, 5(2), 137–142.

Killen, J. D., Fortmann, S. P., Kraemer, H. C., Varady, A., & Newman, B. (1992). Who will relapse? Symptoms of nicotine dependence predict long-term relapse after smoking cessation. *Journal of Consulting and Clinical Psychology*, 60, 797–801.

King, T. K., Borrelli, B., Black, C., Pinto, B. M., & Marcus, B. H. (1997). Minority women and tobacco: Implications for smoking cessation interventions. *Annals of Behavioral Medicine*, 19, 301–313.

Klesges, L. M., Johnson, K. C., Somes, G., Zbikowski, S., & Robinson, L. (2003). Use of nicotine replacement therapy in adolescent smokers and nonsmokers. *Archives of Pediatrics & Adolescent Medicine*, 157, 517–522.

Klesges, R. C., Ward, K. D., & DeBon, M. (1996). Smoking cessation: A successful behavioral/pharmacologic interface. *Clinical Psychology Review*, 16, 479–496.

Kotlyar, M., Golding, M., Hatsukami, D., & Jamerson, B. (2001). Effect of nonnicotine pharmacotherapy on smoking behavior. *Pharmacotherapy*, 21, 1530–1548.

Kotlyar, M., & Hatsukami, D. (2002). Managing nicotine addiction. *Journal of Dental Education, 66*, 1061–1073.

Kozlowski, L. T., Henningfield, J. E., & Brigham, J. (2001). *Cigarettes, nicotine, and health: A biobehavioral approach.* Thousand Oaks, CA: Sage.

Laberg, J. C. (1990). What is presented, and what prevented, in cue exposure and response prevention with alcohol dependent subjects? *Addictive Behaviors, 15*, 367–386.

Lancaster, T., & Stead, L. F. (2002a). Individual behavioral counselling for smoking cessation (Cochrane Review). In *The Cochrane Library* (Issue 4). Chichester, England: Wiley.

Lancaster, T., & Stead, L. F. (2002b). Silver acetate for smoking cessation (Cochrane Review). In *The Cochrane Library* (Issue 1). Chichester, England: Wiley.

Lancaster, T., & Stead, L. F. (2003). Self-help interventions for smoking cessation (Cochrane Review). In *The Cochrane Library* (Issue 1). Chichester, England: Wiley.

Lando, H. A. (1976). Aversive conditioning and contingency management in the treatment of smoking. *Journal of Consulting & Clinical Psychology, 44*, 312.

Lando, H. A. (1993). Formal quit smoking treatments. In C. T. Orleans & J. Slade (Eds.), *Nicotine addiction: Principles and management* (pp. 221–244). New York: Oxford University Press.

Lando, H. A., & Gritz, E. R. (1996). Smoking cessation techniques. *Journal of the American Medical Women's Association, 51*(1–2), 31–34, 47.

Larimer, M. E., Palmer, R. S., & Marlatt, G. A. (1999). Relapse prevention: An overview of Marlatt's cognitive-behavioral model. *Alcohol Research & Health, 23*(2), 151–160.

Laughlin, H. P. (1983). *The ego and its defenses* (2nd ed.). Northvale, NJ: Jason Aronson.

Law, M., & Tang, J. L. (1995). An analysis of the effectiveness of interventions intended to help people stop smoking. *Archives of Internal Medicine, 155*, 1933–1941.

Lawrence, D., Graber, J. E., Mills, S. L., Meissner, H. I., & Warnecke, R. (2003). Smoking cessation interventions in U.S. racial/ethnic minority populations: An assessment of the literature. *Preventive Medicine, 36*, 204–216.

Lawrence, K. G. (2001). Adolescent smokers' preferred smoking cessation methods. *Canadian Journal of Public Health, 92*, 423–426.

Lazarus, R. S., & Folkman, S. (1984). *Stress, appraisal, and coping.* New York: Springer.

Lazev, A. B., Herzog, T. A., & Brandon, T. H. (1999). Classical conditioning of environmental cues to cigarette smoking. *Experimental and Clinical Psychopharmacology, 7*(1), 56–63.

Lee, C. (1989). Perceptions of immunity to disease in adult smokers. *Journal of Behavioral Medicine, 12*, 267–277.

Leeds, J., & Morgenstern, J. (1996). Psychoanalytic theories of substance abuse. In F. Rotgers, D. S. Keller, & J. Morgenstern (Eds.), *Treating substance abuse: Theory and technique*. New York: Guilford Press.

Levine, B. A., (1974). Effectiveness of contingent and non-contingent electric shock in reducing cigarette smoking. *Psychological Reports, 34*, 223–226.

Lowe, M. R., Green, L., Kurtz, S. M., Ashenberg, Z. S., & Fisher, E. B. (1980). Self-initiated, cue extinction, and covert sensitization procedures in smoking cessation. *Journal of Behavioral Medicine, 3*, 357–372.

Lichtenstein, E. (1999). Nicotine Anonymous: Community resource and research implications. *Psychology of Addictive Behaviors, 13*(1), 60–68.

Ma, G. X., Shive, S., Legos, P., & Tan, Y. (2003). Ethnic differences in adolescent smoking behaviors, sources of tobacco, knowledge and attitudes toward restriction policies. *Addictive Behaviors, 28*, 249–268.

MacHovec, F. J., & Man, S. C. (1978). Acupuncture and hypnosis compared: Fifty-eight cases. *The American Journal of Clinical Hypnosis, 21*(1), 45–47.

Mahoney, G. N., & Al-Delaimy, W. (2001). Measurement of nicotine in hair by reversed-phase high-performance liquid chromatography with electrochemical detection. *Journal of Chromatograph B, 753*, 179–187.

Malcolm, R., Currey, H. S., Mitchell, M. A., & Keil, J. E. (1986). Silver acetate gum as a deterrent to smoking. *Chest, 90*(1), 107–111.

Mallin, R. (2002). Smoking cessation: Integration of behavioral and drug therapies. *American Family Physician, 65*, 1107–1114.

Marlatt, G. A. (1996). Models of relapse and relapse prevention: A commentary. *Experimental and Clinical Psychopharmacology, 4*(1), 55–60.

Marlatt, G. A., & Gordon, J. R. (Eds.). (1985). *Relapse prevention: Maintenance strategies in the treatment of addictive behaviors*. New York: Guilford Press.

Mayer, J. D., & Eisenberg, M. G. (1988). Mental representation of the body: Stability and change in response to illness and disability. *Rehabilitation Psychology, 33*(3), 155–171.

McCarthy, W. J., Collins, C., & Hser, Y. I. (2002). Does cigarette smoking affect drug abuse treatment? *Journal of Drug Issues, 22*, 61–80.

McConnaughy, E. A., Prochaska, J. O., & Velicer, W. F. (1983). Stages of change in psychotherapy: Measurement and sample profiles. *Psychotherapy: Theory, Research and Practice, 20*, 368–375.

McKay, J. R. (1999). Studies of factors in relapse to alcohol, drug and nicotine use: A critical review of methodologies and findings. *Journal of Studies on Alcohol, 60*, 566–576.

McNeill, A., Foulds, J., & Bates, C. (2001). Regulation of nicotine replacement therapies (NRT): A critique of current practice. *Addiction, 96*, 1757–1768.

Miceli, M., & Castelfranchi, C. (2001). Further distinctions between coping and defense mechanisms? *Journal of Personality, 69*, 287–296.

Miller, M., Hemenway, D., Bell, N. S., & Rimm, E. (2000). Cigarettes and suicide: A prospective study of 50,000 men. *American Journal of Public Health, 90*, 768–773.

Miller, N. S., & Cocores, J. A. (1991). Nicotine dependence: Diagnosis, pharmacology and treatment. *Journal of Addictive Diseases, 11*(2), 51–63.

Miller, S. A. (1987). Promoting self-esteem in the hospitalized adolescent. *Issues in Comprehensive Pediatric Nursing, 10,* 187–194.

Miyata, H., & Yanagita, T. (2001). Neurobiological mechanisms of nicotine craving. *Alcohol, 24,* 87–93.

Mizes, J. S., Sloan, D. M., Segraves, K., Spring, B., Pingitore, R., & Kristeller, J. (1998). The influence of weight-related variables on smoking cessation. *Behavior Therapy, 29,* 371–385.

Moolchan, E. T., Ernst, M., & Henningfield, J. E. (2000). A review of tobacco smoking in adolescents: Treatment implications. *Journal of the American Academy of Child & Adolescent Psychiatry, 39,* 682–693.

Moolchan, E. T., Radzius, A., Epstein, D. H., Uhl, G., Gorelick, D. A., Cadet, J. L., & Henningfield, J. E. (2002). The Fagerstrom Test for Nicotine Dependence and the Diagnostic Interview Schedule. Do they diagnose the same smokers? *Addictive Behaviors, 27,* 101–113.

Morgan, M. J., Davies, G. M., & Willner, P. (1999). The questionnaire of smoking urges is sensitive to abstinence and exposure to smoking-related cues. *Behavioral Pharmacology, 10,* 619–626.

Morrow, R., Nepps, P., & McIntosh, M. (1993). Silver acetate mouth spray as an aid in smoking cessation: Results of a double-blind trial. *Journal of the American Board of Family Practitioners, 6,* 353–357.

Murray, J. B. (1990). Nicotine as a psychoactive drug. *The Journal of Psychology, 125*(1), 5–25.

Naquin, M. R., & Gilbert, G. G. (1996). College students' smoking behavior, perceived stress, and coping styles. *Journal of Drug Education, 26,* 367–376.

Nathan, P. E., Stuart, S. P., & Dolan, S. L. (2000). Research on psychotherapy efficacy and effectiveness: Between Scylla and Charybdis? *Psychological Bulletin, 126,* 964–981.

Niaura, R., Abrams, D. B., Shadel, W. G., Rohsenow, D. J., Monti, P. M., & Sirota, A. D. (1999). Cue exposure treatment for smoking relapse prevention: A controlled clinical trial. *Addiction, 94,* 685–695.

Nides, M. A., Rakos, R. F., Gonzales, D., Murray, R. P., Tashkin, D. P., Bjornson-Benson, W. M., et al. (1995). Predictors of initial smoking cessation and relapse through the first two years of the Lung Health Study. *Journal of Consulting and Clinical Psychology, 63*(1), 60–69.

Niederdeppe, J., Farrelly, M. C., & Haviland, M. L. (2004). Confirming "truth": More evidence of a successful tobacco countermarketing campaign in Florida. *American Journal of Public Health, 94,* 255–257.

Ockene, J. K., Emmons, K. M., Mermelstein, R. J., Perkins, K. A., Bonollo, D. S., Voorhees, C. C., & Hollis, J. F. (2000). Relapse and maintenance issues for smoking cessation. *Health Psychology, 19*(1), S17–S31.

Orleans, C. T., Schoenback, V. J., Wagner, E. H., Quade, D., Salmon, M. A., Pearson, D. C., et al. (1991). Self-help quit smoking interventions: Effects of self-help materials, social support instructions, and telephone counseling. *Journal of Consulting and Clinical Psychology, 59,* 439–448.

Paffenbarger, R. S., Lee, I. M., & Leung, R. (1994). Physical acitivity and personal characteristics associated with depression and suicide in American college men. *Acta Psychiatrica Scandinavia, 377*(Suppl.), 16–22.

Parrott, A. C. (1999). Does cigarette smoking cause stress? *American Psychologist, 54,* 817–820.

Parrott, A. C., & Garnham, N. J. (1998). Comparative mood states and cognitive skills of cigarette smokers, deprived smokers and non-smokers. *Human Psychopharmacology, 13,* 367–376.

Parrott, A. C., & Joyce, C. (1993). Stress and arousal rhythms in cigarette smokers, deprived smokers, and non-smokers. *Human Psychopharmacology, 8,* 21–28.

Parrott, A. C., & Kaye, F. J. (1999). Daily uplifts, hassles, stresses and cognitive failures: In cigarette smokers, abstaining smokers, and non-smokers. *Behavioral Pharmacology, 10,* 639–646.

Patkar, A. A., Gopalakrishnan, R., Lundy, A., Leone, F. T., Certa, K. M., & Weinstein, S. P. (2002). Relationship between tobacco smoking and positive and negative symptoms in schizophrenia. *The Journal of Nervous and Mental Disorders, 190,* 604–610.

Patten, C. A., Ames, S. C., Ebbert, J. O., Wolter, T. D., Hurt, R. D., & Gauvin, T. R. (2001). Tobacco use outcome of adolescents treated clinically for nicotine dependence. *Archives of Pediatrics & Adolescent Medicine, 155,* 831–837.

Patten, C. A., Gillin, J. C., Golshan, S., Wolter, T. D., Rapaport, M., & Kelsoe, J. (2001). Relationship of mood disturbance to cigarette smoking status among 252 patients with a current mood disorder. *Journal of Clinical Psychiatry, 62,* 319–324.

Patten, C. A., & Martin, J. E. (1996). Measuring tobacco withdrawal: A review of self-report questionnaires. *Journal of Substance Abuse, 8*(1), 93–113.

Payne, T. J., Smith, P. O., McCracken, L. M., McSherry, W. C., & Antony, M. M. (1994). Assessing nicotine dependence: A comparison of the Fagerstrom Tolerance Questionnaire (FTQ) with the Fagerstrom Test for Nicotine Dependence (FTND) in a clinical sample. *Addictive Behaviors, 19,* 307–317.

Perkins, K. A. (1999). Nicotine self-administration. *Nicotine and Tobacco Research, 1*(Suppl. 2), S133–S138.

Perkins, K. A., & Stitzer, M. (1998). Behavioral pharmacology of nicotine. In R. E. Tarter, R. T. Ammerman, & P. J. Ott (Eds.), *Handbook of substance abuse: Neurobehavioral pharmacology* (pp. 299–317). New York: Plenum Press.

Perz, C. A., DiClemente, C. C., & Carbonari, J. P. (1996). Doing the right thing at the right time? The interaction of stages and processes of change in successful smoking cessation. *Health Psychology, 15,* 462–468.

Piasecki, T. M., Jorenby, D. E., Smith, S. S., Fiore, M. C., & Baker, T. B. (2003). Smoking withdrawal dynamics: Pt. 1. Abstinence distress in lapsers and abstainers. *Journal of Abnormal Psychology, 112*(1), 3–13.

Picciotto, M. R. (1998). Common aspects of the action of nicotine and other drugs of abuse. *Drug and Alcohol Dependence, 51*, 165–172.

Pickworth, W. B., Fant, R. V., Nelson, R. A., Rohrer, M. S., & Henningfield, J. E. (1999). Pharmacodynamic effects of new de-nicotinized cigarettes. *Nicotine & Tobacco Research, 1*, 357–364.

Piper, M. E., Piasecki, T. M., Federman, E. B., Bolt, D. M., Smith, S. S., Fiore, M. C., & Baker, T. B. (2004). A multiple motives approach to tobacco dependence: The Wisconsin Inventory of Smoking Dependence Motives (WISDM–68). *Journal of Consulting and Clinical Psychology, 72*(2), 139–154.

Pirie, P. L., Rooney, B. L., Pechacek, T. F., Lando, H. A., & Schmid, L. A. (1997). Incorporating social support into a community-wide smoking-cessation contest. *Addictive Behaviors, 22*(1), 131–137.

Poirier, M. F., Canceil, O., Bayle, F., Millet, B., Bourdel, M. C., Moatti, C., et al. (2002). Prevalence of smoking in psychiatric patients. *Progress in Neuro-Psychopharmacology & Biological Psychiatry, 26*, 529–537.

Pollay, R. W. (1997). Hacks, flacks, and counter-attacks: Cigarette advertising, sponsored research, and controversies. *Journal of Social Issues, 53*(1), 53–74.

Pomerleau, C. S., Carton, S. M., Lutzke, M. L., Flessland, K. A., & Pomerleau, O. F. (1994). Reliability of the Fagerstrom Test for nicotine dependence. *Addictive Behaviors, 19*(1), 33–39.

Pomerleau, C. S., Marks, J. L., & Pomerleau, O. F. (2000). Who gets what symptom? Effects of psychiatric cofactors and nicotine dependence on patterns of smoking withdrawal symptomatology. *Nicotine & Tobacco Research, 2*, 275–280.

Pritchard, W. S., Robinson, J. H., Guy, T. D., Riley, A. D., & Stiles, M. F. (1996). Assessing the sensory role of nicotine in cigarette smoking. *Psychopharmacology, 127*, 55–62.

Prochaska, J. O., & DiClemente, C. C. (1983). Stages and processes of self-change of smoking: Toward an integrative model of change. *Journal of Consulting and Clinical Psychology, 51*, 390–395.

Prochaska, J. O., & Goldstein, M. G. (1991). Process of smoking cessation: Implications for clinicians. *Clinics in Chest Medicine, 12*, 727–735.

Procyshyn, R. M., Patel, K., & Thompson, D. L. (2004). Smoking, anticholinergics and schizophrenia. *Schizophrenia Research, 67*, 313–314.

Prokhorov, A. V., Hudmon, K. S., deMoor, C. A., Kelder, S. H., Conroy, J. L., & Ordway, N. (2001). Nicotine dependence, withdrawal symptoms, and adolescents' readiness to quit smoking. *Nicotine & Tobacco Research, 3*, 151–155.

Prokhorov, A. V., Koehly, L. M., Pallonen, U. E., & Hudmon, K. S. (1998). Adolescent nicotine dependence measured by the Modified Fagerstrom Tolerance Questionnaire at two time points. *Journal of Child & Adolescent Substance Abuse, 7*(4), 35–47.

Quintero, G., & Nichter, M. (1996). The semantics of addiction: Moving beyond expert models to lay understandings. *Journal of Psychoactive Drugs, 28*, 219–228.

Rawson, R. A., Obert, J. L., McCann, M. J., & Marinelli-Casey, P. (1993). Relapse prevention models for substance abuse treatment. *Psychotherapy, 30*, 284–299.

Regier, D. A., Farmer, M. E., Rae, D. S., Locke, B. Z., Keith, S. J., Judd, L. L., & Goodwin, F. K. (1990). Comorbidity of mental disorders with alcohol and other drug abuse: Results from the Epidemiologic Catchment Area (ECA) study. *Journal of the American Medical Association, 264,* 2511–2518.

Resnick, M. P. (1993). Treating nicotine addiction in patients with psychiatric co-morbidity. In C. T. Orleans & J. Slade (Eds.), *Nicotine addiction: Principles and management* (pp. 327–338). New York: Oxford University Press.

Reynolds, P., Hurley, S., Goldberg, D. E., Anton-Culver, H., Bernstein, L., Deapen, D., et al. (2004). Active smoking, household passive smoking, and breast cancer: Evidence from the California Teachers Study. *Journal of the National Cancer Institute, 96*(1), 29–37.

Riedel, B. W., Robinson, L. A., Klesges, R. C., & McLain-Allen, B. (2002a). Characteristics of adolescents caught with cigarettes at school: Implications for developing smoking cessation programs. *Nicotine & Tobacco Research, 4,* 351–354.

Riedel, B. W., Robinson, L. A., Klesges, R. C., & McLain-Allen, B. (2002b). What motivates adolescent smokers to make a quit attempt? *Drug and Alcohol Dependence, 68,* 167–174.

Robins, L. N., Helzer, J. E., Cottler, L., & Golding, E. (1989). *National Institute of Mental Health Diagnostic Interview Schedule* (3rd ed.). St. Louis, MO: Washington University Press.

Robinson, J. H., & Pritchard, W. S. (1995). The scientific case that nicotine is addictive. *Psychopharmacology, 17,* 16–17.

Rohde, P., Lewinsohn, P. M., Brown, R. A., Gau, J. M., & Kahler, C. W. (2003). Psychiatric disorders, familial factors and cigarette smoking: Pt. 1. Associations with smoking initiation. *Nicotine & Tobacco Research, 5,* 85–98.

Rose, J. E., Behm, F. M. Westman, E. C., & Johnson, M. (2000). Dissociating nicotine and non-nicotine components of cigarette smoking. *Pharmacology, Biochemistry, and Behavior, 67,* 71–81.

Royce, J. M., Corbett, K., Sorensen, G., & Ockene, J. (1997). Gender, social pressure, and smoking cessation: The Community Intervention Trial for Smoking Cessation (COMMIT) at baseline. *Social Science & Medicine, 44,* 359–370.

Russell, T. V., Crawford, M. A., & Woodby, L. L. (2004). Measurements for active cigarette smoke exposure in prevalence and cessation studies: Why simply asking pregnant women isn't enough. *Nicotine & Tobacco Research, 6*(Suppl. 2), S141–S151.

Rustin, T. A. (2001). Techniques for smoking cessation: What really works? *Texas Medicine, 97*(2), 63–67.

Rustin, T. A., & Tate, J. C. (1993). Measuring the Stages of Change in cigarette smokers. *Journal of Substance Abuse Treatment, 10,* 209–220.

Sacks, J. J., & Nelson, D. E. (1994). Smoking and injuries: An overview. *Preventive Medicine, 23,* 515–520.

Sargent, J. D., Mott, L. A., & Stevens, M. (1998). Predictors of smoking cessation in adolescents. *Archives of Pediatrics & Adolescent Medicine, 152,* 388–393.

Sayette, M. A., Martin, C. S., Hull, J. G., Wertz, J. M., & Perrott, M. A. (2003). Effects of nicotine deprivation on craving response covariation in smokers. *Journal of Abnormal Psychology, 112*(1), 110–118.

Sees, K. L., & Clark, H. W. (1993). When to begin smoking cessation in substance abusers. *Journal of Substance Abuse Treatment, 10,* 189–195.

Seligman, M. E. (1995). The effectiveness of psychotherapy: The *Consumer Reports* study. *American Psychologist, 50,* 965–974.

Selye, H. (1974). *Stress without distress.* New York: Signet.

Shadel, W. G., Niaura, R., Brown, R. A., Hutchison, K. E., & Abrams, D. B. (2001). A content analysis of smoking craving. *Journal of Clinical Psychology, 57*(1), 145–150.

Shadel, W. G., Shiffman, S., Niaura, R., Nichter, M., & Abrams, D. B. (2000). Current models of nicotine dependence: What is known and what is needed to advance understanding of tobacco etiology among youth. *Drug and Alcohol Dependence, 59* (Suppl. 1), S9–S21.

Shaffer, H. J. (1991). Toward an epistemology of "addictive disease." *Behavioral Sciences and the Law, 9,* 269–286.

Shields, M., & Shooshtari, S. (2001). Determinants of self-perceived health. *Health Reports, 13*(1), 35–52.

Sherwood, N. E., Hennrikus, D. J., Jeffery, R. W., Lando, H. A., & Murray, D. M. (2000). Smokers with multiple behavioral risk factors: How are they different? *Preventive Medicine, 31,* 299–307.

Shiffman, S. (1988). Behavioral assessment. In D. M. Donovan & G. A. Marlatt (Eds.), *Assessment of addictive behaviors* (pp. 139–188). New York: Guilford Press.

Shiffman, S. (1989). Tobacco "chippers"—individual differences in tobacco dependence. *Psychopharmacology, 97,* 539–547.

Shiffman, S., Elash, C. A., Paton, S. M., Gwaltney, C. J., Paty, J. A., Clark, D. B., et al. (2000). Comparative efficacy of 24-hour and 16-hour transdermal nicotine patches for relief of morning craving. *Addiction, 95,* 1185–1195.

Shiffman, S., Engberg, J. B., Paty, J. A., Perz, W. G., Gnys, M., Kassel, J. D., & Hickcox, M. (1997). A day at a time: Predicting smoking lapse from daily urge. *Journal of Abnormal Psychology, 106*(1), 104–116.

Shiffman, S., Fischer, L. B., Zettler-Segal, M., & Benowitz, N. L. (1990). Nicotine exposure among nondependent smokers. *Archives of General Psychiatry, 47,* 333–336.

Shiffman, S., Gnys, M., Richards, T. J., Paty, J. A., Hickcox, M., & Kassel, J. D. (1996). Temptations to smoke after quitting: A comparison of lapsers and maintainers. *Health Psychology, 15,* 455–461.

Shiffman, S., Gwaltney, C. J., Balabanis, M. H., Liu, K. S., Paty, J. A., Kassel, J. D., et al. (2002). Immediate antecedents of cigarette smoking: An analysis from Ecological Momentary Analysis. *Journal of Abnormal Psychology, 111,* 531–545.

Shiffman, S., Kassel, J. D., Paty, J., Gnys, M., & Zettler-Segal, M. (1994). Smoking typology profiles of chippers and regular smokers. *Journal of Substance Abuse, 6,* 21–35.

Shiffman, S., Read, L., Maltese, J., Rapkin, D., & Jarvik, M. E. (1985). Preventing relapse in ex-smokers: A self-management approach. In G. A. Marlatt & J. R. Gordon (Eds.), *Relapse prevention: Maintenance strategies in the treatment of addictive behaviors* (pp. 472–520). New York: Guilford Press.

Shiffman, S., Shadel, W. G., Niaura, R., Khayrallah, M. S., Jorenby, D. E., Ryan, C. F., & Ferguson, C. L. (2003). Efficacy of acute administration of nicotine gum in relief of cue-provoked cigarette craving. *Psychopharmacology, 166,* 343–350.

Silagy, C., Lancaster, T., Stead, L. F., Mant, D., & Fowler, G. (2003). Nicotine replacement therapy for smoking cessation (Cochrane Review). In *The Cochrane Library* (Issue 1). Chichester, England: Wiley.

Silagy, C., & Stead, L. F. (2003). Physician advice for smoking cessation (Cochrane Review). In *The Cochrane Library* (Issue 1). Chichester, England: Wiley.

Sims, T., & Fiore, M. (2002). Pharmacotherapy for treating tobacco dependence: What is the ideal duration of therapy? *CNS Drugs, 16,* 653–662.

Slade, J. (1993). Nicotine delivery devices. In C. T. Orleans & J. Slade (Eds.), *Nicotine addiction: Principles and management* (pp. 3–23). New York: Oxford University Press.

Smith, R. C., Singh, A., Infante, M., Khandat, A., & Kloos, A. (2002). Effects of cigarette smoking and nicotine nasal spray on psychiatric symptoms and cognition in schizophrenia. *Neuropsychopharmacology, 27,* 479–497.

Smith, T. A., House, R. F., Croghan, I. T., Gauvin, T. R., Colligan, R. C., Offord, K. P., et al. (1996). Nicotine patch therapy in adolescent smokers. *Pediatrics, 98,* 659–667.

Sobell, L. C., Toneatto, T., & Sobell, M. B. (1994). Behavioral assessment and treatment planning for alcohol, tobacco, and other drug problems: Current status with an emphasis on clinical applications. *Behavior Therapy, 25,* 533–580.

Society for Research on Nicotine and Tobacco. (2002). Biochemical verification of tobacco use and cessation. *Nicotine & Tobacco Research, 4,* 149–159.

Soteriades, E. S., DiFranza, J. R., Savageau, J. A., & Nicolaou, M. (2003). Symptoms of nicotine dependence and other predictors of student smoking at school: Implications for school smoking policy. *The Journal of School Health, 73*(4), 154–158.

Spiegel, H. (1970). A single-treatment method to stop smoking using ancillary self-hypnosis. *International Journal of Clinical and Experimental Hypnosis, 18,* 235–250.

Spitzer, R. L., Williams, J. B. W., Gibbon, M., & First, M. B. (1992). The Structured Clinical Interview for *DSM–III–R* (SCID): Pt. 1. History, rationale, and description. *Archives of General Psychiatry, 49,* 624–629.

Stead, L. F., & Lancaster, T. (2002). Group behavior therapy programmes for smoking cessation (Cochrane Review). In *The Cochrane Library* (Issue 4). Chichester, England: Wiley.

Stitzer, M. L., & Walsh, S. L. (1997). Psychostimulant abuse: The case for combined behavioral and pharmacological treatments. *Pharmacology, Biochemistry and Behavior, 57,* 457–470.

Stricker, G., Bologna, N. C., Robinson, E. A., Abrahamson, D. J., Hollon, S. D., & Reed, G. M. (1999). Treatment guidelines: The good, the bad, and the ugly. *Psychotherapy, 36*(1), 69–79.

Stubbs, J., Haw, C., & Garner, L. (2004). Survey of staff attitudes to smoking in a large psychiatric hospital. *Psychiatric Bulletin, 28,* 204–207.

Sutherland, G. (2002). Current approaches to the management of smoking cessation. *Drugs, 62*(Suppl. 2), 53–61.

Sutton, S. (1996). Can "Stages of Change" provide guidance in the treatment of addictions? In G. Edwards & C. Dare (Eds.), *Psychotherapy, psychological treatments and the addictions* (pp. 189–205). New York: Cambridge University Press.

Swadi, H. (1992). A longitudinal perspective on adolescent substance abuse. *European Child and Adolescent Psychiatry, 1,* 156–170.

Swan, G. E., Jack, L. M., & Ward, M. M. (1997). Subgroups of smokers with different success rates after use of transdermal nicotine. *Addiction, 92,* 207–218.

Tate, J. C., & Schmitz, J. M. (1993). A proposed revision of the Fagerstrom Tolerance Questionnaire. *Addictive Behaviors, 18,* 135–143.

Teneggi, V., Tiffany, S. T., Squassante, L., Milleri, S., Ziviani, L., & Bye, A. (2002). Smokers deprived of cigarettes for 72 hours: Effect of nicotine patches on craving and withdrawal. *Psychopharmacology, 164,* 177–187.

Tiffany, S. T., & Cepeda-Benito, A. (1994). Long-term behavioral interventions: The key to successful smoking cessation programs. *Health Values, 18*(1), 54–61.

Tiffany, S. T., & Drobes, D. J. (1991). The development and initial validation of a questionnaire on smoking urges. *British Journal of Addiction, 86,* 1467–1476.

Upadhyaya, H., Deas, D., Brady, K., & Kruesi, M. (2002). Cigarette smoking and psychiatric comorbidity in children and adolescents. *Journal of the American Academy of Child and Adolescent Psychiatry, 41,* 1294–1305.

U.S. Department of Health and Human Services. (1988). *The health consequences of smoking: Nicotine addiction. A report of the surgeon general* (DHHS Publication No. CDC 88–8406). Washington, DC: U.S. Government Printing Office.

U.S. Department of Health and Human Services. (1989). *Reducing the health consequences of smoking: 25 years of progress. A report of the surgeon general* (DHHS Publication No. CDC 89–8411).Washington, DC: U.S. Government Printing Office.

U.S. Department of Health and Human Services. (1990). *The health benefits of smoking cessation: A report of the surgeon general* (DHHS Publication No. CDC 90–8416). Washington, DC: U.S. Government Printing Office.

U.S. Department of Health and Human Services. (1994). *Preventing tobacco use among young people: A report of the surgeon general.* Atlanta, GA: Author.

U.S. Department of Health and Human Services. (1998). *Tobacco use among U.S. racial/ethnic minority groups—African Americans, American Indians and Alaska*

Natives, Asian Americans and Pacific Islanders, and Hispanics: A report of the surgeon general. Atlanta, GA: Author.

U.S. Department of Health and Human Services. (2000a). *Reducing tobacco use: A report of the surgeon general.* Atlanta, GA: Author.

U.S. Department of Health and Human Services. (2000b). *Treating tobacco use and dependence: Clinical practice guideline.* Rockville, MD: Author.

U.S. Department of Health and Human Services. (2001). *Women and smoking: A report of the surgeon general.* Washington, DC: Author.

U.S. Department of Health, Education, and Welfare. (1964). *Smoking and health: Report of the advisory committee to the surgeon general of the Public Health Service* (DHEW Publication No. PHS 64–1103). Washington, DC: U.S. Government Printing Office.

Vaillant, G. (1977). *Adaptation to life.* Boston: Little, Brown.

Vaillant, G. (2000). Adaptive mental mechanisms: Their role in a positive psychology. *American Psychologist, 55*(1), 89–98.

Vickers, K. S., Thomas, J. L., Patten, C. A., & Mrazek, D. A. (2002). Prevention of tobacco use in adolescents: Review of current findings and implications for healthcare providers. *Current Opinion in Pediatrics, 14,* 708–712.

Vilhjalmsson, R. (1998). Direct and indirect effects of chronic physical conditions on depression: A preliminary investigation. *Social Science & Medicine, 47,* 603–611.

Vollrath, M. (1998). Smoking, coping and health behavior among university students. *Psychology and Health, 13,* 431–442.

Walters, G. D. (1992). Drug-seeking behavior: Disease or lifestyle? *Professional Psychology: Research and Practice, 23*(2), 139–145.

Walton, R., Johnstone, E., Munafo, M., Neville, M., & Griffiths, S. (2001). Genetic clues to the molecular basis of tobacco addiction and progress towards personalized therapy. *Trends in Molecular Medicine, 7*(2), 70–76.

Wampold, B. E. (1997). Methodological problems in identifying efficacious psychotherapies. *Psychotherapy Research, 7*(1), 21–43.

Wang, M. Q., Fitzhugh, E. C., Eddy, J. M., & Westerfield, R. C. (1998). School dropouts' attitudes and beliefs about smoking. *Psychological Reports, 82,* 984–986.

Wang, M. Q., Fitzhugh, E. C., Westerfield, R. C., & Eddy, J. M. (1994). Predicting smoking status by symptoms of depression for U.S. adolescents. *Psychological Reports, 75,* 911–914.

Watkins, S. S., Koob, G. F., & Markou, A. (2000). Neural mechanisms underlying nicotine addiction: Acute positive reinforcement and withdrawal. *Nicotine & Tobacco Research, 2,* 19–37.

Wechsler, D. (1981). *Wechsler Adult Intelligence Scale—Revised.* New York: Harcourt Brace Jovanovich.

Weinstein, N. D. (1999). What does it mean to understand a risk? Evaluating risk comprehension. *Journal of the National Cancer Institute, 25,* 15–21.

Welsch, S. K., Smith, S. S., Wetter, D. W., Jorenby, D. E., Fiore, M. C., & Baker, T. B. (1999). Development and validation of the Wisconsin Smoking Withdrawal Scale. *Experimental and Clinical Psychopharmacology, 7,* 354–361.

West, R. J. (1984). Psychology and pharmacology in cigarette withdrawal. *Journal of Psychosomatic Research, 28,* 379–386.

West, R. J. (1992). Nicotine addiction: A re-analysis of the arguments. *Psychopharmacology, 108,* 408–410.

West, R., & Hajek, P. (1997). What happens to anxiety levels on giving up smoking? *American Journal of Psychiatry, 154,* 1589–1592.

Westman, E. C., Behm, F. M., Simel, D. L., & Rose, J. E. (1997). Smoking behavior on the first day of a quit attempt predicts long-term abstinence. *Archives of Internal Medicine, 157,* 335–340.

Wetter, D. W., Fiore, M. C., Gritz, E. R., Lando, H. A., Stitzer, M. L., Hasselblad, V., & Baker, T. B. (1998). The Agency for Health Care Policy and Research Smoking Cessation Clinical Practice Guideline: Findings and implications for psychologists. *American Psychologist, 53,* 657–669.

Wetter, D. W., Fiore, M. C., Young, T. B., McClure, J. B., deMoor, C. A., & Baker, T. B. (1999). Gender differences in response to nicotine replacement therapy: Objective and subjective indexes of tobacco withdrawal. *Experimental and Clinical Psychopharmacology, 7*(2), 135–144.

Wetter, D. W., Kenford, S. L., Smith, S. S., Fiore, M. C., Jorenby, D. E., & Baker, T. B. (1999). Gender differences in smoking cessation. *Journal of Consulting and Clinical Psychology, 67,* 555–562.

White, A. R., Rampes, H., & Ernst, E. (2003). Acupuncture for smoking cessation (Cochrane Review). In *The Cochrane Library* (Issue 2). Chichester, England: Wiley.

Wills, T. A. (1986). Stress and coping in early adolescence: Relationships to substance use in urban school samples. *Health Psychology, 5,* 503–529.

Wool, M. S. (1990). Understanding depression in medical patients: Part 1. Diagnostic considerations. *Social Work in Health Care, 14*(4), 25–38.

World Health Organization. (1990). *International classification of diseases and related health problems* (9th rev., Vol. 1). Geneva, Switzerland: Author.

World Health Organization. (1992). The *ICD–10* classification of mental and behavioral disorders: Clinical descriptions and diagnostic guidelines. In *International classification of diseases and related health problems* (10th rev., Vol. 1, chap. 5). Geneva, Switzerland: Author.

World Health Organization. (1993). *Composite International Diagnostic Interview* (Authorized Core Version 1.1). Washington, DC: American Psychiatric Press.

Ziedonis, D. M., & Williams, J. M. (2003). Management of smoking in people with psychiatric disorders. *Current Opinion in Psychiatry, 16,* 305–315.

Zinser, M. C., Baker, T. B., Sherman, J. E., & Cannon, D. S. (1992). Relation between self-reported affect and drug urges and cravings in continuing and withdrawing smokers. *Journal of Abnormal Psychology, 101,* 617–629.

Zucker, D., Hopkins, R. S., Sly, D. F., Urich, J., Kershaw, J. M., & Solari, S. (2000). Florida's "truth" campaign: A counter-marketing, anti-tobacco media campaign. *Journal of Public Health Management and Practice*, 6(3), 1–6.

Zwar, N., & Richmond, R. (2002). Bupropion sustained release: A therapeutic review of Zyban. *Australian Family Physician*, 31, 443–447.

INDEX

ABOUT THE AUTHOR

Charles E. Dodgen, PhD, is a clinical psychologist in private practice in Caldwell, New Jersey. Dr. Dodgen received his doctoral degree from Fairleigh Dickinson University. He authored *What Should I Know About Someone Who Abuses Alcohol or Other Drugs?* and coauthored *Substance Use Disorders: Assessment and Treatment.* He is the former director of psychology and clinical coordinator of the Adult Inpatient Substance Abuse Treatment Unit at a private psychiatric hospital in Summit, New Jersey. Dr. Dodgen is currently on staff at St. Barnabas Medical Center, Department of Psychiatry, in Livingston, New Jersey.